DATE DUE

PRINTED IN U.S.A.

MUSLIMS AND THE NEW MEDIA

Scholars from an extensive range of academic disciplines have focused on Islam in cyberspace and the media, but there are few historical studies that have outlined how Muslim '*ulama*' have discussed and debated the introduction and impact of these new media.

Muslims and the New Media explores how the introduction of the latest information and communication technologies are mirroring changes and developments within society, as well as the Middle East's relationship to the West. Examining how reformist and conservative Muslim '*ulama*' have discussed the printing press, photography, the broadcasting media (radio and television), the cinema, the telephone and the Internet, case studies provide a contextual background to the historical, social and cultural situations that have influenced theological discussions; focusing on how the '*ulama*' have debated the 'usefulness' or 'dangers' of the information and communication media. By including both historical and contemporary examples, this book exposes historical trajectories as well as different (and often contested) positions in the Islamic debate about the new media.

Muslims and the New Media
Historical and Contemporary Debates

GÖRAN LARSSON
University of Gothenburg, Sweden

ASHGATE

Published by
Ashgate Publishing Limited
Wey Court East
Union Road
Farnham
Surrey, GU9 7PT
England

Ashgate Publishing Company
Suite 420
101 Cherry Street
Burlington
VT 05401-4405
USA

www.ashgate.com

British Library Cataloguing in Publication Data
Larsson, Göran.
Muslims and the new media : historical and contemporary debates.
 1. Mass media–Religious aspects–Islam. 2. Mass media–Technological innovations–Social aspects–Islamic countries. 3. Islam in mass media. 4. Ulama–Attitudes.
 I. Title
 303.4'833'088297-dc22

Library of Congress Cataloging-in-Publication Data
Larsson, Göran.
Muslims and the new media : historical and contemporary debates / Göran Larsson.
 p. cm.
Includes bibliographical references and index.
ISBN 978-1-4094-2750-6 (hardcover) – ISBN 978-1-4094-2751-3 (ebook) 1. Mass media–Religious aspects–Islam. 2. Islam in mass media. I. Title.
BP185.7.L37 2011
297.2'66–dc22

2011008609

ISBN 9781409427506 (hbk)
ISBN 9781409427513 (ebk)

Printed and bound in Great Britain by
TJ International Ltd, Padstow, Cornwall.

Contents

List of Tables

Preface

The research for this book was mainly carried out during my time as a post-doctoral researcher in the academic program LearnIT, funded by the Swedish Knowledge Foundation (KK-stiftelsen). It goes without saying that my years in the LearnIT program have changed my view of academic work and how to do research. My interest in Islam and Muslim cultures has never been questioned, nor has my ability to contribute to the group ever been placed in doubt. I would therefore like to thank all members of the LearnIT group for their openness, interest, knowledge, kindness and generosity. My special appreciation goes to Professor Roger Säljö, Professor Ulf P. Lundgren, research colleagues Dr Jonas Linderoth, Dr Thomas Karlsohn and Dr Ove Jobring, Dr Anna-Karin Ramsten, Dr Louise Lindberg and the 'mother' of the project, Doris Gustafson. Besides these key members, I must also thank all the participants in the extended network of LearnIT and the Knowledge Foundation.

I would also like to express my gratitude to a number of colleagues at the Department of Literature, History of Ideas, Religion of University of Gothenburg . Some colleagues have made greater efforts than others, and I would like to express my deepest gratitude to Professor Åke Sander, Professor Bertil Nilsson, Professor Gudmar Aneer (now at Högskolan Dalarna), Dr Daniel Andersson, Associate Professor Henrik Bogdan, Dr Ferdinando Sardella, PhD candidate Simon Sorgenfrei and the other participants in the higher seminar. Besides the religious scholars at the University of Gothenburg, I would also like to express my gratitude to PhD candidate Aurora Tellenbach and Dr Mats Björkin of the Department of Culture, Aesthetics and Media and the Centre of Middle Eastern Studies, as well as Muhammad Muslim, Assistant Professor Heidi Campbell at the Department of Communication, Texas A&M University for important information about Jewish opinions on the cell phone, and Robert Parkin at Oxford University. They have all contributed to this project in various ways.

Over the years, I have also been fortunate to present some of the preliminary results of this book at conferences and academic meetings. The comments I have received during these meetings have been invaluable for the development and refinement of this study. Opportunities to attend a number of international conferences and meetings were made possible by the generous support of LearnIT and the Knowledge Foundation. I thank both organisations for all their support.

During the process of writing this book, I was invited to stay as a guest researcher at the Department of Religious Studies at the University of Leiden, the Netherlands. During my stay I had the great opportunity, and pleasure, to work under the guidance of Professor P.S. van Koningsveld and Dr Amr Ryad. I thank Sjoerd for his kind hospitality and academic professionalism and Amr for inviting me to Cairo and helping me arrange contacts at IslamOnline. My stay in Leiden was made possible by a generous scholarship from STINT.

More recently I have been given support and encouragement from the Linnaeus Centre for Research on Learning, Interaction, and Mediated Communication in Contemporary Society (LinCS), a national centre of excellence funded by the Swedish Research Council. Yet again I would like to thank Professor Roger Säljö for accepting me on to this project too.

This book is truly the outcome of a creative research environment, but the results would have been impossible without the work and efforts of earlier scholars working in the broad academic fields of religion, media and Islamic studies. It goes without saying that all the shortcomings in this book are solely my own.

All Arabic and Oriental language quotes are given in a simplified form. This transliteration is also used for quotes within the book.

Göran Larsson
Gothenburg

Introduction

Hence, do not utter falsehoods by letting your tongues determine [at your own discretion], 'This is lawful and that is forbidden', thus attributing your own lying inventions to God: for, behold, they who attribute their own lying inventions to God will never attain to a happy state! (Q 16:116)

An important aspect of the academic study of religions is to contextualise and situate how and why various religious leaders discuss, understand and develop their interpretations and arguments in specific ways. By focusing on how a number of influential and well-known '*ulama*' in both historical and contemporary periods debate and discuss the introduction and expanding use of new media such as print, broadcasting, photography and film, and most recently the Internet, this study seeks to show how Muslims relate to and come to terms with technological and social changes. Like most discussions of Islamic theology, Muslim debates about how to understand and use the new information and communication technologies are complex and often contradictory.

Even though a considerable number of articles and books have been written focusing on Islam and Muslims and the history and introduction of various information and communication technologies, to the best of my knowledge there is no volume which attempts to apply a broad historical perspective and which includes several technologies for analysis in one volume. The overall aim of the study, however, is not to analyse the various media per se. Rather, my interest consists in showing how a number of '*ulama*' belonging to different traditions, interpretations and localities have discussed and debated the introduction of the printing press, photography, the cinema, broadcasting media, the telephone and the Internet. From this point of view, this study aims to examine how the '*ulama*' interact with and understand technological developments and social changes that are related to the introduction of new media and, furthermore, how these discussions have, among other things, been informed by theological dogmas and prevailing political and social contexts. It is my aim to provide a broad historical outline that helps us to contextualise the answers and discussions of the '*ulama*' that relate to questions about new media. How do the '*ulama*' argue when it comes to new media? To what extent are the answers of these '*ulama*' informed by theological traditions (for example, the law schools and modes of interpretation) that are directly or indirectly influenced by prevailing local contexts? An overall ambition is to highlight historical trajectories and to identify similarities and differences in the various arguments employed by the selected '*ulama*'.

Muslim religious leaders

By Muslim religious leaders, I am primarily referring to the group of religious scholars known as the '*ulama*'. Through the force of their religious education or their social or political status, they are able to pass on religious knowledge, issue judicial recommendations and interpret Islam. To put it in the words of Claude Gilliot, in a Sunni Muslim theological context the '*ulama*' are 'regarded as the guardians, transmitters and interpreters of religious knowledge, of Islamic doctrine and law', in which position they have a responsibility to judge, preach and fulfil religious functions in the community.[1]

The word '*ulama*' is derived from the root consonants '*-l-m*, a root that, among other things, is associated with 'knowledge' and 'learning'.[2] Even though the position and importance of the '*ulama*' may vary over time and place, they have occupied influential and important positions throughout the history of Islam. Among other things, they were responsible for outlining the interpretation of Islam in given contexts. Accordingly, it was the '*ulama*' who had to determine how Islam 'should' be adjusted or interpreted to fit a new situation, that is, a situation not found in either the Qur'an or the *hadith* literature.[3] For this study, the '*ulama*' are of special importance because they discuss and formulate Islamic responses and answers to meet the possibilities, as well as problems, which emerge with the introduction and expanding use of the new media. To grasp the importance of this material, it is essential to stress that I primarily view the answers as ideal positions (that is, how Muslims should ideally deal with the new media) and not as showing what they actually follow or how they apply the answers formulated by the '*ulama*'.

Even though the great majority of the '*ulama*' included in this book have acquired their theological training and knowledge in classical and prestigious Islamic institutions of higher learning (for example, al-Azhar in Cairo, Mecca/Medina, or Lucknow in India), a number of so-called lay preachers are also included in my analysis. A lay preacher is generally defined as a religious authority who lacks the formal training mentioned above, but it can also be used for Muslims who challenge the established order and who have received some formal theological training. Due to his autonomy, it is possible, and often even easier, for the lay preacher to question the prevailing religious and/or worldly order. In this position, it is normal for lay preachers to be perceived as threats to the religious elite and the worldly power. A powerful way of solving this potential problem is to label autonomous Muslim scholars heretics or renegades. Already in medieval times it is clear that this category of preachers were viewed as competitors to the '*ulama*' in power. This is a reminder of the fact that interpreting Islam is closely

---

1   Gilliot 2002, p. 801.

2   Wehr sv. '-l-m, p. 635. For a thorough discussion of knowledge in Islamic traditions, see Rosenthal 1970.

3   Gilliot 2000.

related to the question of power.[4] According to my definition, to be in power is to have an advantage and to be in a position that makes the individual more likely to set boundaries in understanding the 'true' essence of Islam. The concepts of 'orthodoxy' and 'heresy' are, however, complex and difficult to use as heuristic tools. As I have expressed the matter elsewhere:

> Orthodoxy is rather seen as a phenomenon closely related to the articulation and distribution of power. But it is also possible for the group out of power to mark itself as being orthodox. Alterations in the political structure often, though not invariably, tend to affect the current interpretation of orthodoxy. However, it must be stressed that, for their part, the so-called heretical movements argued that they and no one else had access to the true belief and to proper Islamic interpretation. From this perspective the discursive struggle is not reducible to objective evidence or hard proof, since it is the discursive context as such that provides the truths. By whom and when the essence of orthodoxy was formulated is more important than the concept itself. The discursive struggle over how to define Islam could therefore be described as a battle between contesting and contradicting opinions.[5]

Even though the contemporary debates are very different from those of the medieval period, it is clear that the '*ulama*' are still engaged in the struggle over how to define 'true' Islam. Although '*ulama*' or so-called lay Muslims used other methods for questioning authority and the definitions it imposed during the medieval period, today it is common to find Muslims using the latest information and communication technologies to question and challenge the religious order. While questioning those in power is not a new phenomenon, it seems as if the new media have made it both easier and safer (for example, by providing a kind of anonymity) to question the authority to interpret religious traditions and the privilege of doing so. As illustrated by a growing number of sociologists, anthropologists and political scientists, such as Peter Beyer and Manuel Castells, the Internet is of particular importance in this development. Indeed, compared to earlier periods, it is plausible to argue that the struggle over authority and power has become more visible due to the new media.

This is an important reminder of the fact that the debate over the new information and communication technologies is closely related to questions of power and authority. The possibilities, but also the problems, of the new media are also discussed and questioned by lay Muslims using, for example, the Internet to seek alternative interpretations. One illustrative example is a *fatwa* on

---

4   The concept of power is, however, very complex and difficult to define, and its influence is even more difficult to measure. A thorough discussion of power can be found in Lukes 1974.

5   Larsson 2003, p. 22.

'Online Muftis: Who is Eligible?',[6] published on the webpage of IslamOnline. net. Even though Sano Koutoub Moustapha, the *mufti* who is answering this specific question and who has issued a *fatwa* on the topic, never clarifies or specifies the relationship between the new technologies and the authority to make interpretations, he is sincerely worried by the fact that some people are prepared to make interpretations without a proper religious education. Peter Mandaville comes to the same conclusion when he writes:

> Due to the largely anonymous nature of the Internet, one can also never be sure whether the authoritative advice received via these services is coming from a classically trained religious scholar or a hydraulic engineer moonlighting as an amateur *'alim*.[7]

As noted earlier, the link between technologies, power and the authority to interpret religious traditions is not a new topic.[8] Furthermore, it is also evident that the discussion about information and communication technologies is often linked to hopes and fears. While some academic scholars, such as Dale F. Eickelman and Jon W. Anderson, argue that the new media have the potential to democratise public debates and open up the public sphere for suppressed minorities, it is evident that other voices in academic discussions, as well as in the public debates that engage both religious and political voices, view the new media as a potential threat. On the one hand the new media could be linked to utopian dreams about a more democratic society, but on the other hand the information and communication technologies are also seen as potential tools for surveillance and control and bringers of a dystopian nightmare.

Responses against modernity

This study is not about the rise of modern society or the impact of globalisation. However, including a discussion of these processes when discussing and analysing Muslim debates about information and communication technologies is unavoidable. Modernity is a concept that is difficult to define, but most scholars nonetheless tend to associate it with a number of tendencies, changes or processes that are taking place in society. It is debatable whether these changes can be traced to a specific period – for example, developments in seventeenth- and eighteenth-century Europe – or whether modernity should be viewed as an open category. It

---

6   Sano Koutoub Moustapha, 'Online Muftis: Who is Eligible?', retrieved from http:// www.islamonline.net/servlet/Satellite?cid=1218558415726&pagename=IslamOnline-English-Ask_Scholar%2FFatwaE%2FFatwaEAskTheScholar (printed 2008-08-18).

7   Mandaville 2001, p. 183.

8   The connection between technology and power is also evident in the introduction of the railroad and the printing press in the Middle East. See Landau 1971, pp. 12–13.

is, however, evident that modernity is 'intimately connected with such notions as capitalism, industrialisation, urbanisation and modernisation'.[9] As Donald Wiebe stresses:

> the transformation of the social structures of society was associated not just with material changes brought about by technology but also, and necessarily with changes in consciousness involving the rejection of traditional religious structures of authority and the espousal of individualism. The birth of the modern revealed a new way of thinking about the human condition that involved a critique of traditional social hierarchies and a promotion of progress and emancipation.[10]

Even if we may agree with Wiebe's description, there is no consensus over how to measure degrees of modernity.[11] Despite this fact, however, it is clear that cultural, material and economic as well as 'mental' changes must be taken into account if we want to understand modernity. Hence, it is essential to pay attention to, for example, changes within the educational system, political reforms and the degree of urbanisation and social differentiation (that is, differentiation between and autonomisation of the public and private spheres). The latter process was crucial for the rise of the 'modern' society and its institutions. With the separation between the public and private spheres, the church (or other religious institution) in the West generally had less control and power over a number of essential social functions, such as politics, economics, science, education, law, art, health and the family.[12] These processes also empowered the individual to take control of his or her own life, which in itself was a drive for rationalisation, individualisation or privatisation and functional differentiation.[13] These developments were of course closely related to the development and introduction of the new media, and the rise of the printing press, radio and television are at the very core of the discussion about modernity.

Although the degree of change is open to debate, it is clear that the 'Muslim world', like the rest of the world, went through a number of important adjustments from the end of the eighteenth century. This was on the one hand the beginning of the Enlightenment, rationalism and liberty, but on the other hand also of colonialism, imperialism and technological developments.[14] From the nineteenth and twentieth centuries, the educational system was changed in most countries

---

9   Wiebe 2000, p. 354.

10   Wiebe 2000, p. 354.

11   A thorough discussion of modernity and religion can be found in Lambert 1999.

12   Lambert 1999.

13   Lambert 2003, p. 69. A similar development is also clearly seen in the Middle East today. On this development, see, for example, Charles Hirschkind (2006), who provides a clear, illustrative discussion of Islam in contemporary Egypt.

14   An excellent study of colonialism and imperialism can be found in Mitchell 1991.

that were dominated by Muslim and Islamic traditions. A process of urbanisation[15] was also started in what is today called the Middle East, and more people gained access to Western forms of education in countries such as Egypt, Lebanon, Syria and Turkey. This influence is, for example, clearly highlighted by David Waines in his outline of the impact of the British and French colonial systems on the Middle East:

> While private mission schools were allowed to flourish, colonial governments' overall control of education further encouraged the marginalization of Islamic knowledge. Like Muslim legal systems were reformed and largely replaced by the introduction of European codes (especially, French, Swiss and German) lock, stock and barrel. In both cases it meant that those trained in traditional Islamic knowledge, the '*ulama*', were disenfranchized and replaced socially by a new secularized Muslim elite.[16]

All in all, this period challenged the 'traditional' order and the established religious authority of the '*ulama*', who had to come up with various modes of interpretation in order to be able to respond to the rise of modern society.

As pointed out earlier by Donald Wiebe, it is important to consider the material, cultural and ideological changes that were brought about by the process of modernisation when we analyse how the '*ulama*' debate new communication technologies. On the basis of the historical records that have been preserved, however, it is often very difficult to describe or substantiate why an individual who belongs to the class of the '*ulama*' takes a specific position, for example, with regard to a new technology. It is nonetheless clear that criticism of the new information and communication technologies was often disguised as a form of criticism of the growing Western presence – symbolic, material and intellectual – in the society.[17] This tendency is, for example, clearly evident in discussions concerning the printing press in Istanbul, Cairo and Teheran from the end of the eighteenth century, a topic I address in greater detail in the next chapter. To destroy or hinder the introduction of the printing press could easily be understood and presented as a symbolic action against Western interests in the Middle East. Similar ways of arguing are also found in relation to later developments. The negative attitude to the cinema in, for example, post-revolutionary Iran in the 1980s is also relevant because it was often associated with Western and non-Islamic values.

When analysing criticisms based on the religious motives of the new media, it is important to remember that similar attitudes can be found in the West too. For example, the intellectual climate that led up to the revolution in Iran – which I will

---

15   When analysing urbanisation processes in the Middle East, we should remember that we often suffer from a lack of reliable statistical and demographic data. According to Gabriel Bear (1968), large-scale urbanization only took off after World War I in Egypt.

16   Waines 2002, p. 194.

17   See, for example, Peters 1986.

discuss in relation to the introduction of the cinema in Chapter 3 – should therefore also be analysed together with similar intellectual debates in the West. According to Torben Rugberg Rasmussen, 'we are merely dealing with different cultural strategies of escaping, healing, or even revolting against modernity'.[18] While the response to modernity in the West has been discussed, debated and criticised by intellectuals such as Jean Paul Sartre, Albert Camus, Pierre Bourdieu and Michel Foucault, the Iranians found support in religious and political leaders such as Ali Shariati (1933–1977) and Ayatollah Ruhullah Khomeini (1902–1989). The call for 'authenticity', a return to past ideologies or an idealised era identified by its 'pure' interpretation of a religion is, however, nothing but a product of modernity. Again it is important to quote Rugberg Rasmussen here:

> In modern times authenticity, even if it is based on Revelation and Holy Scriptures, is no less modern than modernity itself. To reject modernity and search for identity-saving panaceas in tradition, the sphere of religion, or some invented mythical past, presupposes participation in, or knowledge of modern culture, and the Iranian revolution was in all respects a modern revolution.[19]

Against this backdrop, it is evident that the Enlightenment and the subsequent rise of the British and French colonial systems and their domination and control of the Middle East gave rise to various reactions and responses.[20] Some Muslims, following the pattern of Christian and Jewish communities in Europe and the United States, became convinced atheists and strong believers in scientism and rationalism. Others were concerned and troubled by the new subaltern and inferior position of the Middle East. Why had Muslims lost their powerful and glorious position to the non-Muslims? Was it because they had abandoned God, or was it God who had abandoned them? Besides embracing atheistic, secular, socialist or rationalistic ideas, some Muslims began to explore new ways of approaching the Qur'an. Although interpreting the Qur'an is not a new phenomenon (for example, the *tafsir* tradition), from the end of the nineteenth century it became possible to talk about a reform movement attempting to find a middle way by interpreting the traditional sources of Islam through the prism of modernity. According to '*ulama*'

---

18   Rugberg Rasmussen 1994, p. 171.

19   Rugberg Rasmussen 1994, p. 172.

20   As Yves Lambert and others have pointed out, globalisation and modernity could receive different and often contradictory responses: 'It could lead to religious decline (atheism, agnosticism, scientism, materialism), as well as to reinterpretations (demythologisation, critical exegesis, 'this-worldliness'), fundamentalist reactions (creationism), or religious innovations (deism, para-scientific beliefs and New Religious Movements: modern astrology, telepathy, notions of positive and negative waves, and notions of cosmic energy)' (Lambert 2003, p. 67). The rise of 'modern' society may therefore foster religious decline and reinterpretations as well as fundamentalisms, and innovative new bricolages, including 'old' and 'new' religious forms of expression (i.e. New Age and New Religious Movements).

such as Muhammad 'Abduh (1849–1905) and Muhammad Rashid Rida (1865–1935), to whom I return at several points in the subsequent chapters, Islam was not the problem: it was only the interpretation and implementation of Islam that should be adjusted to fit with the modern world and its requirements. By adjustment, they are not saying that Islam should change – on the contrary. For example, in their answers and discussions about information and communication technologies, it is possible to see how this theological understanding was implemented and put into practice. They argued, for example, that, by applying a 'sound' reading of the sources, it had become possible to go back to the very essence of Islam. Hence, the perception arose that it was possible to find interpretations illustrating and supporting the view that a belief in Allah could be combined with a modern scientific and rational world view. But this way of interpreting the sources – which in some senses resembles the Jewish *Haskhalah* (Enlightenment) movement that had started in Europe in the eighteenth and nineteenth centuries – did not go unchallenged.[21]

For example, according to the Wahhabi interpretation of Islam that emerged on the Arabian Peninsula in the eighteenth century, the decline of the countries dominated by Islamic and Muslim traditions had to do with the fact that Muslims had accepted non-Islamic rituals and local customs. To solve the challenges of the modern world, Muslims had to return to a so-called authentic interpretation of Islam. Consequently, the veneration of saints, amulets and other forms of popular belief were some of the problems that 'true' Muslims had to fight, since these practices were not in line with how the Wahhabis perceived Islam as having been lived during the Prophet Muhammad's time. Even though the Wahhabi and Hanbali interpretations of Islam that predominate in present-day Saudi Arabia and in the Gulf countries are often portrayed as conservative and 'medieval' forms of Islam, the Wahhabi movement is also a reform movement that is closely involved in debates over modernity, authority and interpretation.[22] Without going into any details about the 'emergence' of the so-called Wahhabi movement, the following chapters will show that the '*ulama*' inspired by Wahhabi tendencies often express strong opinions about the introduction and use of the new information and communication technologies.

In response to the same ideological, political and social changes that the Middle East was going through, the Deobandi movement in India and what later became Pakistan emerged more or less at the same time as the Egyptian reform movement. As with other reform movements, it is very difficult to present the Deobandi School as a homogeneous system. It has been called a traditionalist, fundamentalist, modernist, and even a secularist movement.[23] Like the other

---

21   A discussion of Judaism and modernity can be found in, for example, Kunin 2002.

22   We should, however, be careful to add that the followers of the Wahhabi and Hanbali traditions are against all forms of rational argumentation. See, for example, Abrahamov 1998 for a critical discussion.

23   Waines 2002, p. 195.

movements or ideas discussed in this section, the followers of this tradition were eager to revitalise Islam and to find a solution to the current situation and its new challenges. The Deobandi School was also developed as a response to and a defence against the colonial powers and western domination more generally. Resembling the 'reformers' and the followers of the Wahhabi tendency, the Deoband '*ulama*' also had strong opinions about modern society and the rise of the new media.

From this brief backdrop, we can draw two conclusions. First, it is evident that several Muslim '*ulama*' were seriously engaged in and concerned with debates about modernity. Secondly, it is also clear that it is impossible to talk about a single or monolithic Muslim reaction. While some '*ulama*' were willing to accept certain aspects of Western influence, others were more sceptical regarding the same phenomenon. If we use Tariq Ramadan's typology, it is possible to distinguish six major tendencies 'among those for whom Islam is the reference point of thinking'.[24] However, before presenting the typology, it is important to stress that the boundaries between the different tendencies are often flouted and rendered open to discussion, and that individuals can be informed by more than one tendency. Ramadan distinguishes between the following six tendencies:

1. Scholastic traditionalists who are characterised by a 'distinctive way of referring to scriptural Texts, the Qur'an and the Sunna' and by strict and exclusive references to the so-called classical Schools of Jurisprudence. Even though this tendency includes a large number of individuals and schools of thought, most '*ulama*' who are informed by scholastic traditionalism are less positive in their responses to criticism of established truths, and the focus is often on the maintenance of traditions and customs (for example, dress codes). According to Ramadan there is little room for *ijtihad* or a rereading of the sources, and the focus is on religious practice, not on social, civil or political involvement. This tendency includes, among many groups, the Deobandis and the Barelwis, two tendencies included in my study.

2. Salafi literalists reject the importance of the juridical Schools and approach the sources directly, according to Ramadan. Consequently, the Qur'an should be read literally, and there is no room for interpretation. The followers of this tendency try to emulate the Prophet Muhammad and the first followers of Islam, hence the name Salaf.

3. Salafi reformers are also trying to emulate the first followers of Islam, but instead of focusing on external questions (for example, dress codes and rituals), they are rather trying to find the original guiding principals of Islam. Consequently, they are looking for the purpose and intention of the text and the law, and 'they believe that the practice of *ijtihad* is an objective, necessary and constant factor in the application of *fiqh* in every time and place'. Among this group we find names such as, Muhammad

---

24   Ramadan 2004, pp. 24–29.

al-Afghani, Muhammad Abduh, Muhammad Rashid Rida, Mawlana Mawdudi and Hasan al-Banna.

4. Adherents of political literalist Salafism are followers of the Salafi literalists, but they put a much greater stress on political activism, *jihad* and opposition to the West.
5. Liberals or rationalist reformers often defend the importance of separating religion from public and political life and argue that Muslims should strive for integration and sometimes even assimilation. To uphold religion is generally not of great importance for those who belong to this category.
6. Sufism or mysticism is a large category that could include followers from the other tendencies in Ramadan's typology. However, this category has a distinct interest for the so-called inner life of the individual.[25]

In the following sections, I will mainly return to the followers of the Egyptian reform movement, the Wahhabi tradition and the Deobandi School by examining more closely the individual '*ulama*' whom I have included in this study with the aim of examining how they have debated and positioned themselves when it comes to the introduction of modern information and communication technologies. If we apply Ramadan's typology, this study is mainly focused on '*ulama*' who are informed by scholastic traditionalism, Salafi literalism and Salafi reformism. Before I do so, however, I should first say something in general terms about the sources I have used for this book. This will lead us into a discussion of the issuing of *fatwas*.

The sources

In order to analyse Muslim debates on information and communication technologies, I have used a vast number of different sources. Before I present the major texts or sources for this study, it is essential to say a few words about how I have selected the material. First of all, in order to discuss Muslim responses to information and communication technologies, I have chosen texts and '*ulama*' that have a direct bearing on how Muslims have discussed the introduction of new media. Consequently, the '*ulama*' whom I have included in this study are among the best known when it comes to studies of Islam and new media. Most of the '*ulama*' included are also known from academic studies, as well as the Internet, internal Muslim discussions and theological texts that are relevant for the topic of this study. Secondly, in order to illustrate and analyse internal Muslim discussions and contradictions, it has been my aim to choose '*ulama*' who belong to different local contexts and theological branches of Islam.

The major texts for this study, however, are Islamic legal responses or advice given by Muslim '*ulama*'. In Arabic this literature is known by the term *fatwa*

---

25   All quotations in these six points are taken from Ramadan 2004, pp. 24–29.

(plural *fatawa*, but I will write *fatwas* according to English plural). Besides issued *fatwas* that have relevance to Muslim debates on information and communication technologies, I have also used travel books, historical records and theological treatises to cast light on important periods and events relating to the new media. For example, the report by two Swedish diplomats, Edvard Carlson (1704–1767) and Carl Fredrik von Höpken (1713–1778), provide a first-hand source for the early history of the printing press in the Ottoman Empire. Similar data for Egypt can be derived from 'Abd al-Rahman al-Jabarti's description of the early French expedition to Egypt at the end of the eighteenth century and Edward William Lane's classical description of the manners and customs of the modern Egyptians from the nineteenth century. When it comes to more contemporary periods, I have tried to identify books and pamphlets written by Muslims that have a bearing on discussions about new media. Some publications are very explicit, their very titles indicating that they are dealing with Islamic opinions about a new medium, but other important publications, like, for example, the book *al-Halal wa-al-haram fi al-Islam* by Yusuf al-Qaradawi, also contain important information about Muslim debates on information and communication technologies.

A major proportion of the sources used for the present analysis are also derived from Internet forums and various so-called online *fatwa* sites. I have especially used *fatwas* issued and published by the web pages of IslamOnline.net and Ask-the-Imam. While the first site is mainly associated with reformist interpretations of Islam that had emerged in Egypt by the end of the nineteenth and beginning of the twentieth centuries, the second site is more closely related to the traditions of the Deobandi School of Indian Islam. When it comes to IslamOnline.net, it is important to stress that I have mainly used *fatwas* issued before the year 2010. This information is important for the reader of this book because the website has gone through important changes since 2010 due to internal struggles over authority, and currently it concentrates more on issuing texts in Arabic. At the time of writing this introduction, it is very difficult to analyse the reason behind these changes, but it seems as if the influence and importance of Yusuf al-Qaradawi (whom I return to below) has come under challenge.

As far as possible, I have tried to check whether the *fatwas* have been translated into English, but in several cases it has been impossible to find out if the text was originally issued in Arabic or in other languages. But it should also be stressed that several *fatwas* might have been issued directly in the English language. It is also common for the published texts to have been edited before they are put online (this is, however, also general for printed collections of *fatwas*).[26] Since data taken from the Internet have a tendency to disappear over time, I have given as much information as possible in the notes and supplied the relevant data. Even

---

26 It is also likely that a number of *fatwas* have been fabricated, i.e. the question is not genuine, but devised by the mufti (or the group of theologians) in order to discuss an important question.

though we are working on different periods and topics, I am inclined to agree with
the French sociologist of Islam, Olivier Roy, when he writes:

> The use of the Internet as a source creates many methodological problems; it
> is difficult to check the impact of websites, and to make a sociological study
> of their promoters as well as of their users. Given that the survival of many
> websites is uncertain (especially after 9/11), it is difficult to provide the reader
> with a way to check our quotations (although I keep a printed version). But
> experience shows that the most important texts are circulating on a number of
> websites and could be retrieved even if the site I have given as a reference has
> disappeared or changed its address. Usually it is sufficient to enter in a search
> engine the title of the article quoted to find it on another site.[27]

The source-critical problems highlighted by Roy should be taken seriously, but
the following study is not focused on the impact of websites or their users. My
focus is rather on how a number of selected '*ulama*' discuss the new technologies.
In adopting this approach, I am not trying to verify or document how or whether
Muslims actually use the information and communication technologies. Since the
'*ulama*' included in my study are renowned from printed sources as well as earlier
studies, it is no problem for me to 'make a sociological study of their promoters',
in Roy's words.

When it comes to translations of the Qur'an, if nothing else is indicated I have
used Muhammad Assad's translation, *The Message of the Qur'an*.

The issuing of *fatwas*

As noted in the previous section, the most important category of sources for this
study is the *fatwa*. Outside Muslim and academic circles, the word *fatwa* is generally
associated with the Iranian religious leader Ayatollah Ruhullah Khomeini and his
'death sentence' against the British-Indian author Salman Rushdie in 1989 after
the publication of the latter's novel, *The Satanic Verses*. Hence, it is necessary to
outline and explain some of the basic components, meanings and functions of a
fatwa for Muslims.[28]

---

27   Roy 2004, p. x.

28   According to Jakob Skovgaard-Petersen, the classical founding fathers of the
history of religions, Islamology and Arabic philology rarely made use of *fatwas* in their
studies. However, with new methods and theoretical approaches – for example, a growing
interest in the oral history, ethnography and anthropology of the Middle East – and with
the growing Islamisation of politics from the 1970s, the *fatwa* has become an important
source. During the last decade, a number of academic books have been based on the study
of *fatwas*. A detailed account of earlier studies can be found in Skovgaard-Petersen 1997b.

According to Muhammad Khalid Masud, a *fatwa* is associated with three distinct functions:

> [M]anagement of information about the religion of Islam in general, providing consultation to courts of law, and interpretation of Islamic law.[29]

The Arabic word *fatwa* is derived from the root *fata*, which among other things is associated with the semantic fields of youth, newness, clarification and explanation.[30] The basic theological meaning or function of the word is also outlined in the context of the Qur'an:

> AND THEY will ask thee to enlighten them about the laws concerning women. (Q 4:127)
>
> THEY WILL ASK thee to enlighten them. (Q 4:176)

As pointed out by several scholars (including Max Weber), the word *fatwa* is to be understood in the 'framework of a question-and-answer process of communicating information about Islam'.[31] Hence, giving or asking for a definitive answer corresponds to similar concepts in Roman and Jewish jurisprudence. The Jewish equivalent to the *fatwa* is found in the *responsa* literature.[32]

To grasp the complete meaning of the concept, it is also important to distinguish between the *fatwa* and a court judgment or *qada'* ('decision'). While a *qada'* is binding and enforceable, a *fatwa* is non-binding according to Islamic law.[33] A *fatwa* is best understood as a recommendation or piece of advice given by a knowledgeable and trustworthy religious authority. The person who issues *fatwas* is called a *mufti*, and he bases his answers on traditions and rational argumentation (*ra'y*). Furthermore, when the *mufti* issues a *fatwa*, his recommendation is based on the facts provided by the person who is asking for advice. In a court case, however, it is necessary for the judge to test and validate all the evidence before he can make a decision, which is not the case for a *fatwa*.[34] According to Brinkley Messick, the difference between the 'judgement' and the *fatwa* can be explained in five bullet points:

- A judgement is a performative act ↔ a *fatwa* is a communicative act
- A judgement is binding ↔ a *fatwa* is a recommendation

---

29 Masud 1996, p. 8.
30 Masud 1996, p. 8. Cf. Wehr 1976, p. 696.
31 Masud 1996, p. 8.
32 Shlomo Tal explains that a *responsa* is 'a rabbinic term denoting an exchange of letters in which one party consults another on a halakhic matter'. Tal 1971, p. 831.
33 See Skovgaard-Petersen 1997b, pp. 6–8.
34 Masud 1996, p. 9; Messick 1996, p. 10.

- A judgement is narrowly specific ↔ a *fatwa* is general
- A judge is employed by the state/authority ↔ a mufti is a private scholar
- A judge investigates the evidential fact ↔ a mufti answers an individual questioner, and the question is voluntary[35]

According to Skovgaard-Petersen, it is also important to differentiate between a *mufti* and a *qadi* (judge) because a *mufti* is usually held in higher esteem than a *qadi*. This difference is explained by the fact that the *qadi* generally receives his salary from the state or the ruler in power. The *mufti* should also be knowledgeable in both *furu'* and *'ibadat* (religious practices), but the *qadi* is restricted to the first category. The *qadi* generally only makes a distinction between what is permitted, obligatory and prohibited (*halal*, *fard* and *haram*), while the *mufti* is expected to use more ethical concepts, such as recommended and disliked (*mandub* and *makruh*).

The impact of the mass production of legal advice is another aspect that should be highlighted. With the introduction of printing and later broadcasting technologies, the conditions for the issuing of *fatwas* changed. In the 'classical' medieval setting, a person who wanted a *fatwa* went to the mosque to ask the *mufti* for advice and recommendations. In most cases (at least in the ideal theoretical situation), the *mufti* was acquainted with the individual who was asking for the *fatwa*. Using this knowledge, it was possible for the *mufti* to give an answer that was designed to meet the specific situation and the individual's requirements. This was not, however, a procedure for making a short cut – on the contrary – but a method of applying Islamic law to specific circumstances. In the ideal situation, the answer given by the *mufti* was tailored to fit the particular situation and the individual who was asking for advice. With the introduction of technologies of mass communication and mass production, however, it became impossible (or at least much more difficult) to give a unique answer that could meet a specific situation.

This problem is clearly addressed by Anne Sofie Roald in her study of Yusuf al-Qaradawi's and Ahmad al-Kubaisi's use of Arabic satellite television:

> In satellite TV-programmes where one shaikh is sitting in one part of the world talking to a person sitting in another part and is listened to by individuals in others of the globe, *fatawa* might be taken out of their context. This is exactly what happened in the case of wearing headscarves. In a later programme of *Shari'a and Life*, a woman living in Sweden faxed a question about whether it was true or not that al-Qaradawi had permitted women to take off their headscarves. Embarrassed and irritated, al-Qaradawi explained that he had been talking about specific situations such as the problem of wearing the headscarf in France and, as he said, 'a particular country in North-Africa [Tunisia]'. This event points to the sensitivity in making *fatawa* 'live' on satellite TV-channels.[36]

---

35   My list is based on Messick 1996, p. 10.
36   Roald 2001, p. 41.

The quotation from Roald is an example of how the mass media embody the power to transform the very basis of the art of issuing *fatwas*. When a *fatwa* is disseminated via a mass medium, it is changed from an individually designed answer into a general or universal answer that is tailored to fit many different local settings.

An outline of the book

As should have become evident already, this book is the result of a reading of a vast number of articles, books and various sources that might cast light on the history and debates about new information and communication technologies among Muslim '*ulama*'. Hence, I have used different sources for different chapters. However, the discussion is held together by the fact that the examples and the individuals discussed in the chapters that follow are closely linked to debates about the new media. Here I will provide the biographical and intellectual backgrounds to the most important '*ulama*' included in my study. The aim is not to give a full outline of all the individuals discussed in the book, but it is evident that each chapter is more or less clearly focused on one or two individuals who frequently occur in Islamic discussions about information and communication technologies. The following presentation can also serve as an outline for the book as a whole.

In the first chapter, which deals with the introduction of printing in the eighteenth century, I have mainly analysed the arguments used by Ibrahim Müteferriqa (d. 1745). In comparison to the other 'key players' in this study, he was not a Muslim scholar by training. Hence, it is more correct to describe him as an entrepreneur who worked for the introduction and acceptance of printing in the Ottoman Empire.[37] In his treatise *Wesilet al-tiba'a*, a work I return to in Chapter 1, he argued strongly for the introduction of printing and for the establishment of a printing press in the Ottoman Empire. His attempts to modernise society are also clearly illustrated by his publication *Usul al-hikam fi nizam al-umam* from 1731. In this essay he goes back to his arguments and stresses that the Ottoman Empire must be modernised in order to be able to compete with the European powers, which had become stronger and stronger over time. In order to stay in power and have the upper hand, it was necessary to take into account Western science, government reforms and military innovations, and among other things, printing technology.[38]

---

37 Müteferriqa was born in Kolozsvár (Cluj) in Erdel (Transylvania) of Christian parents and was a convert to Islam. The sources for his biography are meagre, but Niyazi Berkes argues that he was either a Calvinist or a Unitarian Christian who converted to Islam. The reasons for his conversion have been debated, but it is clear that he was a strong critic of the Catholic Church and the doctrine of the Trinity. By 1715 he was enrolled in the Ottoman service and its diplomatic affairs. Besides his active role in the political sphere, he was also a propagator of reforms, especially in the army, and he advocated the employment of European officers to train the Ottomans.

38 On Ibrahim Müteferriqa, see Berkes 1971.

The discussion of images, photography and the representational arts in the second chapter is based on the opinions and discussions of a vast number of *'ulama'*. As compared to the chapter on the printing press, the debate over images, photography and the representational arts is still an important and much debated issue among Muslims today (for example, the Muhammad cartoon crisis in 2005 and the Lars Vilks controversy in 2007/2010).[39] Hence, for this chapter I have used a number of *'ulama'* who arguably can be considered as representatives of the early modern reformist tradition (in Arabic, this movement is often associated with the concept of *islah*). Within this tradition, we find *'ulama'* such as Muhammad Rashid Rida (1865–1935) and Muhammad 'Abduh (1849–1905), two important and influential Muslim reform thinkers who emphasised that it was possible to be modern and Muslim at the same time. They are often seen as the pioneers of the so-called Islamic reform movement that emerged in the Middle East at the end of the nineteenth and beginning of the twentieth centuries.

Besides the 'classical' forefathers of reform discussed above, I have also used contemporary *'ulama'* who openly support the ideology and theology of the previous reformers (for example, the Egyptian Yusuf al-Qaradawi, who is closely associated with the Muslim Brotherhood movement that emerged in Egypt in the 1920s), as well as *'ulama'* who are more sceptical about the rise of modern society. However, when it comes to new media, Yusuf al-Qaradawi is a prolific user of the new information and communication technologies when it comes to spreading his interpretation of Islam.[40] Opinions about his theology are mixed. Some argue that he is an extremist and a promoter of the introduction of *shari'a*, but for others he is a moderate and a reformer who is trying to establish a middle way (in Arabic this position is often called *Wasatiya*), that is, an interpretation that seeks a moderate position avoiding extremism on the one hand and secularism and atheism on the other.[41]

Even though it is very difficult to make a sharp distinction between supporters and critics of the new medias – the difference is mainly a matter of degree and not

39   See Larsson and Lindekilde 2009.

40   Yusuf al-Qaradawi was born in 1926 in a small village in Egypt, and at an early age it is said that he had already learned the whole Qur'an by heart. His was primarily educated at the al-Azhar University in Tanta and later on in Cairo. Even though his publications cover a vast number of different fields, his doctoral thesis was on *zakat* and religious alms. His theology and political outlook are clearly coloured by the philosophy of the Muslim Brotherhood, and he has been imprisoned several times for his association with this movement. In the 1970s he moved to Qatar to take up the position of Dean of the Islamic Department at the Faculties of Shariah and Education, and he has served as chairman of the Islamic Scientific Councils of Algerian Universities and Institutions. Besides his academic positions, he has been one of the driving forces behind the establishment of the European Council for Fatwa and Research and other pan-Islamic organisations.

41   Several academic studies have addressed the importance of Yusuf al-Qaradawi; see, for example, Gräf 2007, 2008; Gräf and Skovgaard-Petersen 2008; Larsson 2010; Mariani 2006; Salvatore 1997; Skovgaard-Petersen 2004.

of interpretative tradition – the 'critics' I discuss include, for example, the Saudi Arabian Sheikh 'Abd al-'Aziz b. Baz (1909–1999) – who among many things was the Grand Mufti of Saudi Arabia from 1993 until his death in 1999, in which position he became one of the most important *'ulama'* for the modern Wahhabi school – and the South African Deobandi scholar Mufti Ebrahim Desai, who heads the *Dar al-Ifta of Madrassa In'amiyyah*, Camperdown, South Africa. Desai earned his degree in India and was trained according to the Deobandi tradition. However, compared to such *'ulama'* who are more inclined to stress the necessity of interpreting Islam in the light of the contemporary context, these *'ulama'* stick even more closely to what they perceive to be the traditions of Islam and stress that it is society that should be adjusted to fit Islamic norms and values, not the other way round. Although I call them critics, as we shall see later in this book they have issued several Islamic answers agreeing that Muslims can actually make use of the latest technologies.

For the third chapter, which deals with Islamic opinions regarding motion pictures, I have analysed both Sunni and Shi'a *'ulama'* (especially the opinions of Ayatollah Ruhullah Khomeini and Yusuf al-Qaradawi) who have discussed and issued *fatwas* that are related to the film medium and the cinema. The reason for including Khomeini – the religious leader of the revolution in Iran 1979 – in the analysis is that he expressed clear opinions about cinema and Islam. Even though his view of the cinema is very specific regarding place and time, my analysis will show that his conclusion and position regarding film media resemble how other non-Shi'a *'ulama'* have analysed the topic.

The *'ulama'* discussed in Chapters 2 and 3 also provide the key to Chapters 4, 5 and 6, which focus on the broadcasting media, the telephone and the Internet respectively. In these three chapters I have tried to uncover and compare the issues on which the selected Muslim scholars have different opinions. I have therefore compared *fatwas* issued by the followers of the reform traditions with those issued by the followers of the Wahhabi and Deobandi traditions. This exercise reveals important theological differences, as well as similarities that bridge and unite *'ulama'* who belong to different schools of thought.

For the last chapter, which is focused on debates on the Qur'an and its connection with information and communication technologies, I have mainly analysed Muslim debates about the phonograph, early recordings of the Qur'an and the digitalisation of the revelation. An important source for this discussion is the *al-Jam' al-Sawti al-Awwal l-il-Qur'an al-Karim, aw al-Mushaf al-Murattal, Bawa'ithuhu wa Mukhattatathu* ('The First Voiced Recording of the Holy Koran: al-Mushaf al-Murattal, Its Purpose and Planning'), published by Labib al-Sa'id in 1967, in which he explains why it was important for the recitation of the Qur'an to be recorded. The author is Professor of Qur'anic Studies at the University of Riyadh, Saudi Arabia.

All in all, the *'ulama'* included in my analysis are united by the fact that they have all discussed, debated and issued Islamic opinions about how so-called true Muslims should understand and use information and communication technologies. As the following chapters will show, there is often a gap between what the '*ulama*' say and what so-called ordinary Muslims do and think about technological developments, and it is not possible to find a single Muslim opinion about information and communication technologies that is shared by all the '*ulama*' included in my study. However, this is not a problem for this study, since my focus is on how the '*ulama*' have analysed and discussed the information and communication technologies in both historical and contemporary periods.

Why this book?

Before I open the historical exposé and outline the argumentation of the '*ulama*' selected for my analysis, it is vital to say a few words about how this book relates to earlier studies on Islam, Muslims and the new media. If it is not already clear, it will soon become evident that this book is based on a vast amount of earlier studies that belong to the fields of the history of religions, sociology, anthropology/ ethnology and media studies.

Even though my study builds on earlier studies and all shortcomings are mine, it is evident that it would have been impossible to write this book without the work of numerous pioneering researchers in a vast number of academic disciplines. Since I will engage more closely with several earlier studies in the following chapters (and in the notes to this book), I will not give a full review of earlier research that relates to the study of Islam, Muslims and the new media. However, when I started to think about the possibility of writing a book on this topic, I soon realised that it was very difficult to find any one volume that both provided the reader with a historical outline and at the same time analysed how representatives of the '*ulama*' have discussed, analysed and approached the challenges and possibilities that followed the introduction of the printing press, photography, the broadcasting media and most recently the Internet. Earlier studies in this field (that is, the study of information and communication technologies) have generally focused on one medium (for example, the printing press or the Internet), and to the best of my knowledge it is rare to find studies that have tried to outline historical trajectories as well as encompassing several media at the same time. Even though there are good reasons for focusing on one medium and a specific epoch or region at a time, I still believe that it is important to approach the study of information and communication technologies and religions from a much broader perspective and to include developments over time and space. At the risk of becoming eclectic and even shallow, the aim of my study is to highlight historical developments and cast light on the debate about Islam and the new media. Furthermore, since the study of religion and the media has mainly been undertaken by sociologists or media and communication researchers focusing on modern history or contemporary discussions, as a scholar of the history of religions, I believe that it is important to bring in a longer historical perspective. As we will see in the following chapters, questions and answers provided by the '*ulama*' on, for example, current topics related to the Internet or satellite television have a striking similarity to the questions and answers that were related to the introduction of the printing press in the Ottoman Empire in the eighteenth century. Answers and questions that at first glance seem to be novel and innovative are seldom as novel and innovative as we might think. Finally it is important to stress that by bringing in a historical perspective it is not my ambition to criticise contemporary research on religion and the media, but it is still my firm belief that a historical dimension will provide us with a greater potential to reveal trajectories and that growing historical awareness will cast light on current discussions. More importantly it will help us to see and understand what is new in the contemporary answers provided by the '*ulama*'.

Chapter 1

The Print Revolution

From oral communication to print media

> Trust in writing will make them remember things by relying on marks made by others, from outside themselves, not on their own inner resources, and so writing will make the things they have learnt disappear from their minds. Your invention is a potion for jogging the memory, not for remembering. You will provide students with the appearance of intelligence, nor real intelligence. Because your students will be widely read, though without any contact with a teacher, they will seem to be men of wide knowledge, when they will usually be ignorant.
>
> (Plato, Phaedrus, 275a)[1]

Even though Johannes Gutenberg (1394/99–1468) of Mainz is often described as the founding father of print technology, he invented neither printing nor movable type, these technological innovations having already been developed in China long before the fifteenth century. His contribution to the history of printing is mainly connected with the fact that he perfected printing with movable type and by doing so brought print technology closer to its modern appearance.[2] According to some estimates, the number of books that had been printed by the year 1500 was close to 13 million.[3] These figures are of course difficult to substantiate and we should treat them with great care. Still it is relevant to talk about a print revolution. But why

---

1   The quotation is taken from Plato's work *Phaedrus*, a dialogue between Socrates and Phaedrus. The quotation is related to a discussion between the Egyptian god Theuth, who among many things is seen as the inventor of writing, and Thamamous. I have used the translation by Robin Waterfield 2002, p. 69.

2   The early history of printing in Europe is obscure and the question of sources very problematic. See Hanebutt-Benz 2002, p. 1 and Kilgour 1998, p. 82.

3   Asa Briggs and Peter Burke write: 'The practice of printing spread through Europe via a diaspora of German printers. By 1500, presses had been established in more than 250 places in Europe – 80 of them in Italy, 52 in Germany and 43 in France. Printers had reached Basel by 1466, Rome by 1467, Paris and Pilsen by 1468, Venice by 1469, Leuven, Valencia, Cracow and Buda by 1473, Westminster (distinct from the city of London) by 1476, and Prague by 1477. Between them these presses produced about 27,000 editions of the year 1500, which means that – assuming an average print run of 500 copies per edition – about thirteen millions books were circulated by that date in a Europe of 100 million people.' Briggs and Burke 2002, pp. 15–16.

were the Ottomans so slow in adopting the technological innovations developed and refined by Johannes Gutenberg?

To come closer to an answer to this large question, it is necessary to delimit and define the scope of this chapter and to specify its aims. The first aim is to give a general background to the introduction of the printing press in the Ottoman Empire. In order to discuss the impact of printing, however, it is essential to consider how the shift from oral to written communication transformed societies dominated by Muslim and Islamic traditions. This is therefore the second aim of the chapter, which also contains general discussions about knowledge, memory and text in Islamic traditions. This backdrop is important because it casts light on how authority was established and conveyed prior to and after the introduction of the printing technology. This general background will also make it easier to understand the debate that followed with the introduction of the printing press in the Ottoman Empire by the beginning of the eighteenth century. The main focus, however, is on how various Muslim authorities have discussed the introduction and rise of the print media.

By printing I am mainly referring to printing with moveable type, a method developed during the second half of the fifteenth century, but my text also contains a brief discussion of lithographic printing, which was invented by G.A. Senefelder in 1796.[4] Most of the examples in the chapter derive from discussions in the Ottoman Empire, and more specifically, the areas of present-day Turkey and Egypt,[5] two of the most important regions in the history of printing in the part of the world that today we call the Middle East. Even though the first sections of this chapter contain examples from the early and formative period of Islam, the great majority of examples date from the eighteenth and nineteenth centuries. Moreover, I will also briefly discuss the development and introduction of print technology in the Indian subcontinent and Central Asia in the eighteenth and nineteenth centuries. All in all, the chapter tries to determine whether the early Muslim '*ulama*' included in my study believed that the introduction of print technology had the potential to change the transmission of Islamic knowledge and challenge the established religious authorities. If so, in what ways? What kinds of pros and cons were identified and discussed in relation to the printing press by the '*ulama*'? For example, does the source material show that the religious authorities (that is, the '*ulama*') felt that they were being challenged by the new technique? If so, in what ways?

Before I try to answer these questions, it is essential to provide a general background to how religious knowledge was established, preserved and transmitted among the '*ulama*' prior to the print revolution. By highlighting the pre-printing epoch, I am not saying that all of these methods for transmitting knowledge and for establishing authority were forgotten and abandoned with the rise of new information and communication technologies. Although with the introduction of

---

4   On the lithographic printing techniques in the Middle East, see Messick 1997.

5   Cf., for example, Ayalon 1995.

print technology the oral transmission of knowledge was supported or combined with such technologies, they made oral communication and its methods for establishing authority easier to challenge.

Knowledge, memory and text

Before the printing press was introduced, 'knowledge', both secular and theological insights, was mainly transmitted orally and memorised by heart. Charles Hischkind argues, for example, that the authority and transmission of the Qur'an is based on a combination of hearing and listening. Religious authority interconnects and engages the ear, the heart and the voice, and it is not possible to apprehend the Qur'an through a single medium. This understanding makes, for example, a printed version of the holy text incomplete when compared to a recitation of the text.[6] In order to understand the Qur'an, many Muslims argue that the believer should observe, pronounce and hear the word of Allah. As part of his creation and divine plan, God has given man 'hearing' and 'sight', as clearly illustrated by Q 16:78:

> And God has brought you forth from your mothers' wombs knowing nothing-
> but He has endowed you with hearing, and sight, and minds, so that you might
> have cause to be grateful.

Like most religious communities, the early Muslim community based their knowledge and authority on oral transmission and memorisation.[7] From this point of view, it should come as no surprise that the introduction and development of printing created a new possibility to establish authority. Hence, the new technology harboured both possibilities as well as threats to the established order. Even though books had been produced long before printing, the ability to mass-produce books at a much lower cost had a tremendous effect on the book market. Printing obviously had a profound potential to transform society and change human consciousness of how authority was established. This represented a shift from a discourse of sounds to a discourse of text, that is, visual representation. Without exaggerating, print could easily be perceived as an attack on the very heart of how Muslims established religious and worldly authority. Even though this issue was much debated at the beginning of the eighteenth century – as we shall see in the following sections on the introduction of the printing press in the Ottoman Empire – it is also possible to find later examples. The reluctance to

---

6   Hirschkind 2003, p. 342.

7   The importance of oral tradition, memorisation and Islamic knowledge is also stressed by, for example, Eickelman 1978; Graham 1987; Nelson 2001; Weiss 1974, pp. 136–138.

accept printing is, for example, vividly illustrated in a much later discussion by the Moroccan theologian, Muhammad al-Siba'i (d. 1914), who writes:

> Printed books cause the abandonment of memorization, forgetting [Islamic] knowledge and diminishing a desire (among students and scholars) to pursue learning.[8]

A similar way of putting the argument is also found in the *Fatawa Deoband* collection of legal answers from India:

> It is essentially impossible to find a person who fulfils all the conditions required for a *mufti*. However, since the books on *hadith* and *fiqh*, duly compiled and classified, have been published in the modern age and since the state of memory is not the same as it used to be in the old days, when a scholar could recall millions of *hadith* in his mind … persons who have an aptitude for *fiqh* and *hadith*, who are skilled in the studies of the Qur'an and *sunna*, and who have studied religious sciences under the guidance of religious scholars in a regular manner of training and discipline, those who have a profound aptitude for legal problems may be entrusted with this responsibility.[9]

If the above-quoted sources are correct in their conclusions, the introduction of printing promoted the erudition of Islamic knowledge, and the memorisation of Islamic texts lost its former importance. According to the Moroccan Muhammad al-Siba'i, it was this technological development that was the driving factor for the changes in the society. However, in this interpretation, al-Siba'i neglects or downplays the social, cultural and economic changes that had occurred in Moroccan society with the impact of modernity. Without developing this argument, al-Siba'i is an example and illustration of how certain '*ulama*' could argue. It was the technology per se that had transformed society and challenged the established religious order. Even though this technologically driven argument is tempting, it is necessary to bring in other explanatory factors as well.[10]

---

8   Quoted in Abdulrazak 1990, p. 149.

9   Quoted from Masud 1984, p. 133.

10   However, al-Siba'i was not alone in his accusation against the technology. For example, in Charles Issawi's book, *The Fertile Crescent 1800–1914: A Documentary Economic History*, it is reported that some people in Aleppo, Syria, believed that the telegraph could transmit sounds and messages because there was 'an evil spirit dwelling in the wire'. The evil spirit was responsible for transmitting the message that was being sent via the telegraph. The critics argued that it was impossible for mankind to send a message from one point to another 'in the twinkling of an eye'. The miracle of the telegraph could only be explained by magic or evil spirits. See Issawi 1988, p. 87. Similar ways of putting the argument could also be found in a much later Islamic context, namely the introduction of the telephone (a topic that I will return to more thoroughly in a later chapter). For example, when the wireless telephone was introduced in the kingdom of Saudi Arabia, William A.

The explanation given by al-Siba'i is therefore not complete. In order to understand the impact of the new information and communication technologies, it is also necessary to consider social, economic and cultural changes in society. Printing made it easier, more efficient and more profitable to mass-produce texts, but it was also necessary to create an audience for the printed books.[11] Along with the introduction of a number of technological innovations (such as, for example, the steamship, factories and the telegraph),[12] novel education systems influenced by the British and French colonial powers were introduced from the early nineteenth century, which, among other things, produced growing literacy, but also new ways of thinking about the world.[13] The influence of the new technology is clearly illustrated by the following quotation from Roderic H. Davison and his analysis of the impact of the telegraph. He writes:

> The telegraph system produced in its first two or three decades a new bureaucracy, many telegraph stations dotted about the empire, a telegraph school, a telegraph factory, an inspection system strung out over thousands of kilometres, many new laws and regulations, international agreements, coordinated weather reports, speed and new pressure in diplomacy and decision-making, westernizing influences of individuals and techniques, and increased use of French, new words in Turkish, a Turkish Morse code, job opportunities for minority group members and for modernizing Turks, a vital adjunct to railroad operation, a boon for merchants, a tool for military planners and warriors, an a means of speedy news for newspapers. And, above all, the telegraph proved to be a powerful instrument of control in the hands of a centralizing government. The essence of the telegraph was the annihilation of distance, the divorce of communication from transportation, the emphasis on speed.[14]

The processes described by Davison fashioned an audience that, among other things, had the necessary means and qualities to consume and absorb information and knowledge related to a vast field of subjects. However, for the political and

---

Eddy reports that several of the '*ulama*' argued that it was *Shaytan* (Satan) or a *jinn* that was responsible for carrying the sound. See Eddy 1963.

11   A prerequisite for print technology was the manufacture of paper. Muslims had learned how to manufacture paper in the eight century, when they conquered Transoxiana and reached the Silk Road. According to Jonathan M. Bloom, paper was introduced in the region by Buddhist missionaries and merchants. The first Muslim paper mills were established in Baghdad in 762 CE. Even though paper was very important for the emerging 'Abbasid bureaucracy and for the development of the administration of the growing empire, the Qur'an was still copied on parchment codices until the end of the tenth century. Bloom 2006, pp. 592–593.

12   See, for example, Peters 1986.

13   For developments and reforms in the Ottoman Empire during the 19th century, see Şeker 2009, pp. 29–34.

14   Davison 1990, p. 155.

religious elite in power, the printing and the growing literacy could also become a problem. For example, with the printing of the Qur'an, the holy text of Islam could easily be circulated and spread among non-Muslims. Hence, it was perceived that the revelation from God could easily end up in 'indecent' localities and contexts. Within these milieus, it was believed that the Qur'an could, for example, be handled in 'improper' ways and without the respect it deserved, a topic I will return to in the last chapter.[15] This possibility was, of course, a problem for many Muslim '*ulama*', and it is evident that many arguments against printing were connected with this issue. For example, the printing of the Qur'an in the Middle East was delayed by these concerns, an Egyptian standard edition only being produced in 1923/1924.[16] For many of the '*ulama*' the printing press was perceived as a threat to both the Qur'an and religious authority. Again it is relevant to quote Charles Hirschkind, who argued:

> In its capacity to reproduce versions of the Qur'an in vast, seemingly infinite quantities, the printing press threatened to unleash the sacred text from the structure of discipline and authority that governed its social existence and ensured its ethical reception.[17]

Even though printing had an effect on society, it should be remembered that the region dominated by Muslim and Islamic traditions was not unique in its reaction to the introduction of the printing press. Similar debates also took place within the Western world, and Christian theologians raised similar objections to the printing press, such as the final document from the Fifth Lateran Council (1512–1517).

In this document – which is only one example – the new technology is associated with a number of problems. For example, printed books could include errors, but more importantly, they could also spread so-called heretical opinions that contradicted the official theology of the Catholic Church.

> That is why, to prevent what has been a healthy discovery for the glory of God, the advance of the faith, and the propagation of good skills, from being misused for the opposite purposes and becoming an obstacle to the salvation of Christians, we have judged that our care must be exercised over the printing of books, precisely so that thorns do not grow up with the good seed or poisons become mixed with medicines. /.../ We therefore establish and ordain that henceforth, for all future time, no one may dare to print or have printed any book or other writings of whatever kind in Rome or in any other cities and dioceses,

---

15   Hirschkind 2003, p. 343.

16   A detailed description of the history of the printing of the Qur'an is found in Albin 2004.

17   Hirschkind 2003, p. 343.

without the book or writings having first been closely examined, at Rome by our vicar and the master of the sacred places …[18]

Still the gathered members of the Council held printing in great esteem and praised the fact that more people could learn from the printed books.

> The skill of book-printing has been invented, or rather improved and perfected, with God's assistance, particularly in our time. Without doubt it has brought many benefits to men and women since, at small expense, it is possible to possess a great number of books. These permit minds to devote themselves very readily to scholarly studies.[19]

Like the *'ulama'*, the Catholic Church also tried its best to control print technology at the beginning of the sixteenth century. It should be remembered, however, that written texts were being produced within the realms of the Ottoman Empire long before the introduction of the printing press, that is, in the form of hand-copied manuscripts. But even though manuscripts were produced and copied by the *'ulama'* or the *qudat* (judges), this was an insecure, slow and expensive procedure.[20] Furthermore, a large number of manuscripts and copied books were also lost because of fire, social turmoil and natural causes. One pre-Ottoman example is the famous and mysterious library of al-Hakam al-Mustansir, the ruler of al-Andalus between 961 and 976. This library is described in Said al-Andalusi's *Kitab al-Tabaqat al-'umam* as follows:

> Toward the end of the first part of the fourth century, al-'Amir al-Hakam al-Mustansir bi-Allah ibn 'Abd al-Rahman al-Nasir li-Din Allah began his effort to support the sciences and befriend the scientists. He brought from Baghdad the best of their scientific works and their most valuable publications whether new or old. He began his activity during the reign of his father and continued this endeavour during the time when he was in power. His collection became equal to what the Banu 'Abbas were able to put together over a much longer period. This was possible only because of his great love for science, his eagerness to acquire the virtue associated with it, and his desire to imitate the sage kings.[21]

---

18   *Fifth Lateran Council (1512–1517)*, p. 633.

19   *Fifth Lateran Council (1512–1517)*, p. 632.

20   According to Reinhard Schulze, who has tried to calculate the difference in cost between a printed and a manuscript copy in the eighteenth-century Ottoman Empire, the discrepancy is striking. While the cost of one printed sheet was fixed at 1 para and sold for 1.5 para, giving a printed book an average cost of 5 piastres, in comparison a manuscript copy of the same text cost 100 to 500 piastres. Schulze 1997, p. 43.

21   Said al-Andalusi, *al-Tabaqat* p. 61.

al-Hakam al-Mustansir's library was, however, destroyed just a few years after his death. Only books dealing with language, grammar, poetry, history, medicine, tradition, *hadith* and other sciences accepted in al-Andalus at the time were preserved.[22] Despite this outcome, Said al-Andalusi gives a detailed and vivid picture of the intellectual milieu in al-Andalus. If his account is to be trusted, and it has been questioned by some scholars, his book is a description of how the bulk of Islamic knowledge was transmitted from Egypt, Syria and Iraq to the outermost regions in the *dar al-Islam*, that is, the territory conquered by Muslims from al-Andalus in the west to India in the east. In his *Kitab al-Tabaqat al-'umam*, Said al-Andalusi pictures the Muslim world as an integrated body embracing all the knowledge known to mankind. From this point of view, al-Andalus could be portrayed as an integrated and equal part of the rest of the Middle East, despite the fact that it was located far from the Muslim heartlands. Trade routes, roads, postal systems, pilgrimages and educational journeys (*rihla/talab al-'ilm*) in the Middle Ages could all be seen as early illustrations of the fact that globalisation is by no means a new phenomenon.

To preserve and establish theological authority and 'sound' knowledge, it was necessary for the Muslim community to develop methods and modalities for the communication and transmission of knowledge. Another important guarantee for the distribution and maintenance of a 'sound' knowledge (*'ilm* in Arabic) was the so-called *ijaza* licence, which was developed during the medieval period. *Ijaza* is, for example, the third of the eight methods of receiving the transmission of a *hadith*.

> It means in short the fact that an authorized guarantor of a text or of a whole book (his own work or a work received through a chain of transmitters going back to the first transmitter or to the author) gives a person the authorization to transmit it in his turn so that the person authorized can avail himself of this transmission.[23]

Still we should be careful when comparing the 'permission granted by one individual to represent a text or body of knowledge' (that is, an *ijaza* licence) with the Medieval Western system (*licentia*) that was developed in Europe. According to Michael Chamberlain and his study of knowledge and social practice in medieval Damascus, Syria, the *ijaza* as a form of 'qualification' had little to do with the fact that the student had studied at a *madrasa*. Instead, he argues:

> The ijaza was rather the sign of an authority that was transmitted within temporary social networks bound together through loyalties of love and services.

22   Said al-Andalusi, *al-Tabaqat* p. 61.
23   Vajda 1971, p. 1020.

This authority was acquired through an ijaza from another shaykh, who himself had acquired it through personal contact.[24]

Even though the function and ways of acquiring an *ijaza* are open to question, this principle is also closely related to the fundamental importance of oral transmission in Islamic history. An oral testimony, a *sama'* ('certificate of hearing'), is an important method of knowledge diffusion, a fact to which I return in the last chapter.[25] The focus on the transmission of knowledge and authoritative traditions were both highlighted by the canonisation of the *hadith* literature and the establishment of the law schools in Islam. The rise of the *madrasa*, the educational system, made it even more urgent to develop a system that could guarantee a sound and reliable transmission of knowledge, that is, from master to student. Two ways of solving this problem were to use the *ijaza* and *sama'* licence as safety guarantees. The 'licence' could answer important questions, such as 'under whom', 'when' and 'where' the sheikh had gained his knowledge about Islam. With the introduction of printing, it seems that many Muslims thought that this basis for the sound transmission of religious knowledge and authority was being threatened. However, before I explore various expressions of Muslim criticisms of print technology, it is first necessary to present in general terms the history of printing in the Middle East.

The introduction of the printing press

Compared with Europe, the Ottoman Empire was slow to adopt new information and communication technologies. For example, the printing press was only introduced in Istanbul at the beginning of the eighteenth century. Ibrahim Müteferriqa (*c.*1674–1754), spent, according to Michael Albin, more than a decade trying to persuade the Ottoman sultan and his sheikhs that the printing press was not a danger to Islamic culture.[26] Among other things, he wrote an essay entitled *Wesilet al-tiba'a*, on the usefulness of printing, in which he endeavoured to demonstrate that the Muslim community would prosper if print technology

---

24   Chamberlain 2002, p. 89.

25   Sellheim 1995, pp. 1019–1020. Cf. Sardar 2003, p. 97. On the theological importance of hearing and deafness in the Qur'an, see van Gelder 2002.

26   Albin 1995, p. 226. Cf. Berkes 1971, pp. 996–998. The establishment of the printing press in Istanbul and its printings were even noticed by two Swedish envoys, Edvard Carlson and Carl Fredrik von Höpken. See Carlson and Höpken 1735, pp. 21–24. The report by Carlson and Höpken also contains a list of thirteen books printed in Istanbul. In total, the press in Istanbul printed seventeen books on different subjects from 31 January 1729 to 17 February 1741. Cf. Rohnström 1988. The history of printing during the eighteenth century in Ottoman Istanbul is thoroughly described and documented by Babinger 1919.

were to be accepted.[27] According to Müteferriqa, the Muslim community was endangered by the fact that a large bulk of Islamic knowledge had been destroyed during periods of turbulence and decay. Examples of this given by Müteferriqa included the anarchy that followed the fall of al-Andalus and the Mongol invasion that put an end to the 'Abbasid dynasty in 656/1258.[28] Another problem, according to him, was the fact that European printers were publishing oriental books, that is, books printed in the Arabic, Turkish and Persian alphabets, with a low standard of printing.[29] First, the books produced in Europe contained many errors and misprints.[30] For example, the non-Muslim printers who printed the Qur'an in Venice in the 1530s and in Hamburg in 1694 had only a limited knowledge of Arabic. Consequently, they produced copies of low quality with a lot of errors.[31] Secondly, the distribution and production of printed books was in the hands of the Europeans, a fact that Müteferriqa strongly disliked.[32] To raise the general intellectual level in the Muslim community and to put an end to the fact that non-Muslim Europeans were translating and printing the Qur'an it was, according to Müteferriqa, necessary to support the introduction of the printing press.

> If this point is studied intensely, with the aim of one's becoming learned in the goodness of religion and the merits of states, then these books, written as if on a tablet created by strength and purpose from emerald, ruby, gold, and silver, are a means for the religion and state of Islam to continue the glory of the state and

---

27   This text was printed together with Ahmed III's ferman (*Khatt-i humajun*) and Mufti 'Abdallah Efendi's *fatwa* on the installation of the printing office and the approvals (*taqarid*) of several '*ulama*' in the first book printed by Ibrahim Müteferriqa. Rohnström 1988, p. 125.

28   *The Firman of Ahmed III*, p. 284 (English translation) and *Wesilet al-tiba'a*, p. 288 (English translation).

29   *The Firman of Ahmed III*, p. 284 (English translation) and *Wesilet al-tiba'a*, p. 291 (English translation).

30   However, if Angela Nauvoo's conclusion is correct, that the printing of the Qur'an in Venice was made for export to the Ottoman Empire, the fear expressed by Müteferriqa is exaggerated. Mahdi 1995, pp. 1–4. A discussion of the printing houses that printed Arabic and Oriental books in Europe from the sixteenth to nineteenth centuries is, for example, found in Pedersen 1946, pp. 131–133. A later, but still striking example of the Arab aversion towards Arabic texts printed by Europeans is found in the Egyptian historian 'Abd al-Rahman al-Jabarti's book *Tarikh muddat al-Faransis bi-Misr*. When Napoleon arrived in Egypt in 1798, he handed over a printed proclamation prepared by French orientalists to the Egyptians. al-Jabarti responded by copying the text by hand and by listing all the printing and grammatical errors in the text. He concludes by saying: 'Here is an explanation of the incoherent words and vulgar constructions which he put into this miserable letter', al-Jabarti, *Tarikh muddat al-Faransis bi-Misr*, Arabic text p. 10/English translation p. 42. See also Mitchell 1991, p. 133, and Sardar 2003, p. 101. On al-Jabarti's reaction and response to Western sciences in Egypt, see Levingston 1997.

31   Bobzin 1993 and Bobzin 2002, p. 154.

32   This information is taken from Bobzin 2002, p. 154.

the good ordering of the important affairs of the community. Books are also a tool for perfecting the nation and the state, a method of increasing the majesty of the empire, and of becoming the protector and preserver, until the last day, of arts and sciences and recorded events from the miscalculations of man. And these writings create a solidarity in the community against factions and disorder, and the laws and regulations preserve the good order of the community from change and innovations. /.../ This [printing of books] is a noble profession and beautiful calling.[33]

According to Ibrahim Müteferriqa there are at least 10 benefits for Muslims and the Ottoman sultan in accepting and introducing printing:

1. It 'answers the needs of the people for Islamic books' and 'creates tremendous educational benefits'.
2. 'The work of the noble compilers and interpreters will become a means of renewal and restoration.' The knowledge of the authors will be more easily disseminated to the people.
3. Printed books are more 'secure' to use because they do not contain any passages that have been destroyed by damp, water or dryness.
4. Printed books become items of commerce and can boost the economy. Furthermore, they are cheap, and both rich and poor students can afford education.
5. Through printing, it is easier to include indexes, tables and summaries that will make the books more user-friendly.
6. The price of books will fall, and more people will be able to afford them. This process will also help the rural population receive education.
7. The printing of books will also be of great importance for the glory and power of the Ottoman Empire.
8. The printing of books is an important part of the Islamic *jihad*.
9. It is important that Muslims produce and print their own books in Arabic, Persian and Turkish. The books printed by Europeans are 'full of misspellings and mistakes, and the letter and lines are not easily read'.
10. 'Printing is a means to enliven and make happy the Muslims' all around the globe.[34]

Finally, in 1727, Sultan Ahmed III was persuaded to issue a *firman*, or royal decree, to Sa'id Efendi and Ibrahim Müteferriqa allowing them to open a printing house in Istanbul using Arabic script.[35] The authorisation to print books was, however, limited and restricted to secular and practical books. Because of

---

33   *Wesilet al-tiba'a*, pp. 286–287.

34   The list of the ten benefits of printing is taken from *The Firman of Ahmed III*, pp. 285–287.

35   Ibrahim Müteferriqa's press operated between 1729 and 1742.

this decree, they were not allowed to print books that dealt with Islamic theology (that is, the Qur'an, *hadith*, *tafsir*).[36] Permission was limited to the printing of 'dictionaries, history books, medical books, astronomy and geography books, travelogues and books about logic'.[37] Neither in the *firman*, nor in the writings of Müteferriqa, is any explanation or reason given for the prohibition. Müteferriqa's printing press was active between 1727 and 1741 and published exclusively 'secular' texts.[38] One detailed account of this printing house dating back to 20 July 1735, is found in the report by the Swedish diplomat Edvard Carlson.

However, to give printing Islamic authority and to legitimise the use of the printing press, the *shaykh al-Islam*, the 'head of all Muslims' during the Ottoman era, issued a *fatwa* on the usefulness of printing.[39] Following the general pattern for a *fatwa*, a *mustafti* asked a question, and the *mufti*, in this case Shaykh Mevlana Abdallah, who functioned as the *Shaykh al-Islam* at that time, gave his authoritative answer.

> Question: If Zeid undertakes to imitate the characters of handwritten books, such as dictionaries, treatises on logic, philosophy, astronomy and other scientific works, by forging letters, making type and printing books conforming absolutely to handwritten models, is he entitled to legal authorization?

> Response: God knows best. When a person who understands the art of the press has the talent to cast letters and make type for printing manuscripts correctly and exactly; when his operation offers great advantages such as clarity of work, the ability to pull a great number of copies, and the low price at which anyone may acquire it; if one can propose persons greatly learned in literature to correct the proofs, the printer cannot but be favoured in his enterprise, which is the most beautiful and praiseworthy.[40]

This *fatwa* was also printed together with the Sultan's decision to support the first official printing house, that is, the first printing press to use movable type in the Arabic/Turkish alphabet, in Istanbul. The first books that were printed by Muslims in the Ottoman Empire in February 1729 were also accompanied by the above

---

36   *The Firman of Ahmed III*, p. 285. According to Bobzin, the Oriental printings of the Qur'an differ significantly from those printed in Europe. He writes: 'they are far more strongly indebted to manuscript models. Indeed, generally up to the present day they have not been set in movable type and then printed, but produced by means of other printing processes, such as photo-mechanical reproductions, that more strongly emphasises the hand-written character of the Koran.' Bobzin 2002, p. 167.

37   *The Firman of Ahmed III*, p. 285.

38   Kreiser 2001, p. 16.

39   On this office, see Repp 1997.

40   Quoted in Skovgaard-Petersen 1997a, p. 73.

named *fatwa*[41] and contained a list of approvals (*taqarid*) of several '*ulama*' who supported and guaranteed the quality of the printed books. In the *firman* of Ahmed III, a number of learned individuals are also listed as proof-readers.

> Copies will be printed of dictionaries, and books about logic, astronomy and similar subjects, and so that the printed books will be free from printing mistakes, the wise, respected and meritorious religious scholar specializing in Islamic Law, the excellent *Kazi* of Istanbul, Mevlana İshak, and Selaniki's *Kazi*, Mevlana Sahib, and Ghalata's *Kazi*, Mevlana Asad, may their merits be increased, and from the illustrious religious orders, the pillar of the righteous religious scholars, the Şeyh of the Kasim Paşa Mevlevihane, Mevlana Musa, may his wisdom and knowledge increase, will oversee the proof-reading.[42]

Even though Ibrahim Müteferriqa's printing press is often presented as the first 'Muslim press', printing as a method was known among Muslims long before 1728. For example, both Bayezid II (ruled 1481–1512) and Selim I had forbidden printing with Arabic characters in the Ottoman Empire as early as 1485 and a second time in 1515.[43] But evidently the prohibition did not apply to Arab Christians, Jews, Armenians and other non-Muslim subjects who lived within the borders of the Ottoman Empire.[44] And after the fall of Granada in 1492, a Jewish printing press was also started in Istanbul.[45] The exact date of this press is debated, but nonetheless it is evidence that print technology was known within the borders of the Ottoman Empire prior to the eighteenth century.[46] But until this century, books were primarily printed by Christians and the authorities of the Eastern Churches.[47] During the seventeenth and eighteenth centuries, small but important printing houses were also set up by Christians in the Ottoman Empire.[48] Also in Persia it is reported that two presses were functioning during the seventeenth century (one in Isfahan and one in Julfa).[49]

---

41   Rohnström 1988, p. 125. According to Babinger, Müteferriqa printed in total 17 books in 23 volumes with a print run of 12,500. Babinger 1919, p. 18.

42   *The firman of Ahmed III*, p. 285.

43   Oman 1991, p. 795.

44   Glass and Roper 2002, p. 177.

45   On Jewish printing houses in Constantinople and Salonika, see Tamari 2001.

46   Cf. Albin 2004.

47   Lewis 1996, p. 23. Cf. Babinger 1919, p. 7.

48   Günay Alpay Kut 1991, pp. 799–800. According to Carsten Walbiner, Aleppo in Syria was the cradle of Arabic printing in the East due to the activities of the Greek Orthodox Church and the Maronities. In 1733 'Abdallah Zakhir opened a printing press in the monastery of St John in al-Shuwayr, Lebanon, which was active from 1733 till 1899 and in all printed 33 titles and 36 reprints. Walbiner 2001, pp. 11–12.

49   Floor 1980.

Block printing

Besides the printing houses discussed in the section above, it should also be noted that so-called xylography or block printing (*tarsh* in Arabic) was already known in the Middle East from the ninth or tenth centuries.[50] For example, Richard W. Bulliet argues convincingly from a poem by Abu Dulaf al-Khazraji that block printing was in use during the tenth century. This writer was a Persian poet and vagabond who frequented the Buyid princes.[51] He was also a member of the so-called Banu Sasan, the Islamic underworld of beggars, tricksters and performers described by C.E. Bosworth. According to Bulliet's interpretation, the following quotation from Abu Dulaf al-Khazraji demonstrates both the existence of block printing and his belonging to the Islamic underworld:

> 'Among us [the Banu Sasan], without publicity (*jahr*) or boasting (*khart*), is the engraver of *tarsh* [variant in two manuscripts *tars*].' The engraver of *tarsh* is he who engraves (*yahfiru*) moulds (*qawalib*, sing. *qalib*) for amulets (*ta'awidh*, sing. *ta'widh*). People who are illiterate and cannot write buy them from him. The seller keeps back (*hafiza*) the design (*naqsh*) which is on it [the *tarsh*] so that he exhausts his supply of amulets on the common people (*nas*) and makes them believe that he wrote them. The mould is called the *tarsh* [variant in two manuscripts *tars*].[52]

Even though block printing existed long before the printing press was introduced in Istanbul, it is clear that this technique had a limited impact. It seems also as if the *tarsh* printing was associated with something that had been destroyed and had been imperfect. To produce a text by printing was, at least according to the poem above, perceived as something negative or even 'false'. As noted in the introduction to this chapter, a message transmitted orally or copied by hand was viewed as more reliable and more perfect than a mechanically produced copy.[53] However, the block printing technique did not disappear because of some kind of religious resistance to printing. According to Bulliet, the block print vanished

---

50 On this technology, Juttan Bernard writes: 'Block printing was introduced in China as early as the first millennium CE, greatly simplifying the work of printing and copying. Here was a means of production that not only offered enormous economy, but also made the first 'mass editions' possible' Bernard 2007, p. 1195. As Karl Schaefer points out, it is not clear whether the Arabic word *tarsh* was the proper term for block-printing. Schaefter 2002.

51 This dynasty originated from the regions of the Caspian Sea and lasted 945–1057. See Turner and Hower 2006.

52 Bulliet 1987, p. 430. It should be noted that Bosworth's translation and interpretation of the same text is different from Bulliet's. Cf. Bosworth 1976, p. 201. The Arabic text of Abu Dulaf al-Khazraji is printed in Bosworth 1976, p. 18.

53 Cf. the earlier discussion about Plato and the written word.

because the clientele of the Banu Sasan disappeared with the rise of the Sufi orders.[54]

Even though Bulliet's outline of the history of block-printing in the regions dominated by Muslim and Islamic traditions is attractive, it is important to stress that his conclusions have been debated. A more source-critical and cautious evaluation, for example, has been provided by Karl Schaeffer, who writes:

> An understanding of the origin, development and ultimate demise of the block-printing art in mediaeval Islam is complicated by several considerations. First, with one known exception, none of the block-prints can be reliably dated. The only clues to their age come from relevant archaeological data – that is, the presence of datable objects in the same location in which the *tarse*s were found – and the style of script used in the text of the amulet. Texts in which the older *Kufi* script is used are assumed to be of greater antiquity. Second, there is almost no reference made to such a craft in any of the contemporary Arabic historical texts. What mention does appear is often ambiguous, even cryptic in nature. There are a few seductive allusions to something which might be interpreted to be printing, but to date no clear description of block printing has been found in mediaeval textual sources. Third, as with many handwritten documents of similar vintage, both the quality of the creator's work and the ravages of time have influenced the legibility of many of the texts.[55]

Hence, whether Bulliet's suggestion can be substantiated or not is beyond the scope of my investigation, and I leave this problem unanswered.

The printing press outside Istanbul

If we return to the early history of printing in the Ottoman Empire discussed above, it is clear that the printing press was soon transmitted to other parts of the Middle East. This development was related to the fact that the Sultan had accepted printing. But the introduction was also closely related to the rise of the colonial system. For example, with the arrival of Napoleon Bonaparte in Egypt in 1798, the printing press with movable types was introduced to an Egyptian readership. The aim of this printing press was to make it easier to circulate information about and among the French administrators and to raise the moral of the soldiers.[56] The French printing house, *Imprimerie Orientale et Française*, that was opened in 1799 was, however, often looked upon with great scepticism and mistrust by

---

54 Bulliet 1987, p. 438.

55 Schaeffer 2002, pp. 124–125.

56 A descriptive history of the establishment of the French printing press in Egypt is to be found in Bustani 1986.

the Egyptians as a symbol of the colonial power. For example, this press was deliberately demolished by an angry mob in the 1800 revolt that erupted in Cairo.[57]

Even though the French press was destroyed in 1800, the printing press was soon re-introduced in Egypt.[58] In 1819–1820 the famous Egyptian Bulak press (*Matba'at Bulaq*) was opened. This printing house was run by the Syrian Niqula al-Masabiki (d. 1830), who had learnt the art of printing in Italy.[59] This press became an essential tool in the transformation and development of Egypt, and it played a key role in the modernisation process that was launched by Muhammad 'Ali Pasha (ruled 1805–1848).[60] Irrespective of the fact that many '*ulama*' in Egypt viewed the printing press as a negative innovation (*bid'a*) and considered it reprehensible (*makruh*) or even forbidden (*haram*) to use 'metal letters or to apply heavy pressure in printing the name of God', Muhammad 'Ali introduced and supported printing.[61] For this leader, the printing press was perceived as an essential tool for modernisation and reform.[62] The technological innovation developed and refined in the West was the epitome of modernity and prosperity. Consequently, the printing of books and journals was a decisive instrument in the modernisation of the society and its governmental system.[63]

However, publication of Husayn al-Marsafi's (1815–1890) *Risalat al-Kalim al-thaman* (Essay of Eight Words) illustrates well that debate and criticism of the printing press was far from over.[64] Although al-Marsafi supported modernisation and the development of an education system – he is even presented as one of the forefathers of the Arabic renaissance (*al-nahda*),which had been initiated by the arrival of the British colonial authorities – he was very sceptical of the mass production of texts. Hence, he was a strong critic of the 'uncontrolled spread of printing', which he believed would erode and damage the authority of the religious

---

57 Glass and Roper 2002, p. 183.

58 Salaheddine Bustani writes: 'During the second revolt in Cairo (March 1800) the printing plants were attacked by rioting mobs. This resulted in serious head injuries for Marchel, Desgenettes and death for some employees and workers.' Bustani 1986, p. 11.

59 During this period, Egypt had extensive contracts and relations with Italy. Italian was, for example, the first foreign language taught to officer cadets in the early Citadel school erected by Muhammad 'Ali, and the first Egyptian students sent abroad in 1809 and 1813 were sent to Leghorn, Milan, Florence and Rome to learn such trades as printing, letter-making and shipbuilding. The first book printed by the *Bulaq* press was an Italian-Arabic dictionary prepared by Father Rafael Zakhur. Vatikiotis 1991, p. 95.

60 Oman 1991, pp. 797–798. Cf. Hammam 1951, p. 156, and Glass and Roper 2002, p. 183. On the relationship between printing and the translation of scientific works from Western languages into Arabic, see Heyworth-Dunne 1940.

61 Albin 2004, p. 270.

62 Ayalon 1995, p. 16, and Hammam 1951, p. 156.

63 Glass and Roper 2002, p. 183, and Mowlana 1995a, p. 302.

64 Husayn al-Marsafi had earned his degree from the al-Azhar university in Cairo and in 1872 was appointed Professor of Arabic Linguistics at the *Dar al-'Ulum*. See Delanoue 1991, p. 602.

leaders.[65] With printing, the oral transmission of religious knowledge decayed. For him, to put it in the words of Timothy Mitchell, 'the only way to read a text and retain its uncertain authority was to hear it read aloud, phrase by phrase, by one who had already mastered it, and to repeat and discuss it with such a master'.[66] This conclusion can partly be explained by the fact that al-Marsafi had been blind since birth, but he was also a strong believer in the traditional Islamic way of transmitting and securing Islamic knowledge and learning.

As al-Marsafi illustrates, the traditional educational system of Islam, the *madrasa*, was placed under great pressure by the arrival of the British and French colonial systems. The traditional educational system was from now on downgraded by both Muslims and Europeans. As a result, European-style institutions for education were set up all over the Muslim world from the nineteenth century onwards. The establishment of new schools was also preferred by a growing number of Muslims, especially by members of the more privileged groups. This process naturally had a profound effect on both Muslim society and the control of the traditional educational system, the classical system of the mosque and the *madrasa*.[67] With these changes, it seems that the oral transmission of Islamic knowledge was put under heavy pressure and the traditional schools of Qur'anic instructions became more and more unpopular. Even the prestigious al-Azhar University in Egypt was forced to abandon its age-old policy of requiring complete memorisation of the Qur'an as a pre-requisite for admission.[68]

Islam and printing

Most printing presses were introduced and set up in the Ottoman Empire and the Middle East during the nineteenth century, that is, almost 500 years after Johannes Gutenberg started his press in Germany. Why was this the case? According to Jakob Skovgaard-Petersen, resistance to the printing press is a complex phenomenon with different and often diverging opinions on the issue. The answer to the question of why Muslims were more sceptical of the introduction of the printing press than Christians in the West should therefore not only be viewed in relation to the opinions of the '*ulama*'. Although the '*ulama*' have often been portrayed as the major obstacle,[69] the answer to the question of why the printing press was not introduced earlier is complex.

As I have tried to demonstrate earlier in this chapter, the regions dominated by Muslim and Islamic traditions could generally be described as having oral literary traditions. For example, it is often stressed that the revelation of God

---

65 Mitchell 1991, p. 132.
66 Mitchell 1991, p. 133. See also Sardar 2003, p. 101.
67 Eickelman 1978, pp. 487–488. Cf. Abdulrazak 1990.
68 Weiss 1974, p. 136.
69 This opinion is, for example, clearly expressed by Sardar 2003, p. 101.

was transmitted orally to the Prophet Muhammad, because of this fact it was not necessary, or dangerous to write down or print the holy text.[70] This opinion is, for example, described by Edward William Lane in his classic work, *The Manners and Customs of the Modern Egyptians*. According to Lane, many Muslims have had problems with the printing of books because they feared that the ink or the paper could be polluted.[71] It was also believed that the contamination could be transmitted from the printing press to the holy books and damage the theological message of Islam. This was a serious problem, especially since most if not all books on Islam printed by Muslims contained (and still contain) the holy invocation ('*Bismillah al-rahman al-rahim*'). Lane summarises the problem by saying:

> They [i.e., the Muslims] have scarcely a book (I do not remember to have seen one) that does not contain the name of God: it is a rule among them to commence every book with the words, 'In the name of God, the Compassionate, the Merciful,' and to begin the preface or introduction by praising God, and blessing the Prophet; and they fear some impurity might be contracted by the ink that is applied to the name of the Deity, in the process of printing, or by the paper to be impressed with that sacred name, and perhaps with the words from the Qur'an. They fear, also, that their books, becoming cheap by being printed, would fall into the hands of the infidels; and are much shocked at the idea of using a brush composed of hogs' hair (which was at first done here) to apply the ink to the name, and often to the words, of God.[72]

According to this opinion, printing was perceived as something dangerous that would destroy, or at least corrupt, the holiness of the Qur'an or the words of the Prophet Muhammad. Consequently, it was forbidden (*haram*) to print the holy Qur'an.[73] In this view, 'true' Muslims do not need books other than the Qur'an; the words of God as transmitted via Gabriel (*Jibril*) to the Prophet Muhammad are more than enough. And when it is forbidden to reproduce the Qur'an by printing, Muslims should of course avoid all printed books. From a general Muslim point of view, the Qur'an should be the main work to be recited. This emphasis is clearly indicated by the meaning of the word Qur'an, which simply means 'to recite, read aloud'.[74] This understanding also explains why all Muslims should learn to memorise the holy text by heart. The Qur'an is essentially a book that one should listen to or recite aloud.[75]

Besides the theological arguments listed above, the resistance to print technology can also be linked to practical and economic considerations. For

---

70   Cf., for example, Albin 2004. Cf., also Plato, *Phaedrus*, p. 69.
71   Cf. Albin 2004, p. 270 and Carter 1943, p. 213.
72   Lane 1908, p. 289. Cf. p. 288.
73   Cf. Albin 2004, p. 270.
74   Cf. Kassis 1983, pp. 912–913.
75   Cf. Graham 1987, pp. 79–115.

example, many calligraphers or copyists were most likely afraid of losing their jobs when this more efficient technology was introduced.[76] There are also indications in the sources that the guild of calligraphers (*warraq*, plural *warraqun*) had a strong position in, for example, Istanbul during the eighteenth century.[77] The resistance of the copyists is described in the correspondence between James Mario Matra (1746–1820), who was secretary to the British Embassy in Istanbul and British consul in Tangier, and Sir Joseph Banks (1743–1808), who was a British botanist and patron of science. In one of his letters to Banks, Matra discusses the possibility of reviving the Turkish printing press. He is here referring to the fact that Ibrahim Müteferriqa's printing press had been closed in 1742. According to Matra, it was vital for the Turks to reopen the printing press in order to become modern. However, in his correspondence, Banks explains why the first press had been abolished:

> A Press had been set up here about sixty years ago in the turbulent reign of Achmet 3d but those who maintained themselves by copying Books, apprehending with reason that their trade would be totally ruined, were so loud in their clamours as to alarm the Seragli, and as they were supported by a seditious Corps of Janizarys, the Sultan apprehending what really did after happen, that as mounted the throne by one insurrection, he might be tumbled from it by another, gave way to their complaints, and suppressed the Press, before anything better than the Koran, Sunna, and some trifling books of mathematics had been struck off.[78]

Although the information is wrong – the Qur'an was, for example, not printed by Müteferriqa – it is clear that the mass production of texts had had an effect on the power structure of Ottoman society.[79] For example, the introduction of the printing press had highlighted the question of authority and the distribution of power. It seems that the new information and communication technology was perceived as a potential threat to the old power structure, that is, the '*ulama*' class.[80] However, according to Jakob Skovgaard-Petersen, it is also possible to find members of the '*ulama*' who supported the use of the new technology.[81] For example, Barbara

---

76   Cf. Rohnström 1988, p. 122. Cf. Babinger 1919, p. 18.

77   Babinger 1919. The history and rise of the Islamic guilds is complex, and I cannot discuss it at length here. It is, however, interesting to note that the guild system was also challenged by the arrival of the colonial powers. Bernard Lewis writes: 'All these organisations, which have survived almost without change into the nineteenth and sometimes even the twentieth century, have not been able to resist the shock of the European invasion. Everywhere in the Muslim lands the old forms of production are giving way to new ones, and inevitably the old guilds are falling to pieces. Often they are transformed into trade unions (*naqabat*) of the European type.' Lewis 1937, p. 35.

78   Quotation in Clogg 1979, p. 68.

79   Cf. Rohnström 1988.

80   Cf., for example Abdulrazak 1990, pp. 151–152.

81   Skovgaard-Petersen 1997a, pp. 77–78. Cf. Mandaville 2001, p. 176.

Metcalf's and Francis Robinson's research on Muslims in the Indian subcontinent and Central Asia demonstrated that some of the '*ulama*' were actually supporters of the first printing presses and publishing houses.[82] The same development has also been observed by Adeeb Khalid for Tsarist Central Asia and by Fawzi A. Abdulrazak for Morocco.[83] However, support for printing in the latter country was also closely related to the fact that the Sultan and the state had decided to approve the new technology. If the '*ulama*' wanted to continue to enjoy an influential position and stay in power, they had no option but to accept the introduction of the printing press.[84]

Other reasons why some Muslim '*ulama*' were reluctant to accept early print technology seems to be related to cultural and artistic norms and values. For example, Brinkley Messick has demonstrated that handwritten manuscripts were more highly appreciated than printed texts in the Yemeni highlands. In this case, the aversion to printed books could be explained by the simple fact that the first printing presses had great problems in manufacturing Arabic characters of good quality. From an artistic point of view, it was therefore easier for the Yemeni community to accept lithographic printing,[85] which, according to Messick, preserved the artistic feelings associated with handwritten or copied texts to a higher degree. In contrast to the machine-produced text, the lithography left the impression that the product had been copied, even though it was mass produced.[86] But this explanation is questioned by Klaus Kreiser and his analysis of the development of the first printing house in Istanbul at the beginning of the eighteenth century. According to Kreiser, the early printing industry in the Ottoman capital was developed in close cooperation with representatives from the copyist craft. It should also be stressed that the first printed book resembles in many ways the work of the copyists. For example, the books printed by Ibrahim Müteferriqa were more or less designed in the same way as a classical manuscript and used the same leather bindings as the copyists did.[87] From this point of view, the introduction of the printing press in the Ottoman Empire did not erode the traditional occupation associated with the guild of manuscript copyists. On the contrary, it could even be argued that the press created new possibilities for the best copyist. At this point in time, the work of the most refined copyist became a true art form, and their works could now be measured and compared with mechanically and mass-produced books.[88] For Abdulrazak, whom we discussed above in relation to developments in Morocco, it is also doubtful that the early print technology was seen as a real threat to the

---

82 Metcalf 1982, pp. 198–210, and Robinson 1993.

83 Khalid 1994, p. 190 and Abdulrazak 1990, pp. 148–149.

84 Abdulrazak 1990, p. 149.

85 Messick 1997, pp. 158–176. Cf. Pedersen 1946, p. 138.

86 On the difference between lithographic and typographic printing, see Messick 1997, p. 168 and Bobzin 2002, p. 167.

87 Kreiser 2001, p. 14.

88 Skovgaard-Petersen 1997a, pp. 52–53.

guild of copyists. As long as the technology was primitive and rather expensive, it raised few problems for the '*ulama*'.[89] Nonetheless it should be stressed that the introduction of the printing press and the development of the educational system gave rise to a new market for books and journals, and for the '*ulama*' who supported the printing or lithographic press, the technology could also be used to defend and spread Islam. For example, the new technology could be used as an apologetical tool protecting Islam against Western influences, Christian missionaries, colonialism and imperialism.[90]

The social impact of printing

An inevitable side-effect of the introduction of the new print technology was that the power position of the religious elite was broken.[91] Even though this was a slow development that included a number of complex processes, it is clear that the mass production of texts and the reform of the educational system, which had a strong effect on overall literacy levels in the region we today call the Middle East, changed the conditions for the transmission of Islamic knowledge and the establishment of religious authority.[92] In Mecca between 1884 and 1885, the Dutch orientalist Christiaan Snouck Hurgronje noted and reported how the educational methods for acquiring Islamic knowledge had been changed with the introduction of printing:

> All students now bring to lecture printed copies of the text which is being treated, which circumstance has entirely changed the mode of instruction. Formerly the teacher had first to dictate the text, in the margin of which the students then noted down his glosses. Now, on the contrary, the student notes down only a few oral remarks (*taqarir*) of the professor, and often has nothing to write at all.[93]

As clearly illustrated by Snouck Hurgronje's quotation above, the introduction of printing in the countries dominated by Muslim and Islamic traditions made the Islamic education system and its pedagogy more similar to the nineteenth-century way of organising education in the West.

Slowly, it became more rewarding to hold a doctoral degree from a Western university than to have a similar degree from an Islamic educational institution. Naturally this challenge had a deep impact on the transmission and preservation of Islamic knowledge. For instance, during the reign of Muhammad 'Ali, al-Azhar

---

89   Abdulrazak 1990, p. 149.

90   Cf. Hirschkind 2003, p. 343; Robinson 1993, pp. 242–243; and Abdulrazak 1990, p. 149.

91   Mandaville 2001, p. 177.

92   Cf. Eickelman 1978.

93   Snouck Hurgronje 1970, p. 192.

University in Egypt became affected and influenced by the increasing contact with the West. Between 1871 and 1872, Khedive Isma'il (ruled 1863–1880) tried to change the curriculum in al-Azhar to make this Islamic university more like a Western university. In resembling other European universities, al-Azhar was to have employed professors granting diplomas and degrees (*'alimiya*).[94] These reforms were strongly opposed by several individuals at al-Azhar, and most of these changes were never imposed,[95] but new reforms were soon to be inaugurated. For example, the sheikh of al-Azhar became closely affiliated to the Egyptian state in 1895. From now on he was recognised as the head of all Egyptian *'ulama'*. Because of this change, it became easier to impose new reforms in 1908 and 1911. In sum, these reforms transformed al-Azhar into a modern institution resembling most contemporary Western universities, with a centralised administration and a leadership that was in charge of a nationwide Islamic educational system.[96]

Even though many of the administrative and educational reforms were questioned by the religious elite, the changes imposed from the end of the nineteenth century gave rise to new ways of understanding and debating Islamic theology. According to Jalal al-Din al-Afghani (1839–1897), Muhammad 'Abduh (1849–1905)[97] and Muhammad Rashid Rida (1865–1935),[98] for example, it was necessary for all Muslims to respond to the challenges posed by modernity and imperialism. Although 'Abduh had earned his first training and education at al-Azhar, he was strongly opposed to what he called the harmful effects of *taqlid* (adherence to tradition). For 'Abduh, it was necessary to liberate Islam from the mentality of *taqlid* and return to what was believed to be an authentic way of interpreting Islam.[99] With the help of reason and *ijtihad* (independent judgement) it was, according to him, possible to find authoritative and new ways of letting 'God be God'. For 'Abduh it was irrational not to listen to the interests (*maslaha*) of the community and embrace scientific developments in the form of new scientific discoveries and innovations.[100] From this point of view, 'Abduh, together with al-Afghani and Rashid Rida, was one of the leading figures in Islamic modernism and the early Salafiyya movement, that is, those who wanted to go back to the ways of Muhammad's early followers.

---

94   Skovgaard-Petersen 1997a, p. 45.

95   Cf. Zettersteen 1914, p. 12. A description of the history of al-Azhar and its role as an Islamic institution for education can be found in, for example, Jomier 1960; Skovgaard-Petersen 1997a and Zeghal 2007.

96   Skovgaard-Petersen 1997a, p. 46.

97   For 'Abduh, see Cragg 1995, pp. 11–12.

98   For Rashid Rida, see Shahin 1995, pp. 410–412.

99   A description of the 'old' educational system of al-Azhar can be found in Skovgaard-Petersen 1997a, pp. 47–51.

100   'Abduh's support for science is, for example, manifest in his *Risalat al-tawhid*, English translation by Musahad and Cragg 1980, pp. 48–49.

This movement [that is, the *salafiyya*], provoked by the stagnant and vulnerable conditions of the Muslims, sought to reinvigorate Islam; it stressed the need for the exercise of reason and the adoption of modern natural science, for agitation against tyranny and despotism and resistance to foreign domination, and the promotion of Muslim solidarity.[101]

The ideas of 'Abduh played a vital role in the development of modern Egypt. His ideas were of special importance during his last six years, when he functioned as the grand *mufti* of Egypt. But the ideas of al-Afghani, 'Abduh and Rashid Rida were also important for another reason. Their books, articles and theological answers were, for example, mass-produced, presented and distributed to a large audience outside the realm of the *'ulama'*. With the help of influential journals, such as, al-Manar ('Lighthouse') and *al-'urwah al-wuthqa* ('The Strongest Link', that is, the Qur'an), the ideas of the reformists reached a much larger audience.[102] For example, the latter journal was published by al-Afghani and 'Abduh in Paris in 1884 and was distributed free among Muslims. According to Nikki R. Keddie, this newspaper was most likely subsidised by an English Arabophile and poet, Wilfrid Scawen Blunt (1840–1922). Even though the *al-'urwah al-wuthqa* was only published for one year, it was important in spreading the ideas of Islamic modernism, especially the idea of Pan-Islamism and anti-imperialism/colonialism.[103]

For these Muslim modernists and reformers, the press and print technology presented no problems, but rather provided a solution. For example, in one of the first issues of *al-Manar*, the editor Rashid Rida stated that the press had three aims: ta'lim, khataba wa ihtisab: to teach, to preach and to 'promote good and forbid evil'.[104] The press should therefore serve the whole *umma* and show the Muslim community the road to salvation, prosperity and freedom from Europe.[105] From this point of view, I am inclined to follow Jacob Skovgaard-Petersen and Reinhard Schulze, who argue that the establishment of the early press separated the 'old' *'ulama'* from the new Muslim intellectuals that dominated Egypt during the nineteenth and twentieth centuries.[106] Contrary to the large number of *'ulama'* who rejected the printing press, the new Muslim intellectuals embraced the technology and put it effectively to use for their own interpretations and political agendas.[107] This could be seen as one of the first examples of how the new information

---

101   Shahin 1995, p. 410.
102   Cf., for example, Ayalon 1995, p. 49 and pp. 54–55. See also Bæk Simonsen 2008, p. 326. On the importance of *al-Manar* in Egypt, as well as in other countries such as India and Indonesia, see Shahin 1994, pp. 10–13.
103   Keddie 1995, p. 25.
104   Quoted in Skovgaard-Petersen 1997b, p. 79.
105   Skovgaard-Petersen 1997b, p. 79.
106   Skovgaard-Petersen 1997b, p. 80 and Schulz 1990.
107   Cf. Abdulrazak 1990.

and communication technologies had a direct impact and influence on theological debate and discussion in the Middle East. This also clearly illustrates the fact that the mass production of texts could be analysed as a threat to the 'old' *'ulama'* class and its religious authority.[108] From now on, it was also the Muslim intellectual who published his ideas or *fatwas* in the press and who educated the great majority of Muslims, not only the traditional *'ulama'* who was associated with the mosque and its institutions. But the mass production of texts also had an effect on Islamic learning and exegesis. Schulze writes:

> Unlike a manuscript penned by a learned man, the printed book was sold to an anonymous public. The scholar, who had been used to propagating the ideas in a specific text by reading it out to his pupils, now had to face the fact that the book, once it left the printing office, was beyond the sphere of his direct authority. It was no longer possible for him to influence the readers or have an effect on their attitudes towards the text. On the other hand, the reader of a book – who had now lost contact with the scholars – frequently ignored the commentaries, and concentrated solely on the original.[109]

From this point of view, the new information and communication technology could be described as an agent that started a process in which the authority and hegemony of the 'old' *'ulama'* came to be questioned.[110] The printing technology and the development of the press also paved the way for interpreters who favoured *ijtihad* above *taqlid*.[111] Instead of putting the traditional *'alim* at the centre, the importance of the individual was stressed by those who favoured *ijtihad*. From this point of view, the introduction of the printing press and the mass production of texts could be analysed as an important step towards the privatisation of religion, and even secularisation in Egypt.

Conclusions

With the introduction of the new information and communication technologies, the authority and power of the 'old' *'ulama'* was placed in question and later broken. However, it is difficult to demonstrate or substantiate whether this development should be explained by the introduction of the new information and communication technologies or by the general social changes that were taking

---

108   In the late Ottoman period, for example, the press in Lebanon and Syria was used as a vehicle for spreading nationalistic and anti-Turkish feelings. Cf. Tauber 1990.

109   Schulze 1997, p. 48.

110   Cf. Abdulrazak 1990, pp. 151–155.

111   The Arabic press was also important for educating and implementing awareness of the new technologies, such as the printing press, photography and general developments in the field of science. See Ayalon 1995, pp. 33, 53.

place in the Midlle East from the eighteenth century onwards. Irrespective of how we answer this question, it is clear that the introduction of the printing press in the eighteenth and nineteenth centuries was much debated among Muslim *'ulama'*. While some argued that printing had a harmful effect on the authority of Islam and the *'ulama'*, other Muslims saw opportunities and potential in the new technology. For example, Jalal al-Din al-Afghani, Muhammad 'Abduh and Muhammad Rashid Rida embraced and adopted the printing press. For them, the technology was not a problem per se. The task of the *'ulama'* was to lay down the necessary guidelines for using printing as a tool for spreading and upholding Islam. From this point of view, al-Afghani, 'Abduh and Rida specified the foundations of the so-called modernist or reform Islam. Like Yusuf al-Qaradawi and Tariq Ramadan, whom we will discuss in more detail in the following chapters of this book, they were eager to find a middle way between extremism (that is, a denial of everything modern) and secularism (that is, a full-blown adaptation of everything non-Islamic that derives from the West). As already indicated in this chapter – and we will see more of this in the following centuries – on the one hand a number of *'ulama'* had begun to argue in the eighteenth century, and still do so today, that it is necessary to be more sceptical about the introduction and use of information and communication technologies. On the other hand, we also find a growing number of *'ulama'* arguing that it is necessary to find interpretations that are in line with modernity and technological innovations.

Chapter 2

Muslim Conflicts over Images, Photography and the Representational Arts

I have gone to them many times and they have shown me all these various things and among the things I saw there was a large book containing the Biography of the Prophet, upon whom be mercy and peace. In this volume they draw his noble picture according to the extent of their knowledge and judgement about him. He is depicted standing upon his feet looking toward Heaven as if menacing all creation. In his right hand is the sword and in his left the Book and around him are his Companions, may God be pleased with them, also with swords in their hands. In another page there are pictures of the Rightly Guided Caliphs. On another page a picture of the Midnight Journey of Muhammad and al-Buraq and he, upon whom be mercy and peace, is riding upon al-Buraq from the Rock of Jerusalem.[1]

This quotation is taken from the Egyptian historian 'Abd al-Rahman al-Jabarti's chronicle of the first seven months of the French occupation of Egypt in 1798. The particular passage is a description of the author's visit to one of the libraries that the French occupation government set up in Egypt. Besides the images of the Prophet Muhammad described in the quotation, al-Jabarti writes that he is also looking at pictures of several mosques (for example, the mosques of Aya Sofya, Sultan Muhammad, Sultan Sulayman and Abu Ayyub al-Ansari) and detailed pictures of how Muslims celebrated the Prophet's Birthday (*Mawlid al-Nabi*).[2] The quotation is interesting for several reasons, especially when we consider the Muslim reactions that followed the publication of the Danish Muhammad cartoons in 2005/2006 and the Swedish artist Lars Vilks' drawing of Muhammad as a dog in 2007; both the cartoons and the drawing were reprinted in order to defend freedom of speech after the artists had received death threats.

With the publication of the satirical cartoons of the Prophet Muhammad in the Danish morning newspaper, *Jyllands-Posten*, questions concerning Islam, images and representational art became hot topics on a global scale.[3] The violent reactions that followed in Syria, Jordan, Lebanon and Pakistan in February 2006, leading to the burning of a number of Nordic embassies in the Middle East and boycotts

---

1 al-Jabarti, *Tarikh* Arabic text p. 91/English translation p. 116.

2 al-Jabarti, *Tarikh* Arabic text p. 91/English translation p. 116–117. A detailed description of *mawlid* can be found in Kaptein 1993.

3 The drawings were published in September 2005, but the debate and conflict only erupted in February 2006.

of Danish products, were ignited on the pretext that the Prophet Muhammad was being deliberately portrayed as a terrorist and barbarian in order to test the boundaries of freedom of expression. For many Muslims the cartoons had nothing to do with testing the limits of the freedom of expression but were perceived merely as an open provocation and an attack on Islam and Muslim doctrines.[4] This attitude is illustrated in the following quotation about Islamic opinions concerning images, photography and the representational arts.

> Some Muslims consider this subject [i.e., the debate about pictures] out of the scope of the religion, stating that religion has nothing to do with art, cinema, theatre and so forth. However, this attitude exposes the utter ignorance of these people regarding the religion. It also demonstrates their admiration of the West, which is characteristic of defeatism. This is due to the military, economic and political inferiority the Muslims suffer from when compared to the West.[5]

Although the theological dimension of the conflict is important, the reactions that followed should not only be analysed in the light of religion. The response could also be seen as an illustration of the frustration, anger and inferior position that many Muslims consider they are living under in both the Orient and the Occident.[6]

However, the conflict over the representational arts and freedom of expression did not cease with the publication of the Muhammad cartoons. In 2007 the Swedish artist Lars Vilks provoked the large majority of Muslims by depicting Muhammad as a dog (*rondellhund*). Even though the conflict was handled differently in Sweden than in Denmark, many Muslims were angry with how non-Muslims were presenting and representing the Prophet of Islam.[7] The conflict over this drawing resurfaced in 2010 after Lars Vilks' received death threats and a plot against him was revealed.

---

4   A number of reactions were, for example, reported on the homepage of IslamOnline. net. Sheikh Yusuf al-Qaradawi expressed strong criticism, but he also emphasised that: 'The sabotage done by some Muslims in some [Arab] capitals in response to the offensive cartoons is unacceptable and should be denounced'; see http://islamonline.net/English/News/2006– 02/06/article01.shtml (printed 2006–02–21). A similar opinion is also expressed in a *fatwa* issued by Maher Hafhout, Jamal Badawi and Muhammad Nur Abdullah for IslamOnline. net, 'Are Violent Protests Against Anti-Prophet Cartoon Acceptable?', retrieved from http:// www.islam-online.net/servlet/Satellite?pagename=IslamOnline-English-Ask_Scholar/ FatwaE/FatwaEandcid=1139318348431 (printed 2008–09–24). See also Dr Abdulla Al-Faqeeh's *fatwa*, 'Muslims' position towards the Danish insulting cartoons', retrieved from http://www.islamweb.net/ver2/Fatwa/ShowFatwa.php?lang=EandId=91149andOption=Fa twaId (printed 2008–09–24).

5   *The Ruling on Tasweer* 2002, p. 8.

6   An insightful analysis of the debate that followed the publication of the caricatures of the Prophet Muhammad in Denmark is given by Tayob 2006, p. 5. See also Högfeldt et al. 2008.

7   See, Larsson and Lindekilde 2009.

The aim of this chapter is not to analyse the particular conflicts that followed the publication of the *Jyllands-Posten* cartoons or Lars Vilks' drawings, nor to explore the reasons behind the eruption of violence and frustration among Muslims. The first aim of the chapter is to give a general background to some of the most important theological opinions concerning the debate over Islam and the representational and visual arts. The theological opinions discussed in this chapter are taken mainly from the *hadith* literature and from a number of early modern and contemporary *fatwas* that discusses questions related to the representational arts, especially debates about photography. The second aim is to analyse how a number of Muslim '*ulama*' view and debate photography. What kinds of arguments are used in these debates?

In order to draw up the boundaries of my research, I have mainly examined opinions that have been articulated by Sunni Muslim '*ulama*', and more specifically their opinions on the art of photography (an issue that is also discussed in relation to the representational arts). An indirect aim of my text is also to demonstrate that there has been no consensus among Muslims about how the representational and visual arts should be regarded.[8] To do so, I will analyse two types of *fatwas*. First, there are those that have been issued by Muslims who belong to the so-called reform movement (especially '*ulama*' who can be associated with the modern and contemporary Salafiyya movement in Egypt, for example, Muhammad Rashid Rida (d. 1935), but also contemporary authorities such as Yusuf al-Qaradawi and Tariq Ramadan; the relationship between these three will also be discussed further in the chapter.[9] Secondly, I will analyse a number of *fatwas* that have been issued

---

8   According to Abid Hussain's pamphlet, 'An Islamic perspective on Visual Arts', which is distributed via the Internet, it is possible to present two different and contradictory Islamic opinions on the visual arts. He distinguishes between two schools of thought: 'The first viewpoint is based on the fact that photography did not exist during the time the Prophet Muhammad PBUH, therefore it is not prohibited under Islam. The second suggests that the Islamic rulings on the representation of animate beings in traditional visual arts can be extended to photography as both results in the depiction of the life caught on canvas or on print.' Hussain Abid is listed as a Cultural Diversity Officer ACE Midlands Westminster, UK. See Abid 2005, p. 5. The pamphlet was downloaded from: www.faithandthearts.com/images/8_20061201143729.pdf (printed 2006–04–26).

9   The word *salaf* refers to the past in the Qur'an (cf. Q 5:95; 8:38), and in Arabic lexicons the *al-salaf al-salih* refers to 'the virtuous forefather', i.e. the first three generations of Muslims. According to Emad Eldin Shahin, it is possible to distinguish between the pre-modern (that is, the Hanbali- and Wahhabi-influenced movement) and the modern Salafiyya. Muhammad Rashid Rida clearly belongs to the modern Salafiyya, which was started in Egypt at the end of the nineteenth century. According to Shahin, the prime objectives of the modern movement 'were to rid the Muslim Ummah of a centuries-long mentality of *taqlid* (blind imitation) and *jumud* (stagnation), to restore Islam to its pristine form, and to reform the moral, cultural, and political conditions of Muslims. It is distinguished from the classic Salafiya by its essentially intellectual and modernist nature and by the diversity and expanse of its objectives'. See Shahin 1995, p. 464.

by '*ulama*' who have been informed by the Wahhabi interpretation (especially the opinions of the Saudi Arabian Sheikh 'Abd al-'Aziz b. Baz (d. 1999), but also Sheikh Muhammad Salih al-Munajjid).[10] However, it should be stressed that I am not aiming here to give a presentation that is representative or valid for all '*ulama*'. The aim of the chapter is rather to discuss some ideal positions in the debate over photography, to use the vocabulary of sociologist Max Weber.

In addition, I will argue that the different opinions on photography that are represented among the '*ulama*' mentioned above are closely related to how they view the *hadith* literature. The '*ulama*' who can be associated, directly or indirectly, with the Islamic reform movement can generally also be presented as belonging to the *ahl al-ra'y* (that is, those who support logical reasoning). This opinion is crucial for how they view photography and the representational arts in general. Similarly, it is important that Sheikh 'Abd al-'Aziz b. Baz can be described as a follower of the *ahl al-hadith*, those who strongly emphasis the importance of the *hadith* literature in Islamic jurisprudence. However, as we shall see later on in this chapter, the boundaries between the two groups (or rather positions) are not that strict, and the differences between the selected '*ulama*' are debatable.[11] My third aim in this chapter is therefore to consider whether the two concepts (that is, *ahl al-hadith* and the *ahl al-ra'y*) can be used as heuristic tools to demonstrate and explain differences among '*ulama*' regarding how they view the art of photography.

The historical background

Even though Islam is often conceived and presented as a religion that prohibits pictures, there are important differences between various regions, times and religious interpretations when it come to the question of the representational and visual arts.[12] Before these differences are outlined, it is also necessary to stress that

---

10   Sheikh Muhammad Salih Al-Munajjid was born on 30/12/1381 AH and is a student of Sheikh 'Abd al-'Aziz b. Baz. A full bibliography in English can be found at http://www.islam-qa.com/words/munajed/munajid_eng.html (printed 2006–04–28).

11   For example, if Muhammad Rashid Rida belongs to the modern Salafiyya movement, the ideas of the Wahhabi '*ulama*' belong to the pre-modern Salafiyya movement, according to Shahin 1995, p. 464. It is also clear that Muhammad Rashid Rida changed his ideas on the Wahhabi movement. W. Ende writes: 'Until his death in 1935 he repeatedly explained how and why his judgement of the Wahhabiyya had changed: in his youth, under the influence of Ottoman propaganda, he had regarded the Wahhabis as fanatical sectarians; after his arrival in Egypt, however, through reading the chronicle of al-Djabarti and works of other authors and through direct information, he had understood that it was the Wahhabis, not their opponents, who defended true Islam, even if they were inclined to certain exaggerations.' Ende 1995. See also Abrahamov 1998.

12   From a general point of view, it is important to stress that a religion per se cannot have any agency of its own, but only its followers. For example, it is humans who accept or reject images, photography and representational arts, not a religion.

prohibitions against so-called graven images is a recurring theme in Near Eastern contexts, as well as in the Hebrew Bible (cf., for example, Exodus 20:25; Leviticus 19:4; 26:1). However, if we return to the discussion about Islam, it is clear that it is possible to find several different and often contradictory opinions. For example, Shi'a Muslims have generally been more positive regarding representations and images of the Prophet Muhammad and the imams, while most Sunni Muslims have been more eager to prohibit images.[13] This distinction between the two major branches of Islam is, however, questionable. For example, the Sunni Muslims in Istanbul had no problems in accepting miniature paintings that depict Sultans and important individuals.[14] Irrespective of regional or theological differences, the Qur'an does not contain any explicit ban against paintings or the representational arts (for example, drawings). However, it is quite explicit in its prohibition of idols and sculptures (*timthal*), and several different Arabic words are used for designating idols, for example, *awthan* and *asnam*.[15] The prohibition also includes objects (stones) raised to be worshipped as gods (*nusub* or *ansab*):[16]

> You worship only [lifeless] idols [*awthan*] instead of God, and [thus] you give visible shape to a lie! Behold, those [things and beings] that you worship instead of God have it not in their power to provide sustenance for you: seek, then, all [your] sustenance from God, and worship Him [alone] and be grateful to Him: [for] unto Him you shall be brought back! (Q 29:17)

> AND WE BROUGHT the children of Israel across the sea; and thereupon they came upon people who were devoted to the worship of some idols [*asnam*] of theirs. Said [the children of Israel]: 'O Moses, set up for us a god even as they have gods!' He replied: 'Verily, you are people without any awareness [of right and wrong]!' (Q 7:138)

---

13   An interesting and illustrative analysis of shi'a depictions of the Prophet Muhammad is found in Ceutlivres and Ceutlivres-Demmunt 2006, pp. 18–19. In shi'a literature, 'Ali ibn Abi Talib, the fourth Caliph, is often depicted. See, for example, Markussen 2006, p. 163, and Thurfjell 2003 (Cover). A Turkish printer interviewed by Hege Irene Markusen in Istanbul says that he has no problems with printing posters of Imam 'Ali or other Shi'a imams, but he refuses to print posters of the Prophet Muhammad because he is a Sunni Muslim. See Markussen 2006, p. 171. A discussion about the iconography of the Islamic Republic of Iran is found in Gieling 1998, p. 16. A useful collection of Islamic images is also found on the homepage of the University of Bergen, Norway. See http://www.hf.uib.no/religion/popularikonografi/default_eng.html.

14   Şeker 2009, p. 35.

15   Cf. Q 22:30; 29:17, 25 (for *awthan*) and Q 6:74; 7:138; 14:35; 21:57 and 26:71 (for *asnam*). Cf. Hawting 2002, pp. 481–484.

16   Cf. Q 5:3; 70:43 (for *nusub*) and Q 5:90 (for *ansab*). Cf. Hawting 2002, p. 481–484. According to Fahd (1995), the *nusub* 'denotes the blocks of stone on which the blood of the victims sacrificed for idols (*awthan, asnam*) was poured, as well as sepulchral stones and those marking out the sacred enclosure (*hima*) of the sanctuary'. Fahd 1995, p. 154.

As Nimet Şeker has pointed out, however, it is possible to find many different interpretations of the word *ansab*. It can, for example, be understood as a word for a sacrificial stone (Opferstein) in the pre-Islamic era, but in a more general sense it has become a synonym for polytheism (Idolatrie).[17]

Irrespective of the prohibition against images in the *hadith* literature, reservations against the legality of paintings and the representational arts only date back to late Umayyad or early 'Abbasid times.[18] Archaeological materials, book illustrations and miniatures from this period all demonstrate that there is a gap between theory and practice, and it is evident that the prohibition was not put into practice in all parts of the Muslim world. For example, the great Umayyad Mosque in Damascus, the Dome of the Rock in Jerusalem and palaces in Muslim Spain (al-Andalus) all demonstrate that pictures and ornaments, including flowers and animals, were used, irrespective of theological debates over the representational arts.[19] For example, Edward William Lane provides us with an illustration of the tension between theory and practices in his famous book on Egypt:

> Painting and sculptures, as applied to the representation of living objects, are, I have already stated, absolutely prohibited by the religion of El-Islám: there are, however, some Muslims in Egypt who attempt the delineation of men, lions, camels and other animals, flowers, boats, &c., particularly in (what they call) the decoration of a few shop-fronts, the doors of pilgrims' houses ...[20]

Irrespective of the difference between theory and practice, that is, that images were used under the Umayyads and the early 'Abbasids, it is clear that the prohibition against three-dimensional objects and paintings (in modern discussions, this ban includes pictures as well as photographs) does not rest on the Qur'an, but on a large number of *hadith* traditions ascribed to the Prophet Muhammad.[21] For example, *Sahih Muslim*, by Imam Muslim (d. 875) and al-Bukhari (d. 870), two of the most important collectors of traditions, tells us that angels do not enter a house in which there is a dog or a picture.[22] It is also reported in the *hadith* traditions that Muhammad pulled down curtains decorated with pictures in the house of 'A'isha bin Abi Bakr's, one of the Prophet Muhammad's wives.[23] The *hadith* traditions

---

17   Şeker 2009, p. 16.

18   Soucek 2000, p. 361.

19   See, for example, Grabar 1954 and 1959, and Dodds 1992.

20   Quotation taken from Lane 1973, p. 308. See also pp. 95–96.

21   An extensive index of *hadith* traditions about images can be found in Wensinck 1927, p. 108.

22   al-Bukhari, *Sahih Bukhari*, Hadith no. 5949 (vol. 7, p. 438); Hadith no. 5958 (vol. 7, pp. 441–442) and Hadith no. 5960 (vol. 7, pp. 442–443).

23   al-Bukhari, *Sahih Bukhari*, Hadith no. 5954 (vol. 7, p. 440). Cf. Hadith no. 5955 (vol. 7, p. 441); Hadith no. 5957 (vol. 7, p. 441) and Hadith no. 5961 (vol. 7, p. 443).

also tell us that the image-makers will be punished in hell because they imitate Allah's act of creation:[24]

> ibn 'Umar reported that Allah's Messenger (may peace be upon him) had said: Those who paint pictures would be punished on the Day of Resurrection and it would be said to them: Breathe soul into what you have created.[25]

The reason for the restrained attitude towards images and pictures is 'basically in tune with the stark monotheistic doctrine that there is no creator but God: to produce a likeness of anything might be interpreted as an illicit arrogation of the divine creative power by humans', to quote Annemarie Schimmel.[26] It is believed that it is only Allah who can be the fashioner of form (*musawwir*), that is, it is God who is the creator (cf. Q 3:6; 59:24). Therefore, it is perceived as idolatry (*shirk*) to put something or someone in the place of God.[27] This way of putting the argument is clearly illustrated in both *Sahih Bukhari* and *Sahih Muslim*: on the Day of Resurrection the image-makers will be asked to breathe soul into what they have created, but they will fail entirely, since it is only God who has the power either to create life or to end it (cf. quotation above).[28] From a large number of traditions that are found in the *hadith* literature, it is possible to find support for opinions arguing that Muslims should avoid images, pictures and the representational arts.[29] However, in the discussion about images, one can also find the '*ulama*' trying to distinguish between images that were two- or three- dimensional. Generally two-dimensional images of humans and animals that cast no shadow were not a problem for the '*ulama*', but the three-dimensional images were more problematic because they came closer to a reproduction of creation. But as the following sections will illustrate, it is evident that the '*ulama*' soon came up with arguments that solved this problem, and three-dimensional images of humans were soon accepted.[30]

---

24   Traditions about images and image makers are, for example, found in *Sahih Muslim*, English and Arabic text pp. 406–413.

25   *Sahih Muslim* English trans. p. 411/Arabic text p. 412.

26   Schimmel 1987, p. 65. Cf. al-Qaradawi 1985, pp. 108–115.

27   The 'associaters', i.e. those who associate something or someone with God, are called *mushrikun* in the Qur'an.

28   See also al-Bukhari, *Sahih Bukhari*, Hadith no. 5950 (vol. 7, p. 439); Hadith no. 5951 (vol. 7, p. 439); Hadith no. 5954 (vol. 7, p. 440); Hadith no. 5957 (vol. 7, p. 441); Hadith no. 5961 (vol. 7, p. 443); and Hadith no. 5963 (vol. 7, p. 444).

29   Cf. Wensinck 1927, p. 108.

30   Şeker 2009, pp. 21–27.

Theory and practice

The suppression of pictures and the representational arts resulted in the development of an abstract ornamental design and calligraphy and a rich Islamic architectonic and symbolic 'language'. The development of the Islamic iconography also shows that the prohibitions against pictures and representations were flexible and dynamic. For example, it was quite common for medieval manuscripts, such as the world history of Rashid al-Din (d. 1317), or medical treatises to contain illustrations.[31] For example, Thomas W. Arnold's classic study, *Painting in Islam: A Study of the Place of Pictorial Art in Muslim Culture*, contains several illustrations depicting the Prophet Muhammad. In this book there are paintings of the Prophet when he delivers his farewell sermon, discusses affairs with Abu Bakr and receives the message of God from the angel Jibril. In many cases the face of the Prophet is visible and uncovered, but in others he is veiled or his face is omitted from the picture.[32] In Iran, India, Pakistan and Afghanistan, at least prior to Taliban rule, pictures of Muhammad's night journey (*isra', mi'raj*) or scenes from the *Qisas al-anbiya'* literature (Stories of the Prophets) were also popular. Muslims in Pakistan have also made drawings of *al-Buraq* (the flying steed on which Muhammad is said to have ridden when he made his miraculous night-journey) lawful by referring to Qur'anic commentators, such as 'Abd al-Haqq al-Haqqani and his reading of Q 34:12–13.[33] Wall decorations from the *hajj* – the obligatory pilgrimage to Mecca – and posters of politicians, state chiefs and religious leaders are also ubiquitous and very popular in many parts of the world dominated by Muslim and Islamic traditions.[34] Although it is difficult to demonstrate when the representational arts were accepted in the Middle East, it is clear that images became more ubiquitous and popular from the time of Western colonialism, and especially since the rise of the Arab press at the beginning of the twentieth century.[35] This development was stimulated by technological developments, the rise of higher mass education and

---

31 Schimmel 1987, p. 65.

32 Arnold 1965, p. 89 and p. 93. Cf. Grabar and Natif 2003.

33 Baljon 1994, p. 479. Q 34:12–13 reads: 'And to Solomon the wind; its morning course was a month's journey, and its evening course was a month's journey. And We made the Fount of Molten Brass to flow for him. And of the jinn, some worked before him by the leave of his Lord; and such of them as swerved away from Our commandment, We would let them taste the chastisement of Blaz; fashioning for him whatsoever he would – places of worship, statues, porringers like water-troughs, and anchored cooking-pots. "Labour, O House of David, in thankfulness; for few indeed are those that are thankful among My servants." ' (Translation Arberry 1964, p. 438). It should also be remembered that the Sunni might have been accustomed to images of the Prophet Muhammad and al-Buraq; see, for example, al-Jabarti, *Tarikh*, Arabic text p. 91/English translation pp. 116–117.

34 A large number of *hajj* paintings can be found in Parker and Neal 1995.

35 Ayalon 1995, p. 81. The transformative effect of the new media on the culture, mentality and taste of the audience in the Middle East is discussed by Mirbakhtyar 2006, p. 37.

growing literacy, as well as by changes in mentality, a topic I will return to in the next chapter on Islamic opinions regarding motion pictures.[36]

A contemporary example is that many mosques in the West have accepted photographs and certain images as parts of an Islamic design. This practice has not always been accepted or approved of, as the Dutch Orientalist Snouck Hurgronje demonstrated. In his classical study of Mecca at the end of the nineteenth century, he reports the Muslim theologian Sheikh al-Haqqi complaining about the expanding of use of images. He writes:

> Among the things that lead into Hell is this that the devils in these times have put into the heads of Christians and other God-abandoned people to place on all wares that are used by man pictures of living creatures so that there is now hardly a house, shop, market, bath, fortress, or ship without pictures [an allusion perhaps to the often indecent pictures on Austrian matchboxes] while to the Angels of Grace no room is left without pictures for them to descend into, except the mosques and a few other places preserved by God. Even into our mosques pictures come, for most people, when they come to prayer, have their little packets of cigarettes and tobacco on which there are pictures; so I warn you O brethren![37]

The trend described by al-Haqqi has clearly been developed further through increased contact with Europe and North America. However, photographs and posters of religious environments, such as the Ka'ba in Mecca or the Masjid al-Aqsa in Jerusalem, have today become standard features in the design of mosques in the West. According to both Saphinaz-Amal Naguib, who has especially studied mosque interiors in Norway, and Barbara Daly Metcalf, who has studied the making of Muslim space in the United States, the representational arts play a central role today in the creation of Muslim sacred spaces in Diaspora environments. This development is analysed by both Metcalf and Naguib as examples of the emerging transitional or global character of Islamic sacred spaces. Pictures and posters of the Ka'ba, the Dome of the Rock and the mausoleum of Hussein in Kerbela all function as important vessels of communication that help believers to create Islamic sacred spaces. This function is, for example, very important in a Diaspora context when Muslims are likely to live as a religious and cultural minority.[38] For example, by putting up posters and calligraphy in basement mosques, an atmosphere that articulates Islamic values and norms can be created. Consequently, one way of changing and transforming a rundown basement or an industrial unit into a mosque or a *musalla* (prayer room) is to decorate it according

---

36 See, for example, Ayalon 1995 and Eickelman 1992.

37 Sheikh Haqqi, quoted in Snouck Hurgronje 1970, p. 165.

38 Naguib 2001, pp. 80–85 and Metcalf 1996a. Another example is Markussen's analysis of Muslim barber shops in Bergen, Norway. See also Markussen 2005 and Hirschkind 2003.

to an aesthetic Islamic norm. Even though this conclusion is most likely correct, it is an illustration of the fact that Muslims too have accepted certain types of image. The observation made by Naguib, Metcalf or indeed anybody who has visited a mosque in the West thus demonstrates that al-Haqqi's criticism, reported in Snouck Hurgronje's book from Mecca at the end of the nineteenth century, had little effect on the Muslim community.

The examples from both history and more recent periods demonstrate clearly that there has always been a difference between theory and practice when Muslims have discussed images and the representational arts, that is, whether they are *halal* (lawful) or *haram* (prohibited). While images and the representational arts have been condemned by many '*ulama*', various forms of Islamic representation and even photographs have played a role in both historical and contemporary periods. For example, Annemarie Schimmel's analysis of Islamic iconography shows that the so-called popular religion, that is, religious ideas and practices accepted and followed by the 'common' Muslim, have been more open to pictures and representations than the institutionalised form of Islam developed by the '*ulama*'.[39] However, as we shall see in the next section, many different opinions are also present within the Muslim community, as well as between different '*ulama*' and 'common' Muslims, about how photography and the representational arts should be regarded.

Photography in the Middle East

With the development of the art of photography, the debate about Islam, pictures and representations was renewed. The issue became even more problematic due to the fact that the art of photography had been introduced by Westerners, the first to pick up the new technology in the Ottoman Empire being non-Muslims living in Istanbul.[40] Like printing, this technological innovation was also closely related to colonialism and Western interests in the Middle East.[41] Irrespective of this background, however, the technology was soon put to use, and it is reported that the first photography from the region, dated to 7 November 1839, was shot in Alexandria, Egypt.[42] Although the art of photography was introduced by Westerners, it was slowly accepted by the presumably Muslim public. For example, the Ottoman Sultan Mahmud II (who ruled 1808–1839) was the first Sultan to have his portrait displayed publicly, thus breaking the taboo on human representations. Nonetheless it is important to stress that the Ottoman rulers had

---

39 Schimmel 1987.

40 Şeker 2009.

41 Cf. Denny 1995; Larkin 1999, Thompson 2000 and Thompson 2001.

42 Chevedden 1984, pp. 151–152, and Landau 2000, pp. 363–364. It is, of course, difficult to verify or prove that this date for the first photography in the Middle East is correct.

already accepted images of humans and animals by not forbidding miniature paintings and medallions with human faces.[43] But Mahmud II was still sceptical about photography. For example, he forbade the selling of photographs of holy buildings, especially ones that show the *Ka'ba*, and of unveiled women.[44] Although the art of photography was supported by his predecessor, especially by 'Abd al-'Aziz (ruled between 1861–1876) and 'Abd al-Hamid II (ruled between 1293/1876–1327/1909), Mahmud II was not alone in his criticism. For example, in 1908 Muhammad Rashid Rida expressed criticism of the new technology. Although advocating that Muslims must use *ijtihad* rather than *taqlid* when interpreting the Qur'an and the Islamic tradition, he issued a *fatwa* that rejected the taking of pictures.[45] As Nimet Şeker has pointed out, Muhammad Rashid Rida was not alone in his interpretation and acceptance of the taking of certain photographs, provided they were necessary and used for good purposes.[46]

Despite his critical *fatwa*, therefore, Muhammad Rashid Rida argued that certain pictures were acceptable under the right conditions if they were necessary (in Arabic this principle is often called *darura*).[47] For example, he allowed the taking of pictures to be used for passports, driving licences, ID cards, and so on.[48] From the remaining sources (that is, the material published in *al-Manar* and other journals), it is difficult to detect a clear reason why he changed his mind on this issue. Was it because pictures (for example, photographs in newspapers) had become more common from the 1920s, or was it because Muhammad Rashid Rida had now had an opportunity to travel to Europe, India and to other parts of the Middle East?[49] Or could this shift be explained by the fact that he was following an interpretation of Islam close to the opinions of the *ahl al-ra'y*? Whatever was the case, in order to be able to travel outside Egypt, he had to have his picture taken for the obligatory passport and travel documents.[50]

---

43   Şeker 2009, pp. 35–36.

44   Landau 2000, p. 364. Still it is possible to find photos of Mecca and the Ka'ba in both historical as well as more recent periods. A detailed photographic description of the *hajj* ritual and Ka'ba is found in, for example, Snouck Hurgronje 1889.

45   Rashid Rida 1908, pp. 277–278.

46   For more examples, see Şeker 2009, pp. 21–27.

47   See, for example, El Fadl 2001, p. 197. On the concept of *darura*, see Linant de Bellefonds 1965, pp. 163–164.

48   These exceptions to the prohibition of pictures and photographs are accepted by '*ulama*' that follow both the *ahl al-hadith* and the *ahl al-ra'y* positions.

49   It is reported in *al-Manar* that Muhammad Rashid Rida travelled extensively after 1908. For example, he travelled to Istanbul (1909–1910), to India (1912; on his way back to Egypt he visited Musqat and Kuwait), to Hijaz (1916 and again in 1926), to Syria 1919–1920, to Europe (1921–1922) and finally to Jerusalem (1931). Cf. Ende 1995, p. 446.

50   His passport picture is still preserved, and I have actually seen a copy of it in his great grandson's apartment in Cairo, Egypt.

In order to develop the analysis further, one must ask whether the differences between these theological opinions can be understood by relating the question about photography to the difference between the so-called *ahl al-hadith* and *ahl al-ra'y* positions.

Ahl al-hadith and *ahl al-ra'y*

It is evident that most debates in the West about Islam and the representational arts have not been analysed or linked to the division between the *ahl al-hadith* and *ahl al-ra'y*. For example, Rudolph Peters argues convincingly that most law books give two grounds for the prohibition of images. The first argument against images holds that the image-makers must be condemned because they are trying to copy God's creation (*mudahat al-khalq*). The second argument is that the image-makers (or for that matter those who keep images) are imitating the unbelievers (*al-tashabbuh bi'l-kuffar*), that is, the Christians or Westerners who have accepted the taking of pictures.[51] In my view, we have no reason to doubt that Peters' conclusions are correct regarding the 'classical' period, but at the same time it is evident that, for example, Tariq Ramadan relates the question about images and photography to the division between the *ahl al-hadith* and *ahl al-ra'y*.[52] Although Ramadan should not be seen as representative or typical of all *'ulama'*, his way of putting the argument demonstrates the importance of paying attention to the difference between these two movements. But before we try to outline the difference between the two theological positions and use that difference as an analytical tool, it should be stressed that the two positions should be treated as ideal types. Joseph Schacht writes:

> There never was a school of thought in religious law that called itself, or consorted to be called, *ashab al-ra'y* [the partisans of personal opinion] and the distinction between *ahl al-hadith* and *ashab al-ra'y* is to a great extent artificial.[53]

But even though the division between the two theological positions is fuzzy and open to debate, it is possible to outline some specific ideas for each position. According to Schacht's description in the *Encyclopaedia of Islam*, the *ashab al-hadith* (the partisans of traditions) based their opinions on the 'normative custom of the community, which in due course identified with the *sunna* of the Prophet'.[54] For the *'ulama'* who supported this opinion, the traditions of the Prophet Muhammad (that is, the *ahadith*) superseded the 'living tradition', that is, the use of human

---

51   Peters 1996, p. 218. Cf. Snouck Hurgronje 1970, p. 165.
52   Ramadan 2002, p. 205.
53   Schacht 1960a, p. 692.
54   Schacht 1960b, p. 258.

reasoning or personal opinion.[55] According to Schacht, the debate about authority, authenticity and tradition was very intense during the second century of Islam.[56] Although all '*ulama*' were affected or influenced by this debate, it was only Ahmad ibn Hanbal (780–855) who could be described as 'purely traditionalist' among the four law schools.[57] From the 2nd/8th century, the study of *hadith* became a basic part of Islamic theology, and knowledge of the transmission and authenticity of traditions is still elementary to all '*ulama*', regardless of their theological positions. But significantly it was mainly the ideas of Ahmad ibn Hanbal that were in agreement with the opinions of the *ahl al-hadith*. His view (or more correctly the opinions of the Hanbali law school) is also the foundation of the opinions of the Wahhabi interpretation of Islam, that is, the ideological and theological position of Sheikh 'Abd al-'Aziz b. Baz from Saudi Arabia (whom we will return to later in this chapter).[58] But it should be stressed that the followers of the Wahhabi tendency often present themselves as following the Qur'an and the *hadith* literature even more closely than the followers of the Hanbali law school. If an interpretation advocated by the Hanbali law school is not supported by the Qur'an or by the traditions, it is rejected as false. According to Ayman al-Yasini, the Qur'an and *ahadith* constitute the only foundation for Islamic law, and in most cases Wahhabi '*ulama*' reject all interpretations made by the four schools of Islamic jurisprudence.[59]

The Wahhabi mission is primarily based on the oneness of God (*tawhid*) and a determination to uproot all forms of interpretation that are not in agreement with Wahhabi theology. That means all the forms of innovation (*bid'a*), idolatry or polytheism (*shirk*), Sufism and 'sinful ignorance' that, according to them, prevailed during the age of ignorance (*al-jahiliyya*).[60] In fact Wahhabi '*ulama*' are not automatically critical of interpretations based on *ijtihad* (independent informed reasoning), but to be able to use this method, they believe that one must follow a trained and knowledgeable teacher. The conclusions must also be in line with what they perceive to be the basic ideas of the Qur'an and the *Sunna*.[61]

Although it is difficult to draw a firm line between the *ahl al-hadith* and the *ashab al-ra'y* (the partisans of personal opinion), the later are more inclined to accept and follow personal reasoning or personal opinion. The conflict between these two positions was mainly focused on the debate about the authenticity of

---

55   Schacht 1960b, p. 258.

56   The debate and the authority of the reported traditions (*ahadith*) are still fundamental aspects of Islamic theology. See, for example, Juynboll 1969.

57   Schacht 1960b, p. 259. Abrahamov argues that this conclusion should be modified. Even Ahmad ibn Hanbal used reason when arguing about Islamic theology; see Abrahamov 1998.

58   Voll 1987, p. 313.

59   Al-Yassini 1995, p. 308.

60   A short introduction to Wahhabi theology can be found in Shaykh Muhammad 'Abd al-Wahhab, *Kitab al-Tawhid* 1994.

61   Voll 1987, p. 315.

the traditions. According to the *ahl al-hadith*, it was wrong for the followers of personal opinion to argue that traditions reported as coming from the Prophet on the basis of *ra'y* (in this case *ra'y* refers to a 'sound opinion') could be rejected. According to this criterion, Abu Hanifa and Malik b. Anas are often counted as belonging to the *ahl al-ra'y*.[62] As already noted, before we make this conclusion, we should recognise that it is difficult to draw a clear line between the two theological positions, and the literary accounts are mainly illustrations of theological conflicts and polemics.[63] Due to problems with the sources, it is also hard to know whether the accounts provide a correct picture of the actual theological context or whether they are being exaggerated for purposes of debate.

The *ahl al-ra'y* position

The difference between the *ahl al-hadith* and the *ahl al-ra'y* should not be overestimated, and sometimes the concepts were not even used by the '*ulama*'. Nonetheless I believe that the two concepts can be used to outline important differences regarding how various '*ulama*' view tradition, and especially the interpretation of Islam. In this section, I have selected three '*ulama*', one historical example, Muhammad Rashid Rida, and two contemporary, Yusuf al-Qaradawi and Tariq Ramadan, to show how the division can be used as an analytical tool. All three have explicitly discussed whether photography is lawful or prohibited in Islam, and they are all well known and often quoted '*ulama*'. However, before the arguments of these '*ulama*' are considered in some detail, it is important to determine in what ways they are related to each other, and more importantly, to what degree they are comparable. Can all three be viewed as representative of the opinions of the *ahl al-ra'y*?

As mentioned earlier, Muhammad Rashid Rida is linked to the modern Salafiyya movement in Egypt, which struggled for a reform of the interpretation of Islam. Compared to Jamal al-Din al-Afghani (1839–1897) and Muhammad 'Abduh (1849 – 1905), Rashid Rida was portrayed as more conservative. His opinions and interpretations are also a link between the reformist Salafiyya and the activist Muslim Brotherhood in Egypt.[64] His influence over the ideas of Hasan al-Banna

---

62   Schacht 1960a, p. 692.

63   For example, Montgomery Watt writes: 'There was indeed fluidity in the use of both terms [i.e. Ahl al-hadith/As'hab al-hadith and Ahl al-ra'y/As'hab al-ra'y]. The As'hab al-ra'y were sometimes – for example, by ash-Sharastani – identified with Abu-Hanifa and his followers; but in the early period we find, for instance, ibn-Qutayba ascribing Malik and Sufyan ath-Thawri to this group.' Montgomery Watt 1998, p. 181.

64   Shahin 1995, p. 467. According to Richard P. Mitchell's insightful study of the Muslim Brothers, Hasan al-Banna was influenced by the leaders of the Salafiyya movement. But compared to them, al-Banna took his 'cause directly to the people'. Mitchell 1993, p. 211.

(1906–1949) and the Muslim Brotherhood connects him to the ideas and theology of Yusuf al-Qaradawi and Tariq Ramadan. However, as with Muhammad Rashid Rida, it is possible to find different interpretations of Yusuf al-Qaradawi's importance, and he is often given contradictory titles and positions within both contemporary Islamic discourses and public debates about Islam and Muslims (not the least in the West).

According to Muhammad Qasim Zaman, al-Qaradawi is a 'moderate' scholar, while for Gilles Kepel he was one of the leaders of the neo-Muslim Brotherhood.[65] The 'moderate' position is defined by Zaman:

> They [i.e., the moderates] base themselves on the specifics of the law, without however, losing sight of its larger purpose; and they are guided by considerations of public interest, but only insofar as such considerations are not contradicted by the foundational texts.[66]

According to Armando Salvatore and his analysis of al-Qaradawi's theological thinking, al-Qaradawi is mainly trying to apply the Salafiyya ideology, his goal being to reform Muslim society.[67] His aspiration is to awaken the Muslims and raise their society to its former glory. One of the most important aspects of al-Qaradawi's theology is his idea of *al-sahwa al-islamiyya* (an Islamic awakening), the common good (*maslaha*) and *al-wasatiyya wa-l-i'tidal* (balance and moderation).[68] The ideas of al-Qaradawi are summarised in this quotation from Salvatore:

> Even if al-Qaradawi advocates a fusion of Salafiyya and *tajdid* ('reform'), he tends to lay a heavier emphasis on the latter, as this seems to be, at some points, equated with *sahwa*. The evocation of the era of *al-salaf al-salih* ('the reputable ancestors') does not provide the platform for a backward-looking attitude, but serves as a reference to an idealized model of hermeneutic smoothness, given by the time when Muslims were capable of shaping simply crafted, binding interpretations, whilst keeping the degree of conflict within the community to a minimum, and so allowing the unfolding of innovative capacities. The idealized consensus is viewed as focusing on essential questions, and obtained through the real participation of the legitimate holders of the key for interpreting the Law.[69]

---

65   Zaman 2004, p. 136, and Kepel 1985, pp. 127–128. According to Kepel: 'The propaganda of the neo-Muslim Brethren was directed at Egyptians who were well established in social life and wanted to Islamicize social relations by granting religious dignitaries or other elite groups more power than military officers or technocrats'. Kepel 1985, pp. 127–128.

66   Zaman 2004, p. 136.

67   On the so-called *da'wa* movement in the Middle East, see, for example, Hirschkind 2006.

68   See, for example, Gräf 2007, pp. 405–406; Salvatore 1997, pp. 197–209; and Zaman 2004.

69   Salvatore 1997, p. 206.

Although al-Qaradawi's thinking resembles that of the Muslim Brotherhood (or the neo-Muslim Brotherhood, to use Kepel's terminology), Zaman points out that he is not referring to, for example, Rashid Rida when he is discussing and writing about *maslaha* (the common good), and his connection to the movement is complex and often open for debate.[70] However, this might indicate that the ideas of Rashid Rida are not that important for al-Qaradawi. Still, it is evident that both Rashid Rida and al-Qaradawi are seeking a so-called middle way (in Arabic, this position is often labelled *wasatiyya*) in interpreting Islam. This position seeks a balance between extremism on the one hand and a denial of religion (that is, secularisation) on the other. But let us now return to the debate about photography.

Even though most Muslims today do not hesitate to take or look at photographs, the question is still debated by several '*ulama*', and there is no consensus over how to judge the art of photography. For example, in *The Lawful and the Prohibited in Islam* (*al-Halal wa-al-haram fi al-Islam*) and in *Diversion and Arts in Islam* (*al-lahw wa-al-funun al-Islam*), Yusuf al-Qaradawi outlines his idea of an Islamic view of photography. According to Sheikh Muhammad Bakhit (1855–1935), a late Egyptian *mufti* quoted by al-Qaradawi, the taking of pictures cannot be equal to an act of creation.[71] A camera and a photographer do not create something new; they are only capturing an image already created by God. According to al-Qaradawi the photograph is merely a reflection, the photographer a reflector.[72] With the aid of a camera, the user is only capturing an image through light and lens. According to this argument, the photographer is not a fashioner of form (*musawwir*), that is, he is not a creator (Cf. Q 3:6; 59:24). For al-Qaradawi, however, Muslims should ask themselves two questions before they decide whether an image is good or bad. What does the picture depict, and what was the purpose of taking the photograph?

> No Muslim would disagree concerning the prohibition of photographing subjects whose portrayal is against the beliefs, morals, and laws of Islam. Thus there cannot be any doubt concerning the prohibition of photographs, drawings, and paintings of nude or semi-nudes, of those parts of the male or female body which excite lust, or of pictures of men and women in sexy poses such as one sees in various magazines, newspapers, and on the billboards of movie theatres.

---

70   Zaman 2004, p. 137.

71   Sheikh Muhammad Bakhit (1855–1935) was appointed Mufti of Egypt in December 1914, an office he held for five and a half years. According to Skovgaard-Petersen, he issued a large number of *fatwas*, 2,028 of which are recorded in the Dar al-Ifta' and 280 of which have been printed in the *Fatawa Islamiya*. He issued *fatwas* on a large number of different topics, for example, on divorce, banking and insurance, as well as on new technologies such as photography and the telegraph. Skovgaard-Petersen 1997a, pp. 133–140. The *fatwa* discussed by al-Qaradawi is taken from the pamphlet *Al-Jawab ash-Shafi fi ibahat at-taswir al-Futughrafi*. Cf. al-Qaradawi 2001, p. 133.

72   al-Qaradawi, *Diversion ...*, p. 80. This argument was already being used in the 1940s according to Landau 2000, p. 364.

It is *haram* to make such pictures, to publish them, to buy them, to take them into homes, offices or shops, or to hang them on walls. It is *haram* to have the intention of looking at them.[73]

Like al-Qaradawi, Tariq Ramadan, who is the grandson of Hasan al-Banna, emphasises that Muslims must take into account the intentions and contents of drawings, photographs or movies before accepting or rejecting them. If a photograph is lawful, according to his understanding it should not contravene Islamic principles or ethics.[74] Both al-Qaradawi and Ramadan emphasise that it is the individual who must assess his or her intentions and consider the meaning and place of drawings, pictures and movies in his or her life.[75] As a result, it is the individual who has the responsibility to decide whether a specific photograph is forbidden or permissible. Although Ramadan does not use the Arabic term *niyya* (intention), in his book *To be a European Muslim* it is likely that he is indirectly referring to this concept. In 'classical' debates on the *shari'a*, *niyya* is used when the believer declares that he or she has an intention to perform a ritual act (especially before the performance of the *'ibadat*).[76] But it is also clear that the concept of *niyya* could be used in a more general meaning. For example, al-Bukhari uses the word in a much broader way in his first section of the famous *hadith* collection.

I heard Allah's Messenger saying, 'The reward of deeds depends upon the intentions [*bi 'l-niyyati*] and every person will get the reward according to what he has intended'.[77]

The quotation above seems to indicate that it is possible to use *niyya* as a synonym for intention, that is, not only in relation to a declaration to perform a certain ritual. Despite the minor differences between al-Qaradawi and Ramadan, both argue that the intention of the believer is the most important point to be taken into account when deciding whether a photograph is lawful or prohibited in Islam. For example, if a photograph or a poster has been made with the intention of increasing the ego or of obtaining the affection of other personalities (that is, pop stars, sport stars, hero worship), according to this interpretation they are bad and should be prohibited.[78] In other words, is the individual Muslim taking pictures and looking for images for the 'right' reasons, or is he or she searching for images for the 'wrong' reasons?

---

73   al-Qaradawi 1985, pp. 117–118.

74   Ramadan 2002, p. 205. See also Zaman's discussion of al-Qaradawi, Zaman 2004, p. 146.

75   Ramadan 2002, p. 205.

76   Wensinck 1995, pp. 66–67.

77   *Sahih al-Bukhari*, vol. I, English trans. p. 45/Arabic p. 45.

78   Cf. Sheikh Ahmad Kutty, 'Fatwa on Photography', retrieved from http://www.islamonline.net/servlet/Satellite?pagename=IslamOnline-English-Ask_Scholar/FatwaE/FatwaEandcid=1119503545144 (printed 2005–02–15).

Although both al-Qaradawi and Ramadan are well aware of the importance and place of the *hadith* literature (both, for example, quote al-Bukhari and Imam Muslim), they are clearly emphasising the importance of rational arguments regarding tradition, and according to my reading, from this point of view their opinions are more closely related to the *ahl al-ra'y* than to the *ahl al-hadith*.

The *ahl al-hadith* position

Although the views of Yusuf al-Qaradawi and Tariq Ramadan are shared by many contemporary *'ulama'*, there are those who disagree with them. Yet again it is important to stress that the dividing line between the theological schools and the arguments they are using is often open, and it is difficult to make a clear division between them.[79] However, most *'ulama'* who oppose the *ahl al-ra'y* seem today to belong to the Wahhabi-inspired interpretations of the Hanbali law tradition. Two examples are the Grand Mufti of Saudi Arabia, Sheikh 'Abd al-Aziz b. Baz, and Sheikh Muhammad Salih al-Munajjid.[80] According to them no Muslim should keep pictures for memory's sake, and in general images are viewed as something prohibited by Islam.[81] The practices of making pictures and having them in one's possession is regarded either as a useless activity or as a negative attempt to imitate the behaviour of the unbelievers.[82] The strict interpretation of the *hadith* literature (that is, that Muhammad held a negative attitude towards images and the representational arts) is, for example, repeated by 'Abd Allah al-Faqih, the supervisor of the *fatwa* team at *The Islamweb.net*, a webpage that seeks to promote 'balanced and moderate views, devoid of bias and extremism'.[83] His advice is that all believers should avoid pictures or occupations related to the taking of

---

79   Cf. Schacht 1960a, p. 692.

80   Sheikh 'Abd al-Aziz b. Baz was both the Grand Mufti of Saudi Arabia and the President of the Board of Senior Scholars (*Hay'at kibar al-'ulama*). For information on Sheikh 'Abd al-Aziz b. Baz, see http://www.binbaz.org.sa/. For more information about Sheikh Muhammad Salih al-Munajjid, see, for example, http://www.islam-qa.com. This multilingual homepage was started by the Sheikh in 1997.

81   Sheikh ibn Baz 1996, p. 337, and al-Munajjid 2004, pp. 109–111.

82   Cf. Fatwa no. 4979 (printed 2004–02–03 from www.islamweb.net). In this *fatwa*, Abdullah al-Faqih stresses that it is even forbidden to do the impossible, i.e. to take pictures of angels, since it is forbidden to take pictures of living things unless there is a need and a necessity. Examples of cases when photography is necessary include on the one hand the taking of pictures for ID cards, travel permits, passports and driving licences, and on the other hand taking pictures of performances of the *mujahidun* or recording Islamic lectures for purposes of education or *da'wa*. See Fatwa no. 8910; Fatwa no. 8932 and Fatwa no. 10207 (printed 2004–02–03 from www.islamweb.net). The issue of the angels is also found in Fatwa no. 517 (printed 2004–02–03 from www.islamweb.net).

83   A similar criticism can be found in Shaykh Muḥammad ibn 'Abd Al-Wahhab, *Kitab al-tawhid* 1994, pp. 152–153.

photographs.[84] This position is, for example, shared by Sheikh 'Abd al-'Aziz b. Baz and *The Permanent Committee and the decisions of the Fiqh Council* of Saudi Arabia. They say:

> Yes, pictures of all creatures, be they humans or animals, are unlawful, whether they are in the form of a sculpture or in the form of drawings on paper, whether they are stitching in clothes or photographs. Angels do not enter a house wherein there is a picture – this is substantiated by many authentic *Hadiths*. Pictures are permitted, though, for necessity. For examples, pictures of criminals are permitted, so as to help apprehend them. Passports and identity photos are permitted as well, and we hope that these items do not prevent angels from entering our homes due to the necessity to have them. And from Allah do we seek help.[85]

The quotation above is clearly in line with the opinion of the so-called *ahl al-hadith*, who argue that, although all believers have been given an intellect by God, they must obey and follow the guidelines for how to practice Islam, as these are prescribed and laid down in the *hadith* literature. To follow the example of the Prophet Muhammad is therefore regarded as the essence of the *sunna*, that is, the normative consensus for how to behave as a 'proper' Muslim. If the Prophet prohibits images, there are no reasons to accept them according to the position of the *ahl al-hadith*.

The importance of *niyya*

'*Ulama*' who follow the strict, literary interpretation of the *ahl al-hadith* – for example, those who are informed by the Wahhabi tendencies discussed above – must also pay attention to the question of *niyya* or intention. Even 'Abd al-'Aziz b. Baz admits that it is necessary and important to consider the question of intention when deciding whether a photograph should be forbidden or permitted. Regardless of whether the '*ulama*' are followers of the *ahl al-hadith* or the *ahl al-ra'y*, they are united in their condemnation of certain pictures (especially pictures representing the Prophet Muhammad).[86] For example, al-Qaradawi is very clear

---

84   Fatwa no. 17229 and Fatwa no. 8910 (printed 2004–02–03 from www.islamweb. net).

85   *Fatawa Islamiyah: Islamic Verdicts*. vol. 8, p. 154. This volume contains a special section on photography that includes a large number of *fatwas* addressing questions about the representational arts, photography, the media, singing and music; see pp. 152–207.

86   Dr Muzammil H. Siddiqi, former President of the Islamic Society of North America, stresses that no Muslim should have a picture of the Prophet Muhammad. This opinion is, for example, expressed in a *fatwa* published on the homepage of *IslamOnline. net*. See Siddiqi, Muzammil, 'Pictural Images of Prophet Muhamamd (PBUH)', retrieved

regarding what kinds of pictures believers should avoid, and his opinion on this issue is summarised in the following five points. First, it is forbidden to take or possess pictures of nude or semi-nude women. The problem for all Muslims is that pictures of women in semi-nude or 'erotic poses' are ubiquitous in most newspapers, magazines and movies.[87] Second, it is forbidden to possess pictures or photographs of disbelievers, tyrants and evil-doers. Third, Muslims should not possess pictures or photographs of confirmed atheists, that is, those who believe that there is no God. Fourth, it is forbidden for Muslims to have pictures of a Jew or Christian who denies that Muhammad is a true prophet. Fifth, photographs depicting rites of paganism or other religions which Islam rejects are forbidden by consensus.[88]

Despite the objections presented above, most contemporary 'ulama' seem to argue that pictures and photographs are part and parcel of modern life (this includes also the Saudi Arabian 'ulama' who generally strongly condemn the taking and possession of photos). In some cases, it is even necessary (*darura*) to take pictures (for ID cards, travel permits, passports and driving licences), and sometimes it is even encouraged (cf. the opinions of Muhammad Rashid Rida discussed earlier in this chapter).[89] Pictures (both photographs and movies) that could be used for *daw'a* ('missionary work'), educational purposes or for issuing passports for the *hajj* (pilgrimage) are not only recommended, they are viewed by most contemporary 'ulama' as compulsory and as part of Muslim life. The changing views of the 'ulama' are also demonstrated by a *fatwa* issued by Sheikh Ahmad Kutty for *Islam Online.net*:

> Even some of the scholars who had been once vehemently opposed to photography under the pretext that it was a form of forbidden *Tasweer* have later changed their position on it – as they allow even for their own pictures to be taken and published in newspapers, for videotaping lectures and for presentations; whereas in the past they would only allow it in exceptional cases such as passports, drivers' licenses, etc. The change in their view of photography is based on their assessment of the role of photography.[90]

Despite this change, the Saudi Arabian 'ulama' who are published in the volume *Fatawa Islamiyah* are convinced that any Muslim 'must have a sense of hatred

---

from   http://www.islamonline.net/servlet/Satellite?pagename=IslamOnline-English-Ask_
Scholar/FatwaE/FatwaEandcid=1119503543622 (printed 2006–02–21). Siddiqi's opinion is readily accepted by most Muslims, and there are few arguments against this ban.

87   This problem is clearly addressed in the *Fatawa Islamiyah: Islamic Verdicts*, vol. 8, p. 184.

88   al-Qaradawi, *Diversion* ..., pp. 80–81.

89   Cf. *Fatawa Islamiyah: Islamic Verdicts*, vol. 8, p. 154 and p. 162.

90   Sheikh Ahmad Kutty, 'Fatwa on Photography', retrieved from (printed 2005–02–15), www.islamonline.net/fatwa/english/FatwaDisplay.asp?hFatwaID=69010).

in his heart for pictures'.[91] It is also significant that the guidelines presented by, for example, al-Qaradawi do not say anything about images, pictures or the representational arts portraying the Prophet Muhammad. Most likely, al-Qaradawi thinks that it is obvious and therefore unnecessary to stress that Muslims are not allowed to have pictures that depict the Prophet Muhammad.[92]

Conclusions

The examples and analysis in this chapter demonstrate clearly that it is not possible to find just one Islamic opinion on the representational arts and photography. Prohibition and negative opinions regarding the art of photography are mainly derived from several *hadith* traditions and not directly from the Qur'an.[93] The *hadith* material gives a large number of reasons for banning pictures, the representational arts and photography that can be used by the '*ulama*' who want to condemn images. Regardless of theological opinion, most '*ulama*' stress that Muslims should be careful with pictures. It is argued that images and the representational arts could easily lead believers astray. Therefore it is necessary to develop rules and guidelines for how Muslims should handle and view pictures. For example, instead of searching for pictures portraying the Prophet Muhammad, in a *fatwa* published on the homepage of *IslamOnline.net* Dr Muzammil H. Siddiqi, the former President of the Islamic Society of North America, recommends that Muslims should be content with the descriptions of the appearance of the Prophet Muhammad that can be found in the Islamic literature, that is, the so-called *Shama'il* literature, which contains descriptions of the Prophet's physical appearance.[94]

In its own complexity, the discussion regarding the art of photography is a clear illustration of how the interpretation of Islam could be developed, refined and adjusted over time to fit present conditions and demands.[95] For example,

---

91   *Fatawa Islamiyah: Islamic Verdicts*, vol. 8, p. 156.

92   Cf., for example, al-Qaradawi's reactions to the publication of the Muhammad cartoons in *Jyllands-Posten* and Muzammil Siddiqi's *fatwa* on pictures of the Prophet Muhammad. See, http://islamonline.net/English/News/2006–02/06/article01.shtml (printed 2006–02–21) and http://www.islamonline.net/servlet/Satellite?pagename=IslamOnline-English-Ask_Scholar/FatwaE/FatwaEandcid=1119503543622 (printed 2006–02–21).

93   See Wensinck 1927, p. 108 for a detailed list of *hadith* traditions regarding the representational arts.

94   See Siddiqi, Muzammil 'Pictural Images of Prophet Muhamamd (PBUH)', retrieved   from   http://www.islamonline.net/servlet/Satellite?pagename=IslamOnline-English-Ask_Scholar/FatwaE/FatwaEandcid=1119503543622 (printed 2006–02–21). This literature is described in great detail in Schimmel 1985, especially in Chapter 2.

95   Barbara Daly Metcalf has expressed herself very clearly on this point. She says: 'From Muslims in the West, we learn much about how Islam, like any historic tradition, exists in the process of redefinition and reappropriation in new contexts. In

Muhammad Rashid Rida changed his ideas and perceptions of the art of photography over time. Besides accepting necessary photographs, for example, pictures for ID cards or passports, there are also studio photographs of Muhammad Rashid Rida in which he is posing in front of the camera for no obvious reason. This example can hardly be explained away with the help of the principle of *darura* (necessity) according to the Islamic Law.

According to Tariq Ramadan, the opinions of the *'ulama'* are divided along two different and opposing lines of argument. On the one hand, there are the *'ulama'* who advocate the ideas of the *ahl al-hadith*, that is, those who argue that it is necessary to follow and imitate the traditions of the Prophet Muhammad as outlined in the *hadith* literature, and who prohibit images and photographs. This is the literal interpretation, according to Ramadan. On the other hand, we find *'ulama'* who advocate the ideas of the *ahl al-ra'y*, that is, those who argue that an argument must be in line with its objectives. In this view, is it is obligatory to use not only traditions (that is, the literary readings of the *hadith* literature) but also reason to be able to arrive at a 'correct' interpretation.[96] In this chapter I have tried to show that the first opinion is held by many Saudi Arabian *'ulama'* (especially 'Abd al-'Aziz b. Baz and his colleges at *The Permanent Committee and the decisions of the Fiqh Council*). According to my reading, in accordance with the *ahl al-hadith*, 'Abd al-'Aziz b. Baz argues for the importance of a 'sound' tradition. However, the followers of ibn Baz argue that he advocated a 'middle path', that is, he took into account the significance of both *hadith* and *fiqh* (jurisprudence).[97] If this description is correct, it is an illustration of the fact that the boundaries between the *ahl al-hadith* and the *ahl al-ra'y* are superficial and difficult to use as a heuristic tool for explaining different opinions of, for example, photography.[98] Despite this observation, the second opinion, advocating a rationalistic approach, is more clearly found in the writings of Muhammad Rashid Rida, Tariq Ramadan and Yusuf al-Qaradawi. Although the argumentation of the last named scholar is clearly based on a literal reading of the *hadith* literature, he is open to the fact that the situation of the Muslim community has changed and that it is necessary to use reason when approaching Islamic law.[99] He argues that, to be able to cope with the new social and cultural situation (especially for Muslims living in the West),

---

the situations of cultural displacement or marginality in which these populations find themselves, characteristic Islamic themes and processes of cultural negotiation are thrown into particularly high relief. In seeing this, moreover, we witness the vitality, variability and creativity of populations who, in large part, live in settings characterized by racism, prejudice, and grim material realities.' Metcalf 1996b, p. 21.

96   Ramadan 2002, p. 205.

97   See 'Biography of Imaam ibn Baz', http://salafidawah.tripod.com/books/baaz. html (printed 2006–02–21). Cf. Voll 1987 and his outline of the history, ideology and theology of the followers of Wahhabi interpretation of Islam.

98   Cf. Schacht 1960a, p. 692.

99   Zaman 2004, p. 136.

it is necessary to develop and refine the roles and regulations for the Muslim community, thus making it easier to live as a 'true' Muslim (that is, in accordance with al-Qaradawi's understanding). However, this interpretation does not make it lawful to print or publish pictures of the Prophet Muhammad, especially if they are provocative in their nature, as was the case for the publications in *Jyllands-Posten* and by Lars Vilks.[100] It is therefore clear that whether the *'ulama'* follow the opinions of the *ahl al-ra'y* or the *ahl al-hadith*, they unanimously condemn images of the Prophet Muhammad. To understand this 'alliance', I believe it is more fruitful to focus on the discussion of *niyya* (intention). To most Muslims (of no matter what theological tendency), the editors of the *Jyllands-Posten* and Lars Vilks had an evil *niyya* when they published the cartoons and drawing of Muhammad as a terrorist and a dog respectively. According to the debate that followed the appearance of these pictures, it is clear that most Muslims in Europe, the United States, Asia, Africa and the Middle East perceived the drawings as an intentional provocation and an attack on Islam. The cartoons, as well as Vilks' images, were understood as attempts to provoke, upset and hurt Muslims all over the world. But at the same time, it is clear that both the individual and collective Muslim responses to the cartoons also contributed to their further mediation and dissemination. Abdulkader Tayob writes:

> Apart from the newspapers that rushed to reprint the cartoons to demonstrate their commitment to freedom of expression, Muslims themselves played an equally large role in spreading the reach of cartoons. Emails were sent around the globe to gather support for the protest actions, but, ironically, in many cases these very emails contained all the cartoons. The first Egyptian newspaper that carried the story of the cartoon also carried one of the cartoons on its front page.[101]

Besides being an illustration of 'the desacralization at work in public Islam', to quote Tayob, this is a clear illustration of the impact and use of the new information and communication technologies on a global scale.

In this chapter, I have tried to give the background to and an outline of different Islamic debates and positions on the art of photography in both early modern history and contemporary debates. Although the differences between the *ahl al-ra'y* and *ahl al-hadith* positions should not be exaggerated, the different attitudes towards the authenticity and use of the *hadith* literature constitute an important dividing line that can help us differentiate between different *'ulama'* and

---

100   Although the pictures published in *Jyllands-Posten* were strongly condemned by Yusuf al-Qaradawi, he also expressed strong criticism of those Muslims who attacked and burned embassies and churches in Lebanon and Syria. See 'Qaradawi Condemns Violent Cartoon Protests', retrieved from http://islamonline.net/English/News/2006–02/06/article01.shtml (printed 2006–02–21).

101   Tayob 2006, p. 5.

their views on the interpretation of Islam. The next chapter, which deals with the introduction of the motion picture and the building of cinemas in the Middle East and Muslim regions in West Africa, will clearly demonstrate that the debates over images and pictures have not been resolved. With the development of the moving picture and the building of cinemas, the '*ulama*' had to produce new arguments and strategies for how to handle this powerful and seductive new media.

Chapter 3

'*Ulama*' and the Motion Picture:
The Transformative Effect of Information
and Communication Technologies

In spring 2003, the Hollywood science fiction and futuristic film, *Matrix Reloaded*, directed by the Wachowski brothers, was subjected to heavy criticism by the *Department for Monitoring Artistic Products* in Egypt. According to this body, the film was provocative and immoral since it glorified violence and questioned the creation and existence of the 'real' world. Consequently it was banned. In the film, the world is presented as an illusion produced by computers and machines, that is, the matrix. The critics argue that the film questions creation in a decisive way and debates whether humans can have free will. The film was also perceived as an assault on Arab Muslim culture and a biased glorification and defence of Western culture.[1] Yet another problem was the fact that the story takes place in a city called Zion, a name that provokes strong reactions among many Muslims because it is associated with Israel and Zionism.[2] According to the Egyptian censors, the ideas captured in this motion picture could easily lead to decadence and cause a general moral crisis in society.[3] From a Western point of view, the criticism against *Matrix Reloaded* was often difficult to understand, and in most cases the Egyptian reactions were reported in the press as something curious and strange.[4] Nonetheless, the criticism shows that motion pictures and cinema halls are still problematic issues for many Muslims. That said, it should of course also be stressed that many people of Muslim cultural background enjoy films and have few or no problems with going to the cinema.

This chapter focuses on how Sunni and Shi'a '*ulama*' have debated and understood the motion picture as a media for transmitting ideas and values to

---

1   Similar criticism was also voiced against photography, i.e. that Muslims were only imitating Western habits without a critical Islamic evaluation. See, for example, *The Ruling on Tasweer* 2002, pp. 5–6. See also Peters 1996 and Hirschkind 2006, p. 42.

2   The struggle against Israel and Zionism was part of the political discourse in Egypt until Anwar Sadat's peace treaty with Israel in 1978. See, for example, Kepel 1985; Krämer 2006; Lewis 1999 and Mitchell 1993. The Israel–Palestinian conflict is also a popular topic for motion pictures; see, for example, Khatib 2004, pp. 75–79.

3   A general debate on *Matrix Reloaded* and other films with this focus is discussed in Buchele 2003 and Elbendary 2003.

4   Cf., for example, Wennö 2003.

Muslim audiences in the twentieth and twenty-first centuries. The text also includes a discussion about the cinema as a new public space that enhances cultural and social interactions in a new way for Muslims. The first aim, however, is to elucidate and analyse if, how and why certain '*ulama*' perceived and sometimes still perceive the film media as a potential problem for Muslims. To put it differently, why is the film media and the cinema theatre a challenge and even a danger for Muslims? What kinds of answers and solutions do the '*ulama*' included in this chapter present, and how do they think Muslims should respond to the film media? However, before we can comprehend the discussion and compare the different viewpoints of the '*ulama*' in this chapter, we must describe and analyse the social changes that the introduction of the motion picture and the building of cinema theatres gave rise to in countries dominated by Muslim and Islamic traditions.

Before giving the historical background, it is important to stress that it is not my ambition to cover all aspects of film history, nor to analyse films produced or shot in the Middle East from an aesthetic point of view.[5] My interest in this subject is primarily related to questions that could throw some light on the theological discussion, debate and impact of new information and communication technologies on Muslim groups in both the historical and contemporary periods. The reader who is interested in gaining greater insight into the cinematic history of the Middle East, Africa and Asia, or to learn more about certain films or directors, is recommended to consult encyclopaedias that specifically focus on cinema and film. Even though some of these works are included in my references and footnotes, the reader should keep it in mind that my main focus and interest is on the '*ulama*' who have explicitly discussed and issued Islamic opinions on film media and expressed opinions about the motion picture.

The history of cinema and film in the Middle East

The first purposely built cinema in the Levant was set up by the Ottomans in Damascus, Syria, in 1916.[6] Although the time gap between the introduction of the new medium in the Orient and the Occident is relatively short, the cultural and economic situation was and still is different in the Middle East, and the introduction of the motion picture is primarily linked to Western interests and colonialism.[7] The suspicion of film media is clearly articulated by Shahla Mirbakhtyar, who writes about the Iranian cinema:

> The films were shown at night and most patrons were rich aristocrats, with very few ordinary people attending. Apart from the fact that the purchase of a ticket

---

5   Two general introductions to Middle Eastern and North African films are Leaman 2001 and Dönmez-Colin 2007.

6   Thompson 2001, p. 91.

7   Cf., for example, Armes 1997, p. 661.

was out of reach for the majority of people, most viewed this new phenomenon as a Western influence and therefore an agent of corruption, and a threat to traditional Iranian values.[8]

Partly due to the economic and social situation, but also because of the strong cultural resistance to the new media, it took a while before the cinema was developed into a mass medium in the Middle East. As Mirbakhtyar states, opposition to motion pictures was driven by both cultural and religious motives.[9]

When the motion picture was introduced in the late Ottoman Empire at the beginning of the twentieth century, most showings were arranged and used by Europeans or the social elite.[10] Although the French Lumière brothers had shown films as early as 1896 in the Orient (it is of course difficult to fix the date of the first film to be shown in the region) the popularity of the new medium was delayed.[11] From a more general point of view, it is problematic to write the early history of cinema in the Middle East. Different dates for the introduction of the new technology are the rule rather than the exception. According to Roy Armes, public screenings were first made in Tehran and Istanbul in 1905.[12] Films were also shown in Aleppo in 1908 and in Baghdad in 1909.[13] In 1905 there were five cinemas in Cairo, fifty-three in Alexandria, one in Assiout, one in Port Said and one in Mansourah, all in Egypt.[14] Prior to these dates, screenings had also been organised in cities with high percentages of foreign residents, such as Cairo, Alexandria, Algiers and Oran, but these shows were of a private character. However, by the 1930s most newspapers had regular movie columns, and by the outbreak of the Second World War cinemas were selling approximately 44,000 tickets per week in Syria and Lebanon alone. According to Elizabeth Thompson's estimates, this would produce a cinema-going public of more than 20,000 people, indicating that cinema was a public success by the 1930s in the regions named above.[15]

The introduction of the motion picture also had a transformative effect on society that reached far beyond the technological aspect of the media. This transformative effect is clearly illustrated in the following quotation from Viola Shafik. She writes:

---

8 Mirbakhtyar 2006, p. 8. A similar, but less critical way of putting the argument is found in Shafik 2000, pp. 4–5.

9 Cf. Mirbakhtyar 2006, pp. 9–10, and Shafik 2000, p. 10, on opposition to the cinema in Saudi Arabia and Yemen.

10 Most films were not dubbed into Arabic, there were hardly any subtitles in Arabic, and the great majority of the Arabic-speaking audience were illiterate. Cf. Thompson 2000, pp. 198–199.

11 Shafik 2000, p. 10, and Thompson 2000, p. 197.

12 According to Mirbakhtyar, Mirza Ibrahim Sahhaf-bashi started the first cinema to open to the general Iranian public in 1903. See Mirbakhtyar 2006, p. 8.

13 Armes 1995, p. 286.

14 Thoraval 1990, p. 13.

15 Shafik 2000, p. 10 and Thompson 2000, p. 198.

In the frame of this newly appearing cultural structure, whose development has been decisively supported by the mass media, the cultural model of traditional society has become increasingly invalid as has the differentiation between high (elitist) and popular culture. Arab culture is penetrated now by a new dynamic, which has invalidated inherited dialectics and exchange processes. Daily life and living conditions in the Arab countries have become increasingly dominated by mass production and mass consumption. Traditional ways of communication and former arts, like oral narration or shadow plays, die out and are substituted by mass media.[16]

In conformity with the quotation above, the cinema was related to general processes of modernisation, but also to colonialism, imperialism and Western interests in the Middle East.[17] Furthermore, the technology brought new habits and social customs to the region. In his classic study, *The Society of the Muslim Brothers*, Richard P. Mitchell summarises some of the religious criticism of western influence that was voiced by the Muslim Brothers (*Ikhwan al-Muslimun*). He writes:

When the armies of Europe came to Egypt, they brought with them their laws, schools, languages, and sciences; but also their 'wine, women, and sin'. The introduction of the traditions and values of the West has corrupted society, bred immorality, and destroyed the inherited and traditional values of Muslim society. Social and family life is corrupted by the 'cheap' cinema, stage, radio, and music. The moral and sex problems of youth are related to the 'naked' women in the streets, the 'dirty' films, the 'suggestive' popular music, the 'uncontrolled' press and its lewd pictures and the permissibility of wine.[18]

The criticism of so-called negative Western influences described in the quotation above is, of course, closely related to those that the Muslim Brotherhood voiced against imperialism and the colonial power in general. But as we have seen, similar criticism was also voiced earlier against printing and photography.[19] Yet again it is important to remember that the introduction of the film media was a public success and that the great majority of people in the Middle East had few objections to it. Without developing this discussion further, the debate over the cinema as presented in this chapter illustrates the gap between the '*ulama*' and the behaviour

---

16   Shafik 2000, p. 6.

17   The connection between colonialism/imperialism and technology was clearly articulated by the British ambassador to the Ottomans, Stratford de Redcliffe. He believed, for example, that a network of railways and the telegraph was a prerequisite for introducing 'western Civilization' to the East, see Bektas 2000, pp. 680, 691.

18   Mitchell 1993, p. 223. Cf. *The Ruling on Tasweer* 2002, pp. 5–6.

19   Cf. earlier chapters in this book.

and attitudes of the public.[20] Hence, it is obvious that theological criticism of the cinema must be analysed in relation to political and social developments more generally. From this point of view, the information and communication technologies could be viewed as epitomes or symbols of Western influence over the Middle East. The new possibilities and changes that occurred in society at this time could easily be perceived as a threat to the dominant theological order.

The link between the colonial power and the introduction of the new media is, for example, obvious in Egypt. In this part of the Middle East, the Italian-Egyptian company and the *Banco di Roma* invested in the early Egyptian film industry.[21] For the silent movie period, that is, from the beginning of the twentieth century up till the 1930s, Roy Armes concludes:

> Usually the first film productions, like the first screenings, were the work of foreigners: the Frenchman De Lagarne in Egypt in 1912, the Romanian representative of Pathé, Sigmund Weinberg, in Turkey in 1916, two Dutchmen, Kruger and Heuveldorp, in Indonesia in 1926. Such films were based on foreign models. Thus the Armenian Avans Ohanian's first film – shown in 1930 and one of only four Iranian silent films – was an imitation of a Danish silent comedy, and most Turkish films of the 1920s were adaptations of European stage plays.[22]

The pattern described in the quotation above is not typical of countries dominated by Islam and Muslim traditions, since in most parts of the so-called Third World the cinema was introduced by Westerners. For example, in Dakar (Senegal) and Lagos (Nigeria), cinemas were first built by Western businessmen who had started to show movies at the beginning of the twentieth century.[23] Even though the film industry in the Third World was severely challenged by new problems, especially higher production costs and the greater technical demands of producing films with sound, a local market emerged slowly. An early film industry, with the production of locally shot films, was developed in the Arab Middle East, Iran, Turkey, West Africa, India and Indonesia from the 1930s onwards.[24] As a part of the expansion of the *Bank Misr* and the so-called Misr group, *Studio Misr*, one of the most

---

20 A similar gap is also found in the study of Gregory D. Black. In his analysis of the Catholic Church and Hollywood films, he writes: 'They [i.e. the Catholics] stood in church each December and took the Legion pledge [i.e. they accepted the power of the Legion of Decency to censure films] that was administered to everyone who went to Mass. However, taking the pledge in church was one thing; staying away from a movie was quite another. Millions of Catholics ignored the Legion ratings and flocked to see films that were condemned.' Black 1998, p. 241.

21 Shafik 2000, p. 11 and Thoraval 1990, p. 14.

22 Armes 1995, p. 286.

23 Armes 1995, p. 286.

24 For Egyptian film see, for example, Shafik 2000 and Thoraval 1990. For the history of cinema in Iran, see, for example, Gaffary 1991, Akrami 1991a and Tapper 2002. For cinema in Turkey, see Ilal 1987; Kaplan 1997.

famous and influential film studios in the Middle East, was set up in Cairo, Egypt, in 1934/1935.[25] Even though it is not possible to speak about *one* Arab film as a homogeneous genre – there are large variations over time and place, as well as between different producers and the various Arabic dialects used for the medium – the Egyptian film industry has had a strong impact. Due to its popularity, Egyptian film and the Egyptian Arabic dialect therefore spread far beyond the borders of Egypt.[26]

Lacking any pretension to analysing or describing Egyptian film in the 'correct' way, we may say that, like most movies produced in the Arabic-speaking Middle East, it often overflows with singing and dancing.[27] According to Jacob M. Landau, because of these trademarks, films shot in the Muslim world could be classified differently, in accordance with the following typology:

> The main types of films are: *a*. the historical (generally on themes chosen from Arab or Islamic history; in Egypt – also from Pharaonic times). *b*. the social drama or melodrama (once popular for its tear-breaking appeal, later for its social aims). *c*. the musical. *d*. the comedy or slapstick farce (usually on local background). *e*. adventure and detective films.[28]

Despite its commercial power and economic interests, the introduction of the cinema to the Middle East, as in most parts of the Third World, was especially important because the new medium could easily attract and reach out to large, illiterate audiences.[29] At a time when a large part of the population were unable to read and write, visual media, such as the photograph and the film industry, filled an important role in educating citizens, as well as in instilling nationalism and

---

25 Thoraval 1990. See also Davis 1983, pp. 108, 129 and Shafik 2000, p. 12.

26 The 'problem' with the Arabic language and its various dialects is discussed in Sadoul 1966 and Shafik 2000, pp. 26–27, 81–86. The complex interplay between classical and colloquial Arabic in the Egyptian cinema is also discussed in Armbrust 2000, pp. 312–313.

27 Islamic opinions and criticisms of music are discussed and outlined in Otterbeck 2004. See also Ramadan 2002 and al-Qaradawi 2001 on Islamic views on music. The Iranian taste for singing and dancing is illustrated by the so-called Film Farsi genre; see Mirbakhtyar 2006, p. 27. The movies that belong to this genre are clearly influenced by Indian and Hindi films; see Mirbakhtyar 2006, pp. 31–38.

28 Landau 1965, pp. 39–40.

29 Ami Ayalon notes that a 1937 Egyptian census reported a literacy rate of 18 per cent. Even though this figure should not be taken as a verified or absolute number, it is an indication and illustration of the low level of literacy in Egypt. See Ayalon 1995, p. 142. At the same time, the illiteracy rate for Iran was between 80 and 90 per cent according to Lahiji 2002, p. 216. See also *Arab Human Development Report 2003: Building a Knowledge Society*, United Nations Development Programme.

religious morality.[30] This potential represents an opportunity if the technology is used for what is perceived as the correct purpose – that is, in accordance with the dominant cultural, political and religious norms and values – but if it is used to break or challenge the prevailing discourse, it becomes a problem or a threat for those in power. Because of this potential, the media have always been surrounded by strict control and heavy censorship.[31] According to Viola Shafik, all states in the Arabic-speaking world have therefore monitored and controlled how filmmakers have portrayed and debated religion, sex and politics.[32] For example, the movie industry in Iran and Turkey today is still surrounded by strict rules and regulations, and the first aim of film-makers is, at least according to the state, to produce films supporting the present ruler. Another function is to pass judgement on former or competing rulers.[33] For example, many Egyptian films have given voice to the anti-Israeli sentiments that circulate, in spite of the political agenda of the government and the political elite (that is, irrespective of the Camp David accords in 1978 and subsequent political developments in the region). Films such as *al-Hob fi Taba* (*Love in Taba* by Hisham Abdel-Hamid, 1992) and *Fatat min Isra'il* (*Girls from Israel*, by Ehab Rady, 1999) picture Israeli women as seductive and dangerous (they are, for example, presented as carriers of sexually transmitted diseases such as HIV), in contrast to Egyptian women, who are presented as pure and upright. Similar stereotypes of Israeli women are also found in other forms of popular media.[34] The examples given by Lina Khatib above are clear illustrations of the fact that popular culture often functions as an instrument for debating problematic and sensitive issues in society.[35] According to Khatib's analysis, women are presented either as faithful, obedient and loyal mothers/wives, or as traitors or sexually questionable individuals transgressing the moral boundaries of society.[36]

Since film media could be used for debating sensitive issues, censorship has always been an essential aspect of the history of the cinema in countries

---

30   This was, however, seldom the case according to the criticism voiced by, for example, the Muslim Brothers in Egypt. See Mitchell 1993, p. 223.

31   See, for example, Mirbakthyar 2006, p. 18; and Mostyn 2002.

32   Shafik 2000, p. 34.

33   In the mid 1990s, adult illiteracy in the Arabic-speaking world was estimated to be 43 per cent. Rooke 2003, p. 17. The same trend is also found in Syria and Lebanon. See Thompson 2000, p. 199.

34   This tendency is also present in the discussion that followed the arrest of the so-called 'worshippers of the devil' in Cairo on 24 January 1997. On this date, 76 students at the American University, Cairo University and the 'Ayn Shams University were arrested and accused of Satanism. The students had been seduced by secular media and Western commercialism, but they had also been seduced by 'Satanic Israeli female secret service agents' according to the Ministry of the Interior and the al-Azhar University. On this controversy, see Hamzawy 2000, pp. 137–140.

35   Khatib 2004, pp. 75–79.

36   A similar conclusion is found in Dönmez-Colin 2004.

dominated by Muslim and Islamic traditions.[37] That said, it is important to stress that implementation of the rules and regulations has little or nothing to do with the religious views held by the state. Both secular regimes such as Turkey and religiously motivated regimes such as Iran have imposed heavy censorship on both locally and internationally produced films.[38] With the rise of new information and communication technologies such as the Internet and satellite television, this control has become very difficult and expensive in resources for the regimes in power to maintain.[39]

'*Ulama*' and the cinema

As demonstrated in the previous chapter, most '*ulama*' have been sceptical of images and pictures and have even rejected them because it is held that the *hadith* literature imposes a ban against all forms of representation and the visual arts.[40] It is only with the help of the juridical principle of *darura* (necessity) that most '*ulama*' have reluctantly accepted certain images (for example, photographs for ID cards, passports, for capturing criminals, and so on).[41] From this point of view, it is strange or even paradoxical that the same '*ulama*', that is, those who have problems with pictures or photographs, do not have problems with moving images.[42] But there are some exceptions: for example, a pan-Islamic congress was set up in Karachi in 1952 with the aim of imposing a ban on the film medium, and it was argued without success that all cinema theatres should be closed in countries dominated by Muslims. The only country that followed this recommendation was Saudi Arabia, which still has a ban on public screenings.[43] Despite the conference in Karachi, it is obvious that neither television broadcasts nor for that matter motion pictures are held to be dangerous per se. As we shall see in the following discussion, these media only become a problem for the '*ulama*' when they are

---

37   See, for example, Mirbakhtyar 2006, p. 18.

38   For Turkey see, for example, Ilal 1987; for Iran see, for example, Akrami 1987 and Akrami 1991b, pp. 585–586. Viola Shafik writes: 'All Arab governments, be they capitalist or socialist, have reduced the medium's freedom of expression through legal restrictions.' Shafik 2000, p. 33.

39   Eickelman 2003.

40   See previous chapter.

41   See previous chapter on Islamic opinions on photography for references and bibliographical data.

42   For example, Yusuf al-Qaradaw has expressed criticism of photography in his book *Al-Halal wa-al-haram fi al-Islam*. Still, he was one of the first '*ulama*' to make use of satellite television to promote his theological interpretation via the programme *Shari'a wa al-hayat*. On the importance of this programme, see, for example, Mariani 2006 and Skovgaard-Petersen 2004.

43   Mühlböck 1988, pp. 177–179; Shafik 2000, p. 49.

used for promiscuous or leisure purposes.[44] According to Khaled Abou El Fadl, this paradox should be related to questions of the distribution of power, authority and control. He says:

> Apparently, an expatriate may see his family on a television screen from a videocassette, but not in still photographs. Regardless of the consistency of the logic, what is noticeable is the type of social interests that the jurists consider material. Social non-institutional interests are not as weighty or significant as institutional and governmental interests. The expatriate experience with its particular pains is not a part of their sensitivities or consciousness. Consequently, it is fairly easy to dismiss the role of photographs for expatriates who, quite often, cannot afford to visit their families, as a non-necessity. Meanwhile, the photographs of the King of Saudi Arabia, which decorates the C.R.L.O build itself and most other public places, is a necessity.[45]

Although Khaled Abou El Fadl is correct in his observation, most '*ulama*' who discuss Islamic views of motion pictures generally apply the same arguments they use in discussing photography.[46] However, one important difference between photography and cinema is the fact that going to the movie theatre is something different than just taking or looking at a photograph. Going to the movies is a social activity that involves other participants, and for most '*ulama*' this interaction could become a moral problem because it transgresses and crosses the public/ private distinction. According to Yusuf al-Qaradawi, it is primarily the content and purpose of the movie that decides whether a film is 'good' or 'bad' for Muslims. Since the Prophet Muhammad declared that it is obligatory for all Muslims to seek knowledge, it is possible to argue that an informative or 'good' movie could be a perfect tool for increasing the knowledge of believers. Even Deoband '*ulama*', who generally take a very critical and conservative attitude towards, for example, watching television, have argued that the broadcast media can be used to invite people into Islam and to counter unbalanced or wrong presentations of Islam.[47] Hence, if the content and the social setting are correct, the cinema is not a problem at all according to Yusuf al-Qaradawi.[48] However, he is not alone in this opinion. For example, more or less the same arguments are recapitulated in a *fatwa* published on the webpage of *Islamweb.net*, a Saudi Arabian and Wahhabi-influenced site.

---

44 El Fadl 2001, p. 198.

45 El Fadl 2001, p. 198.

46 See previous chapter.

47 Sikand 2006, pp. 48–49. Strong criticism of cinema is, for example, articulated by the followers of the *Tablighi Jama'at*; see Goborieau 2000, p. 39.

48 al-Qaradawi 1985, pp. 306–307.

If the company produces [that is, an Egyptian cinema production and distribution company] good programs that are useful in this life and the Hereafter, and which are free from all prohibitions then working in such a company is permitted and ultimately the earnings from it are lawful. If the company produces bad, immoral serials or dissolute, shameless dramas that are full of obscenity, songs, music, songsters, and so on., a Muslim is strictly forbidden to work in such a company because his work promotes obscenity, and involves forbidden activities.[49]

In line with the argument above, the film medium could be put to use by Muslim groups in Europe and the United States under the condition that the medium is used to spread the word of Islam and to call people to Islam, that is, to make *da'wa*.

Muhammad the last Prophet

When Muslims are portrayed on film in the West, they are often depicted according to stereotypical models. Accordingly they are presented as violent terrorists driven by a compulsive hatred of everything that can be regarded as Western or as stereotypes fulfilling romantic, exotic or Orientalist expectations. As demonstrated by, for example, Jack Shaheen and others, the Hollywood image of Islam and Muslims is seldom balanced or neutral.[50] It is, of course, possible to argue that it is not a prerequisite for Hollywood, or for that matter other film producers, to be neutral or apolitical, since film is only a form of entertainment. But even though it is possible to take this position, it is obvious that film and popular media are very important for how the public view the world, as well as other religions, cultures or parts of the world. Hence, in order to challenge stereotypical and negative representations, some Muslims have started to produce their own films, as well as other forms of popular culture.

One example, which I will analyse more closely in this section, is the animated family movie *Muhammad the last Prophet*.[51] This movie is of great interest because it is an example of how Muslims have tried to use the motion picture to spread and inform others about Islam. In line with the aim of this chapter, therefore, it is important to outline and analyse the arguments used by the producers and the film company. This movie has been produced by the Fine Media Group, Badr International production and RichCrest Media, three commercial companies that have ties with both the United States and the Gulf. It should also be stressed that the film we are talking about is a so-called family movie. This genre can best be described as a category of films that ensure they follow certain moral codes and instil what is believed to be good behaviour in the viewer. For example, if a parent is renting or buying a film from this genre, he or she can be certain that the video or

---

49   Fatwa No. 36782 (printed 2004–02–03 from www.islamweb.net).
50   Shaheen 2001.
51   I have published a longer version of this section in Swedish; see Larsson 2006a.

DVD in question does not contain any nudity, sexuality or offensive language. This kind of family film finds its main market in the United States among Christians, but some Muslim or Islamic films also clearly belong to the genre. While the Fine Media Group is focused on Muslim films, promoting animated films with titles such as *Great Women of Islam*, *Salman the Persian* and *Before the Light*, RichCrest Media has mainly produced so-called Christian films.[52] Even though this is a very interesting and important genre, I am not aware of any academic studies that have focused on so-called religious family movies.

The aim of the animated movie *Muhammad the last Prophet* is clearly stated on the homepage of the Fine Media Group.

THE MOVIE OF ALL TIMES – MUHAMMAD THE LAST PROPHET

From the creators of *The King and I*, *The Fox and the Hound*, and the *Swan Princess* comes the first animated feature length film about Islam's Prophet. This groundbreaking film is set around 1400 years ago during the early ages of Islam. The film relates the events that unfolded and led to the rise of a renewed religion in the Arabian Desert, eventually spanning 7 continents and counting 1.6 billion adherents around the world.

This movie aims to introduce the story of Islam and its Prophet to new generations in the appealing and accessible medium of animation. Though the Prophet is not personified, sound and cinematography are employed in the telling of his story. The film is capped off with a stunning soundtrack by Emmy-award winning composer William Kidd.

Perfect for the family and for encouraging interfaith dialogue, this film is a definite must-see![53]

The movie, which was released in 2004, contained more than 196,000 images and had a budget estimated at 10 million dollars. Production started in 1998, but its release was delayed because of the 11th September atrocities in 2001.[54] The film is now available on DVD and is being promoted by several homepages that sell Islamic books, videos, clothing, and so on.

Without going into any details about this animated movie and its reception, it is evident that it was developed in order to create an Islamic alternative to non-Islamic children's movies and that the film was authorised by Muslim institutions in Egypt and Lebanon. To live up to this standard, before the film was produced the company behind it sought approval from al-Azhar University for its making. From

---

52 Information taken from the homepage of the Fine Media Group; see http://www.finemediagroup.com/pages/coming_soon (printed 2008–09–24).

53 See http://www.finemediagroup.com/home.html (printed 2008–04–16).

54 Larsson 2006a, pp. 104–105.

this point of view, *Muhammad the last Prophet* is an example of how Muslims are seeking ways of making use of the new information and communication technologies in the service of Islam.

An Islamic cinema?

The film *Muhammad the Last Prophet* is, however, not the first example of how the motion picture has been used to spread information about Islam and call people to it. In 1976 the first feature-length film about the Prophet Muhammad was released with two titles, in English, *The Message* and in Arabic, *al-Risalah*. From the very beginning the film by Moustapha Akkad was criticised by Muslim authorities, and a lot of negative rumours, for example, that the American actor Charlton Heston was going to play the role of Muhammad, created tensions and conflicts over the film. Even though Akkad received initial approval to start the shooting of the film from al-Azhar University and the Shi'ite Council of Lebanon after he had promised that the Prophet Muhammad, his wives and children were not going to appear on screen at all, the film still created problems. First of all, the production team was not allowed to complete the film in Morocco because King Hassan II of Morocco was put under pressure by the Saudi Arabian King Faisal. According to the Saudis it was a sin to trick viewers into believing that they were in Mecca when the film was shot in Morocco. After the team was expelled from Morocco, the Libyan leader Muammar Qaddafi invited Akkad to Libya to complete the film. However, when the film was scheduled to premier in the United States, a group of Black Muslim militants occupied the Washington DC building of the Jewish B'nai B'rith organisation and threatened to kill the staff if the film was shown in the country. This crisis was solved, and despite the initial criticisms the film received, the movie is today easily available. For example, during my field studies among Muslims in Sweden, I have often seen the film on display in Islamic shops in mosques and via online shops.[55]

Also, in post-revolutionary Iran the Islamic government tried to develop an Islamic cinema, that is, a cinema that could be used to spread knowledge about Islam and the revolution.[56] In his analysis of the Iranian film industry, Hamid Naficy shows clearly that the clergy actually changed their minds about motion pictures and the cinema over time. Prior to the revolution in 1978/1979, the cinema and movie theatres were viewed as evil and destructive by the opposition to the

---

55   For a detailed outline of this film, see chapter 5 in Bakker 2009.

56   Even though the situation is very different from Iran, a popular theme in, for example, Indonesian cinema is the coming of Islam to Indonesia. This is also an illustration of the fact that the cinema has been used to spread knowledge about Islam, Islamic historiography and Islamic moral and theology for a long period. Cf. Hanan 1997, p. 693. Similar genres, such as movies that try to instil Islamic values and norms, were also developed in Turkey in the 1970s and in India in the 1960s. See Dönmez-Colin 2004, pp. 87–102.

government (for example, Ayatollah Ruhullah Khomeini).[57] On the one hand, the cinema was seen as a representation of the Shah's rule and his sympathies for the West. On the other hand, it was deemed an un-Islamic medium that broke the rules of Islam. The commercial Film Farsi movies showed too much nudity and 'indecent' behaviour (for example, alcohol and sex), while art films were too positive about communism, Marxism and socialism.[58] In the following section, I will provide an analysis of Ayatollah Ruhullah Khomeini's view on cinema. His opinions have been selected for analysis here because they are very specific and detailed, but as we shall see in the following sections of this chapter, his opinions are not unique to Shi'a Muslims, since similar views are also found among Sunni '*ulama*'.

In his *Velayat faqih* ('The governance of the faqih'), Ayatollah Ruhullah Khomeini described, for example, the cinema as an injection of the ill effects of westernisation, namely immorality, dishonesty, prostitution, corruption and dependence.[59] This subject was also addressed in his *Hukumat-i Islami* ('Islamic Government'), which, among many things, contains an analysis of the negative rule of the Shah.[60] But after the revolution, Khomeini changed his mind regarding the nature of the cinema.[61]

---

57 Similar criticism was also voiced in Turkey in the 1970s according to Dönmez-Colin 2004, pp. 91, 96. The Muslim Brothers expressed similar criticisms; see Mitchell 1993, p. 223. For Iran, see Mirbakhtyar 2006, p. 103; for contemporary Egypt, see Hirschkind 2006.

58 Mirbakhtyar 2006, pp. 103, 106.

59 The friction that the cinema caused in Iran is, however, not unique to this country. According to Thompson's analysis of similar developments in Syria and Lebanon, the cinema halls 'became a node of confrontation between colonizer and colonized, between western cultural influence and indigenous audiences'. Thompson 2000, p. 200. Not even the view that Western influence damages and corrupts the people of the Middle East is new. In the 1930s, the Maronite Patriarch Antoine 'Arida argued that 'it is France that perverts our people and introduces immorality to them'. Quoted from Thompson 2000, p. 204. Cf. Mitchell 1993, p. 223. It is also stressed by Amr Hamzawy that the new information and communication technologies have been accused of spreading and promoting Satanism and 'immorality' among Muslims. See Hamzawy 2000, p. 138. The dichotomy between 'Iranian' and 'Western' values invoked by Khomeini in the quotation above is, however, not unique to him. Similar ways of debating modernity, technology and the impact of the West were a much debated topic among intellectuals in the West who embraced the 'spirit of 68'. Hence, it is important to place the Iranian revolution of 1978/1979 in a much broader intellectual context. Torben Rugberg Rasmusen writes: 'the revolution did not take place within an intellectual or theoretical vacuum, but within the context of an antimodernist, nativist, xenophobic, populist and nationalist discourse, which had already come to dominate the intellectual panorama of Iranian society in the 1960s'. Rugberg Rasmusen 1994, p. 173.

60 Khomeini 1981, p. 58.

61 Naficy 2002, pp. 27–28.

We are not opposed to cinema, to radio or to television; what we oppose is vice and the use of the media to keep our young people in a state of backwardness and dissipate their energies. We have never opposed these features of modernity in themselves, but when they were brought from Europe to the East, particularly to Iran, unfortunately they were used not in order to advance civilisation, but in order to drag us into barbarism. The cinema is a modern invention that ought to be used for the sake of educating the people, but, as you know, it was used instead to corrupt our youth. It is the misuse of cinema that we are opposed to, a misuse caused by the treacherous policies of our rulers.[62]

For Khomeini, the motion picture per se was not dangerous, it was the content and the reason for showing movies that was the problem, an argument that resembles Yusuf al-Qaradawi's opinions today.[63] Instead of combating the popular medium, a so-called Islamic cinema, to use Hamid Naficy's terminology, should be developed to foster Islamic and Iranian ideals.[64] The aim of this film genre was to protect Islamic morality in front as well as behind the camera. Hence, it was necessary to introduce new rules for the control of morality and to allocate state funding for morally approved films.[65] The film industry therefore became an important tool for 'improving' morality in the country, especially during the Iran-Iraq war in the 1980s, but also for resolving the trauma that followed with the war.[66] Another important function for the cinema was to criticise the former rule of Reza Shah and present his rule in a negative and un-Islamic light.[67]

But the overarching aim of the Islamic film industry was to instil morality and enhance Islamic education. To reach this goal, it was necessary to present an idealised Islamic society, among other things, that is, a society that upholds strict gender boundaries and high standards of morality.[68] This ideal Islamic society could then be contrasted and compared with a destructive and negative un-Islamic society. Consequently, women were 'shown as modest and chaste characters whose raison d'être was to be obedient wives and dutiful mothers'.[69] Individuals who tried to break free from the social order were consequently punished symbolically both on the film screen and in real life.[70] If Muslims are presented in an idealised

62   Khomeini 1981, p. 258. The quotation is taken from a speech delivered by Khomeini on February 2, 1979 under the title 'Address at Bihisht-i Zahara' at the cemetery outside Tehran where many of the martyrs of the Islamic Revolution are buried.

63   This conclusion is also supported by Mirbakhtyar 2006, p. 103.

64   See, for example, Naficy 2002. See also Shala Mirbakhtyar 2006, p. 172 and p. 100.

65   Devictor 2002, p. 67.

66   An analysis of war cinema in Iran can be found in Varzi 2002.

67   Akrami 1987, p. 140.

68   Cf. Mitchell 1993, p. 223.

69   Dönmez-Colin 2004, p. 99.

70   Cf. Dönmez-Colin's (2004) analysis of women in Iranian and Turkish motion pictures.

way in the Islamic film industry, non-Muslims or 'bad' Muslims are depicted as immoral, weak and dangerous.[71] Although this dramaturgy is highly visible in the so-called Islamic cinema in countries such as Iran, India and Turkey, the plot is not new. According to Dönmez-Colin, Muslim women in general are presented according to stereotypical and unrealistic images in most Turkish and Iranian films.[72] The ideal woman is consequently the chaste and loyal family woman (that is, the daughter or wife), as opposed to the bad woman, who is presented as a renegade or prostitute. Without an 'owner', women are prey to evil, according to Dönmez-Colin's analysis.[73] Women are supposed to uphold and protect family honour, and those who fail to live according to this law are often punished by rape or violence in several Iranian and Turkish motion pictures analysed by Dönmez-Colin.[74]

> The repeated portrayal of women as the sources and recipients of male anger and frustration, and the linking of violence and sex in people's minds, have been food for cinema since its inception.[75]

From a gender perspective, Muslim and Middle Eastern women in general have more or less played the same character in both secular and Islamic movies, according to Dönmez-Colin, Lina Khatib and Shahla Lahiji's analyses of the film industry in Egypt, Iran and Turkey respectively. In their view, women in motion pictures usually both mirror and uphold the cultural norms and values of society, values that are seldom in favour of women's liberation or emancipation. Consequently the prime function of the great majority of motion pictures is not to question or test the boundaries of the Islamic norms and values that are supported and promoted by the men in power.[76]

---

71 Cf. for example Khatib 2004, especially pp. 75–79.

72 Dönmez-Colin 2004, pp. 19–72.

73 Dönmez-Colin 2004, p. 24.

74 Cf. Dönmez-Colin 2004. According to the social anthropologist Julian Pitt-Rivers' definition, honour 'is both internal to the individual and external to him – a matter of his feelings, his behaviour, and the treatment that he receives'. Pitt-Rivers 1968, p. 503. Furthermore, he writes that sexual purity is the essence of honour in women and that the defence of female purity is a male responsibility in many cultures. Pitt-Rivers 1968, pp. 505–506. The analysis suggested by Dönmez-Colin is, however, contested by Shahla Mirbakhtyar. She argues that Iranian filmmakers had to include 'rape and sexual violence' in order to be able to have sex in their movies, otherwise it would have been impossible to include nudity or sex at all. Mirbakhtyar 2006, pp. 30–31. This suggestion is, however, not supported by any convincing data, and it is unlikely that Dönmez-Colin would agree with this analysis.

75 Dönmez-Colin 2004, p. 74.

76 Cf. Dönmez-Colin 2004, Khatib 2004, and Lahiji 2002.

Guidelines for an Islamic cinema in Iran

To be able to use the cinema and transform it into an Islamic tool, the new Iranian regime had to impose controls, rules and regulations that targeted both the audience and the film-makers. To get a grip on the situation, in June 1982 the Ministry of Culture and Islamic Guidance in Iran issued guidelines for the development of an Islamic cinema and for the control and censorship of imported films and videos. (The list below is based on Hamid Naficy's research, and the bullet points are taken from his translation of the basic Persian documents on the motion picture and cinema halls from Iran.)[77] All films and videos shown in Iran must therefore have an exhibition permit issued by this bureau, which can also ban all films and videos which:

- Weaken the principle of monotheism and other Islamic principles or insult them in any manner.
- Insult, directly or indirectly, the Prophets, Imams, the guardianship of the Supreme Jurisprudent (*velayat faqih*), the ruling Council or the jurisprudents (*mujtaheds*).
- Blaspheme against the values and personalities held sacred by Islam and other religions mentioned in the Constitutions.
- Encourage wickedness, corruption and prostitution.
- Encourage or teach dangerous addictions and earning a living from unsavoury means such as smuggling.
- Negate the equality of all people regardless of colour, race, language, ethnicity and belief.
- Encourage foreign cultural, economic and political influence contrary to the 'neither West nor East' policy of the government.
- Express or disclose anything that is against the interests and policies of the country which might be exploited by foreigners.
- Show details of scenes of violence and torture in such a way as to disturb or mislead the viewer.
- Misrepresent historical and geographical facts.
- Lower the taste of the audience by means of low production and artistic values.
- Negate the values of self-sufficiency and economic and social independence.

---

77   In analysing the guidelines, it is important to stress that the Iranian government imposed several rules and set up a number of different institutions for monitoring the cinema industry. As outlined by Devictor (2002) and Naficy (2002), it should be remembered that new guidelines have been issued over the years. Hence, it is not possible to argue that that the Iranian government has one position or model for the film industry. Both liberal and more conservative rules have been imposed, and policies have been liable to change over the years.

Furthermore it was forbidden to question, alter or negate:

- Monotheism and submission to God and his laws.
- The role of Revelation in expressing laws.
- Resurrection and its role in the evolution of man towards God.
- The justness of God in creation and in law.
- The continuity of religious leadership (*Emamat*).
- The role of the Islamic Republic of Iran under the leadership of Ayatollah Khomeini in ridding Muslims and the downtrodden from world imperialism.[78]

With the help of these rules and regulations, it was believed that the cinema should be transformed and uplifted so that it could be used to spread Islam and the values of the Iranian revolution.

However, as indicated earlier in this text, the motion picture is not only problematic for '*ulama*' because of its content. By visiting cinemas, Muslims run the risk of entering a new public space that is not governed or secluded by Islamic rules and regulations. For example, the physical set-up of the cinema was perceived by the '*ulama*' under discussion as a challenge to Islamic norms and values because men and women would be interacting beyond the traditional gender boundaries, making it difficult to uphold a strict gender division inside a cinema hall. To get a grip on the new situation, Muslim '*ulama*' (but also some Christian leaders in the Orient as described by, for example, Elisabeth Thompson below) had to impose restrictions and guidelines for how to control the new moral space and the new possibility of interaction between the sexes.

Cinemas and moral space

The establishment and introduction of the cinema was not only a process associated with colonialism and imperialism: the cinema was also a vehicle for social, cultural and intellectual transformation and change,[79] a medium transforming 'traditional' society into a modern or Western society, according to both Brian Larkin and Elizabeth Thompson. The technology for transmitting and showing moving pictures was seen as a symbol of modernity, but the cinema, and especially the social practice of going to the movies, was often viewed as something un-Islamic and unlawful.[80] Already in the late 1920s it is reported that some '*ulama*' asked for stricter moral censorship of films, especially so-called love films.[81] According

---

78   Translation taken from Naficy 2002, pp. 36–37.

79   On architecture, urban planning and colonialism, see AlSayyad 1992.

80   Cf. Larkin 1999, p. 13; Naficy 2002; Thompson 2000 and Dönmez-Colin 2004, p. 91.

81   However, it should be stressed that the Muslim leaders were not alone in their criticism of the new medium. Anette Kuhn (1989) has clearly demonstrated in her study,

to the protesters, going to the movies was morally questionable, and most films were perceived as not good for Muslims.[82] During the 1930s, it was also reported by the Arab press that on several occasions Muslim groups in Syria, Palestine and Egypt rallied to protest in favour of having women banned from attending film screenings or visiting cinema halls.[83] Even today women have been killed in public squares by family members in Anatolia, Turkey, after they have visited a cinema hall.[84]

In his work on cinema theatres in Nigeria, Brian Larkin illustrates vividly that the introduction of the cinema and the construction of purpose-built halls for screening films transformed and challenged the Muslim Hausa society in many ways.[85] First of all, the medium, that is, the motion picture, was seen as a theological problem because of the fact that images were not accepted by all Muslims.[86] Hence, the film medium per se was viewed as something un-Islamic or even evil. Secondly, the fact that both men and women came together in a dark room to watch movies without any, or only limited, possibilities to maintain gender boundaries became a moral problem for the '*ulama*'.[87] According to them the

---

Cinema Censorship and Sexuality, 1909–1925, that the introduction of the motion picture and the building of cinema theatres in Europe gave rise to heavy debate and moral panic. Resembling the debate in Syria and Lebanon (as discussed by Elisabeth Thompson, 2000), many religious leaders and politicians were calling for stricter rules, control and censorship of the cinema. A specific problem with the new medium in Europe was that it attracted primarily the interest of the working class and children, two uneducated and morally weak groups in society according to the critics. For example, in 1917 the Cinema Commission of Inquiry (Edinburgh) reported that ' "the darkness, combined with the low standard of morality of the individual" leads to indecency' in the cinema theatres. Quotation from Kuhn 1989, p. 120. In general Kuhn's study of censorship demonstrates that the negative criticisms voiced by the Muslim leaders in Elisabeth Thompson's work on greater Syria were more or less shared by European critics of motion pictures in the two first decades of the twentieth century. Cf. Kennerberg 1996, who also describes and analyses how Pentecostal pastors in Sweden condemned the impact of the film industry, and especially of cinemas, as dangerous and sinful places.

82   See, for example, *al-Ayyam*, 26 February 1935, summarised by Vacca 1935, p. 123, and *al-Ayyam*, 20 March 1939, summarised by Vacca 1939, p. 215. A general discussion is found in Landau 1958, pp. 163–164. Cf. Mitchell 1993, p. 223.

83   Thompson 2000, Chapter 12.

84   Dönmez-Colin 2004, p. 7.

85   Cf. Larkin 2002.

86   See previous chapter on photography.

87   This problem is frequently discussed in Dönmez-Colin 2004. In her study of social developments in Syria and Lebanon, Elisabeth Thompson has also demonstrated that many Christians in the Middle East shared this concern with the Muslims and feared that the cinema was a moral problem. For example, the 1935 Catholic youth congress declared that 'The cinema hall is the classic place of romantic rendez-vous [...] It's a closed, dark bottle where moral and physical fermentations reproduce easily'. Quoted from Thompson 2000, p. 204.

building of cinemas created a new moral space that had to be controlled by Islamic rules and regulations. The building of cinemas reshaped the traditional structure of the Nigerian towns and created new public spaces for interaction between the sexes. This new public space could easily become a problem, according to the '*ulama*'.[88]

With the rise of the Western colonial system in Nigeria at the beginning of the twentieth century, the city of Kano was transformed. When the British arrived in 1903 the town was reshaped, and new institutions, such as beer parlours, theatres, public gardens, libraries and cinemas, were introduced.[89] In some cases, as with the building of the Palace cinema next to the Kurmi market in the Old City of Kano, the transformation of the city fuelled a popular uprising by the Muslim community. For many Muslims, the cinema was associated with un-Islamic behaviour and Western imperialism, and was therefore to be confronted.[90] Already the symbolically loaded names of the cinema halls in Kano, such as Rex, Palace and Queens, illustrates how closely related the new technology was to the British imperial power.[91] In his analysis, Larkin draws parallels between the sacred function of the mosque and the non-sacred function of the cinema hall. Those who attended the cinema theatres were even described as *karuwai* (that is, independent women or prostitutes).[92] Thus it seems that the cinema created an invisible boundary between those who attended it and those who did not.

> Cinema theatres took hold in the Hausa imagination as a social space and practice that enacted the moral qualities of the areas in which they were located. They mimicked, in profane form, symbolic and material qualities traditionally associated with mosques and markets. Just as the mosque traditionally marked out the physical boundaries of moral society and the creation of a public arena for ritual and economic activity, the cinema theatre came to take on this role in inverted fashion. Like the mosque, it created an arena for public association, for ritualistic attendance, it drew around it satellite enterprises selling food or books and magazines; and it constituted a landmark of the urban topography.[93]

---

88   This observation is also relevant for Syria and Lebanon, according to Thompson 2000, p. 198.

89   The transformation of Middle Eastern cities and the impact of colonialism, imperialism and Western culture during the period 1900–1950 are discussed in Skovgaard-Petersen 2001.

90   But it was not only in Nigeria that the movie theatres and the cinema were seen as something morally suspect. In Syria in 1932 a regulation ordered that the cinemas should be closed during religious holidays and that it was necessary to control or censure films that included offensive or morally questionable material. In Syria and Lebanon, this opinion, or concern, was shared by both Muslims and Christians, according to Thompson 2001.

91   Larkin 1999, p. 13 and Larkin 2002, p. 323.

92   Larkin 2002, p. 327.

93   Larkin 1999, p. 13.

But this attitude, or more precisely the concern for the fact that both Muslim men and women socialise when they go to the movies is not typical of Nigeria, nor of this period.[94] In both Egypt and Iran, many cinema palaces solved the problem at the beginning of the twentieth century by giving gender-segregated film shows or by creating separate areas for male and female audiences.[95] The importance of gender is clearly illustrated in the following advertisement from Iran in the 1920s:

> The Founder of the Grand Cinema, in order to serve you, has dedicated a section especially for the respected ladies and therefore tonight invites all locals to view new and unequalled films. And in honour of the attendance of the respected ladies, the first and second parts of the famous series 'The Copper Bullet' will be shown for the first time in one night. The entry door for respected ladies is from the Grand Cinema, and for the gentlemen from the Grand Hotel. The employees of the Grand Cinema and also the officers of the Police Department will refuse entry to inappropriately dressed and troublesome youths.[96]

By maintaining a strict division between men and women, cinema owners, audiences and parents could all be 'guaranteed' that the moral boundaries between the sexes would be upheld.[97] However, as Elizabeth Thompson shows, this was a theoretical or idealised solution that was challenged or contested by both men and women.[98] According to Gönül Dönmez-Colin, women in Turkey used to dress in male clothing or as 'Christians' in order to accompany men to the cinema.[99] Women going to the movies therefore continued to be a 'problem' for both Muslim and Christian religious leaders in Syria, Lebanon and Turkey.

The content of the movies was also seen as a problem since many of them were sexually explicit. Movie stars, both female and male, were presented and viewed as 'sex objects' representing an alternative lifestyle that challenged the established moral order and the prevailing customs of society.[100] But the cinema hall became above all a meeting place or an interface between men and women

---

94   Cf. Dönmez-Colin 2004.

95   Cf. Akrami 1987, p. 134; Landau 1965, p. 40, and Mirbakhtyar 2006, pp. 11–13.

96   Quoted in Mirbakhtyar 2006, pp. 12–13.

97   This method is, however, not unique to this period or to the cinema. In, for example, Sweden, Muslim women organisations rent bath houses to ensure that no males are there when Muslim women are dressed in an 'un-Islamic' fashion, i.e. in a bathing suit. Cf. Roald 1999, p. 127.

98   Cf. Thompson 2000, Chapter 12. It is important to note that Muslim and Christian leaders in, for example, Lebanon were often united in their criticisms of the motion picture and of gender-mixed cinemas. According to Richard P. Mitchell, the Muslim Brothers in Egypt made a clear distinction between Eastern and Western Christians (especially regarding missionaries). Compared to the latter, the former were not a serious problem. Mitchell 1993, p. 231.

99   Dönmez-Colin 2004, p. 9.

100 Cf. Thompson 2000, p. 210 and Mitchell 1991, p. 223.

that was beyond the control of both parents and religious institutions. Through this function, the '*ulama*' perceived cinemas as a threat to the Islamic principle of *khalwa* (privacy).[101] As soon as the film started and the lights went out, the room became dark and it was no longer possible to control the sexual and moral boundaries maintained by society, a conclusion supported by both the '*ulama*' and Christian religious leaders at the time of the introduction of the cinema and the building of cinema halls. From this point of view, the cinema transformed both the topography of the city – most cinemas were, for example, located in the centre, and they were often set up between ethnically, culturally, religiously or economically separate quarters of the city – and thus they created new patterns for social activities in the city. Typical male arenas, such as the city centre, meeting halls and squares, were transformed, or at least challenged, by the introduction of the cinema and the 'modern life' that was associated with the new institutions. For example, in Damascus and Beirut the colonial period had a transformative effect on 'classical' urban planning, and from this time on oriental cities were transformed and reshaped into 'modern' cities. From now on the oriental city had a similar structure and the same facilities as most cities in Europe and the United States.[102] For many religious leaders, the new supply and the habits that followed the introduction of the cinema became a problem.[103] For example, in Damascus, riots and violence erupted frequently outside cinemas from the 1920s until 1940s.[104] Cinema halls showing so-called women's movie matinees, that is, screenings attended only by women, were especially targeted. For example, on 20 June 1928, Elisabeth Thompson reports that a cinema hall in Damascus mysteriously caught fire approximately one hour before the premiere of the first women's matinee.[105] Although officials declared that the fire had been an accident, the timing was important. The debate over women who took an active part in public life was frequently aired in the 1920s and 1930s throughout the region. For example, in April 1932 Muslims in Tripoli asked for a ban against women attending entertainment halls and cinemas.[106] Similar steps were taken by Muslim leaders in Aleppo in 1933 and in Latakia in 1935. The goal was to stop women from attending cinemas and to hinder female emancipation. The *mufti* in Hama, Sheikh Sa'id al-Na'sin, even argued that the cinema corrupts the virtue of women. Consequently women should be prevented from watching movies and

---

101   On the concept of *khalwa*, see al-Qaradawi 2001, p. 147.

102   According to historians of urban planning, it is possible to distinguish between three periods: a medieval phase, a pre-modern colonial phase, and a modern phase. See AlSayyad 1995, p. 288.

103   Cf. Thompson 2000, p. 197, and Mitchell 1993, p. 223.

104   Thompson 2000, chapter 12.

105   Thompson 2001, p. 89, and Thompson 2000, p. 205.

106   Thompson 2001, pp. 205–206.

from attending cinema theatres in Syria. The criticism was partly successful, and women were banned from cinemas in Hama and Homs in 1939.[107]

The examples given by Elizabeth Thompson above illustrate clearly the transformative effect that the introduction of new information and communication technologies had on Muslim society and on the Middle East in general. On the one hand, the introduction of the cinema could be seen as a vehicle with the power to reshape and modernise the city (that is, its architectural language and its institutions) as well as its moral norms. On the other hand, the technology continued to transmit deeply rooted moral values, especially gender structures (cf. the earlier discussion about women in Iranian and Turkish motion pictures).[108] But even when the technology could be used for preserving and harbouring established structures and cultural norms, it is evident that the cinema industry also brought new impulses from the West to the colonised regions of the world. The transformative effect of the film industry is vividly described by the Lebanese historian Albert Hourani:

> The process of change is being speeded by one manifestation of Western civilisation above all: the film which expresses a way of feminine life, and a conception of the relations between men and women, which are far from those prevalent in the Islamic world.[109]

Although the introduction of the cinema was very important in the development and transformation of the Middle East, as described by Hourani above, it is difficult to say whether the changes that took place in the 1920s and 1930s were caused by the introduction of the new media or by the general processes of modernisation that the whole region went through during this time. From a media and communication point of view, this is a classic question that is difficult to answer.[110] Irrespective of how we interpret the impact of the new information and communication technologies, it is necessary to be critical of so-called monocausal explanations that describe the shift in society only by referring to technological

---

107   Thompson 2000, pp. 205–207.

108   Cf. Dönmez-Colin 2004 and Lahiji 2002.

109   Hourani 1946, p. 93. A similar way of putting the argument is found in Mirbakhtyar. She writes: 'The Western invasion of Iran in the 1940s brought more than military machines. It also introduced elements of foreign cultures, in particular their films, which introduced Iranians to new lifestyles that sharply contrasted the centuries-old traditional Iranian way of life.' Mirbakhtyar 2006, p. 37. Furthermore, she continues: 'American films opened Iranian popular entertainment to depictions of actions and behavior that, before, would have conflicted with the people's traditional values. Among these were movie scenes with sex, alcohol, bars, cigarettes, and gangs. Concepts like fashion, in the Western sense, were also new to Iranians where traditional dress was the norm, and a reflection of long-held values.' Mirbakhtyar 2006, p. 37.

110   This problem is, for example, discussed in Raymond Williams' classic study of the impact of television; see Williams 2001.

developments. It is clear that one must also consider the social, economic and intellectual developments that reshaped the region if one wants to understand the Muslim debate on information and communication technologies.

Film and Islamic pragmatism

Even though the debates about cinemas and going to the movies are much more peaceful and non-violent today compared to the beginning of the twentieth century, it is clear that the issue still provokes many Muslims. This tension was, for example, illustrated at the beginning of this chapter and in the discussion about the banning of the movie *Matrix Reloaded* in Egypt in 2003. However, the practical problems involved in watching movies or in going to the cinema, as analysed by, for example, Thompson and Larkin, were not solved after the Second World War. Similar opinions are still articulated by Muslims in Europe or the United States. For example, the lawfulness of watching movies is frequently debated on Muslim sites on the Internet, as well as in printed books and pamphlets.[111] Both the contents of films, especially the image of Arabs and Muslims in Hollywood films, and the social practice of going to the movies are on occasion debated and analysed by Muslims.[112] For example, on the webpage of IslamOnline.net, Sheikh Ahmad ash-Sharabasi, formerly a Professor of Islamic Creed at al-Azhar University, issued a *fatwa* in 2003 on the Islamic position on watching and making films. His answer resembles in many ways the opinion expressed by Ayatollah Ruhullah Khomeini after the revolution in 1978/1979. Ash-Sharabasi says:

> basically watching films, plays and artistic works is permissible as long as they do not present, as we see today, what is contrary to Islamic teachings. Art that provokes vices and Fitnah (temptation) is prohibited. It is permissible to watch films that uphold virtue, morality and humane principles while maintaining the rule of lowering gazes. Islam does not go against beautiful art. […] It becomes incumbent upon all Muslim intelligentsia to make use of what Allah endows them with in reforming society. We greatly need, through films or serials, to remind the new generation about the heroic lives of Muslim reformers and fighters. Moreover, society is in great need to present good morals, history of Islam, and to provide solutions for its problems through works of art that strongly affect different classes in society.[113]

---

111   See, for example, Sikand 2006.

112   On Arabs and Muslims in Hollywood films, see, for example, Shaheen 2001.

113   Ash-Sharabaasi, 'Films and dramas in Islamic perspectives', retrieved from http:// www.islamonline.net/servlet/Satellite?pagename=IslamOnline-English-Ask_Scholar/ FatwaE/FatwaEandcid=1119503544786 (printed 2005-09-22). Cf. Fatwa No. 15426 (printed 2004-02-03 from Islamweb.Net).

According to this *fatwa*, the medium per se is not the problem, but rather the content of the film and the intention of the audience.[114] Ash-Sharabasi is clear when he says that Islam forbids all films that could be labelled as *haram* (forbidden).[115] For example, X-rated movies or plays that attack the virtues and truths of Islam are strictly forbidden. But films produced with a so-called good intention, that is, movies of high morality and good taste, are labelled as *halal* (permitted or lawful). Like ash-Sharabasi, Maulana Mahmoud Ahmed Mirpuri, a Pakistani scholar who was formally employed at the al-Madinah al-Munawwara University and who is a key figure in the establishment of the *Markazi Jamiat Ahl-e-Hadith* in the UK, is open to educational films and documentaries that could have a positive influence and foster Islamic norms and values.[116] He says:

> If something contains obscene material and music, there is no doubt for it being wrong and having no benefits. But it is wrong to say that there are no films available without such things, as there are many good documentaries and educational films, science and Islamic videos and so on, available which are beneficial for us. They contain useful and knowledgeable material without obscenity and music, and are easily obtainable.[117]

It is also interesting to note that ash-Sharabasi's *fatwa* on the topic ends with a request for a greater number of Islamic films. According to him, film-makers and film-producers have a divine mission, and their knowledge could play an important role in spreading the words of Allah and in calling people to Islam if it is used wisely.

> What we need now is to employ this sophisticated technology in the service of religion, airing ethical values and spiritual principles, as well as filling the mind of the new generation with patriotism. Azhar scholars urge film directors all over the world to respond to the call of religion, morality, and patriotism and produce pure and serious films that could strengthen principles of good and virtue in man. They also urge the filmmakers to encourage building social relations among people, based on religious principles, for this will help in developing art.[118]

However, it should be stressed that the *'ulama'* are not unique in this position. Several Christian theologians and other religious leaders have shown an interest in the new media: according to Freek L. Bakker, 'the introduction of film caused

---

114   Cf. El Fadl 2001, p. 198.

115   Cf. Maulana Mahmood Ahmed Mirpuri's *fatwa*, 'Films according to Islamic Shari'a'. Mirpuri 1998, p. 276.

116   The biographical data come from the preface to the book *Fatawa Sirat-e-Mustaqeem* 1998, pp. 7–8.

117   Mirpuri 1998, p. 276.

118   ash-Sharabaasi, 'Films and drama ... '.

a great upheaval in all great religions of the world'.[119] Like the '*ulama*' discussed in this chapter, many Christian leaders also express a fear of the film medium,[120] but several theologians are also optimistic and express the hope that the media can be used as a tool for missionary work. The Christian theologian Robert Jewett can serve as an example of this opinion. He writes:

> If we [the Christian priests] wish to follow Paul's cue ... it is essential that ministers, teachers and laypersons interested in the impact of the faith should begin to take more seriously the growing cultural force of the movies.[121]

Even though we should abstain from general conclusions, the quotation above and several *fatwas* discussed in this chapter show that most '*ulama*' have come to terms with the motion picture and the art of photography.

Nevertheless, even though '*ulama*' argue that Muslims are allowed to watch motion pictures that are labelled *halal*, this should not be used as an excuse for neglecting the religious duties (that is, the '*ibadat*) that all Muslims must follow. According to Yusuf al-Qaradawi, going to the movies seems to be part and parcel of Western life, and to his knowledge such a life is often hard to combine with firm religious belief.[122] To prevent Muslims from committing illicit activities in the darkened cinema halls, al-Qaradawi recommends that men and women should be separated when they attend cinemas.[123] This opinion shows and reminds us that going to the movies is still a problematic issue for many Muslims. But it is also important to remember that the consumption of films and the practice of going to the movies is not only a Western phenomenon. Egypt, for example, is the leading producer of films in the Middle East, and the film industry (cinema, television and DVD) is therefore a strong economic sector in the region, as well as a popular activity for most people.

Conclusions

When analysing Islamic debates and opinions about the film media, it is important to remember that the development and introduction of the cinema in Europe and the United States was not unproblematic or uncontested. As in the Middle East and the rest of the world, the cinema in the West blurred and challenged the distinction between the public and private spheres, and the cinema halls created a new social space. This 'room' or 'social space' was also debated and contested

---

119   Bakker 2009, p. 247.

120   Cf. Black 1998.

121   Quotation taken from Wright 2007, p. 17.

122   The tensions between so-called 'modern' Western life and Muslim life are, for example, addressed by Nasr 1999.

123   al-Qaradawi 1985, p. 307.

by strong forces in Europe and the United States. The call for censorship and restrictions on the new film media is therefore not unique for the '*ulama*'.[124] The Hays Code, for example, was implemented in the United States in the 1930s to uphold the moral norms of society. The aim of the Code was to control the relationship between men and women and to preserve a general decency.[125] It should, however, be remembered that the censorship of films and popular cultures is of minor importance in Western society today as compared to the beginning of the twentieth century, though in most countries in the Middle East and the Third World censorship is still important.

Besides the discussion about morality, it is clear that the cinema has been an important tool in stimulating nationalist feelings and a sense of belonging. This function is still today part and parcel of national film institutes and the promotion of films. Furthermore, it is also obvious that, although the representatives of various religions have tried to make use of the film media to promote specific religious beliefs and world views, the media is also used for criticising, mocking and combating religion and religiosity.[126] But it is also easy to find movies that promote various forms of, for example, Buddhism, Christianity, Hinduism or Islam.[127] Hence, I am inclined to agree with Rachel Dwyer, who argues that:

> the worldwide growth of religiosity and its centrality to globalisation; the shift in the boundaries of the public, the private, and the political; the growth of international markets and their dynamic relationship to the centers of cultural production all call for an urgent reexamination of religion in media studies ...[128]

In this chapter I have outlined the history and introduction of the film media and the establishment of cinemas in a number of countries in what is today known as the Middle East. This backdrop has been related to an analysis of a number of both Sunni and Shi'a '*ulama*' who have debated the pros and cons of the film media. Even though the '*ulama*' included in this chapter have been sceptical of images, photography and the representational arts, few have banned the film as a medium. The criticism has mainly been focused on the immoral aspects that can be found in some movies. Several '*ulama*' have consequently been concerned with the portrayal of women in cinemas and the Western influences that are attached to the new media. As demonstrated by several academic studies, women are often portrayed in accordance with cultural and religious stereotypes in Iranian and Turkish movies, this being an example of how the media uphold traditional values. Hence, it is obvious that several '*ulama*' – especially the contemporary ones discussed at the end of this chapter – argue that film can be used as an

---

124   See, for example, Bakker 2009 and Kuhn 1989, chapter 7.
125   Cf. Devictor 2002, p. 71. See also Black 1998.
126   See, for example, Dwyer 2006; and Wright 2007.
127   Bakker 2009.
128   Dwyer 2006, p. 285.

efficient tool for promoting Islam and in missionary work. Even though film may give rise to problems, it seems that most contemporary '*ulama*' have accepted the 'motion picture' as part and parcel of the modern world. It is believed that, if the technology is used wisely – that is, if it not filled with immorality, nudity or other 'un-Islamic' values – it can even be used as a tool for spreading and calling people to Islam.[129] From a pragmatic point of view, the '*ulama*' have become accustomed to the film medium and are using it today as a means to get more individuals to embrace Islam. Hence, they believe that it is not the technology per se that is dangerous: it is what you do with it that matters!

---

129   Cf. Hirschkind 2006 and the use of Islamic cassettes for *da'wa* work.

Chapter 4
From Airwaves to Satellite Television

The great need for discussion of the Islamic perspective concerning the issue of television is clear to us all. Since television has entered the homes of people in every corner of the earth, the rich and the poor, the educated and un-educated, Muslims and non-Muslims – it has become a necessity to address the issue and explain the problems and dangers of television in a clear and concise manner for the benefit of every Muslim who is seeking to please Allah, the Most High, and earn His reward.[1]

The world of communication in the Middle East was revolutionised with the development and introduction of radio and television broadcasting. Radio broadcasting technology was introduced in the region in the 1920s, and television broadcasting was started in the late 1950s and the early 1960s.[2] Although the importance of physical distance had already shrunk with the arrival of the telegraph in the Middle East,[3] the introduction of radio and television broadcasting reduced the significance of physical boundaries and geographical distance even further. With broadcasting technology, news originating in remote regions, or even foreign countries, could now easily be passed on to a much larger audience residing in all parts of the Middle East, a fact of great importance, not least for the emerging press in the Arabic-speaking world.[4] Although radio and television broadcasting was soon controlled and monopolised by the early nation states in the region, this was the beginning of a new epoch in the history of media in the Middle East.

It goes without saying that the introduction of media based on sounds and images was of great significance in cultures with low levels of literacy and an uneven distribution of education. If we consider this aspect of the broadcasting media, it is even possible to argue that the introduction of radio and television was even more important than that of printing.

In the 1990s the situation of broadcasting media changed dramatically yet again due to the introduction of satellite television, after which a large number of private television channels were set up, both inside and outside the Middle East.[5] With this technological development, the nation states began to lose their control

---

1   *The Ruling on Tasweer* 2002, p. 226.

2   Cf. Mowlana 1995b.

3   On the importance of the telegraph in the Middle East, see, for example, Davison 1990; Brown 1849; Bektas 2000; Peters 1986 and Skovgaard-Petersen 1997a, pp. 80–99.

4   Cf., for example, Ayalon 1995, pp. 74–75, 82, 100.

5   Cf., for example, Sakr 2001, al-Nawawy and Iskandar 2002 and Zayani 2005.

over the media landscape, while, with satellite broadcasting, discussed at the end of this chapter, they lost more or less all control over the flow of information. However, it is important to remember that earlier communication media had also been difficult to control. For example, travelling preachers, books and messages transmitted via media such as the telegraph or cassettes could also cause problems for those in power.[6] Similarly, terrestrial radio and television signals were also difficult to control prior to the age of satellite broadcasting.[7] It is therefore clear that information and communication technologies have always contained a political power that could be used for spreading theological and political ideas such as, for example, pan-Arabism or Islamism within the Arab world, or for that matter for challenging the legitimacy of other states or for revolutionary activities within a specific country.[8]

Besides their potential to bridge physical and geographical distance, radio and television broadcasting also created new forms of social behaviour that had a strong impact on the organisation of ordinary life; it could even be argued that broadcasting media had the power to alter past traditions and to establish new ways of organising family life. With the arrival of broadcasting media, social life was changed for many individuals and families in the Middle East, as it was in other parts of the world. The radio, and later on the television set, became important artefacts that symbolised modernity and prosperity. The technology also embodied a power that could bring the family together and create new behaviours and routines and make families think and interact with the world in new ways.[9] But with the radio, and ever more so with the television, new consumption patterns were soon created. In order to adapt to these new demands, most coffee-house owners bought a radio or television set to attract old and new customers.[10] From this point in time, the television set became the centre and fixed point that rearranged both the private and public spheres. All around the world, homes were from now on decorated, structured and organised in order to accommodate a place for the television set in the room. All in all, there are plenty of examples showing that the radio and television are powerful tools that embody the power to change our understanding and perception of the world.[11]

The focus in this chapter is on a selected number of Muslim responses to the introduction and use of radio and television. My examples date from the early period of the first radio and television broadcasts in the region, but my main focus is on the most recent decades, and especially on contemporary Muslim debates

---

6   Cf. Hirschkind 2006, p. 36, and Sreberny-Mohammadi and Mohammadi 1994.

7   See Boyd 1975, p. 646.

8   Cf. Boyd 1982, pp. 5–6 and Abu-Lughod 2006.

9   To put it in the words of Silverstone et al. 1992, the information and communication technologies should be situated and analysed in relation to the so-called moral economy of the household.

10   Cf. Boyd 1982, pp. 6–7 and Mowlana 1995b, p. 405.

11   Cf. Williams 2001, pp. 10–14.

about television. Important questions are as follows: What kinds of questions are the new media giving rise to among the '*ulama*', and what kind of responses do they produce that can be related to broadcasting medias? Before I can discuss these questions, it is essential to provide the reader with an overview of the history of radio and television broadcasting in the Middle East and discuss these technologies in relation to social and cultural changes in society there.

Historical background

The introduction of both the radio and television coincided to a large extent with a great economic and social transformation of the Middle East. The Middle East went through a period of strong development and modernisation from the beginning of the twentieth century up until the Second World War. Even though some of these processes had already started during the nineteenth century, the following century became much affected by such changes as urbanisation and extensive modernisation.[12] The focus of the economy was also changed from agriculture to industry, and trade with Europe grew rapidly.[13] Moreover, this was also a period that challenged and altered the intellectual and cultural foundations of society. Ideas associated with secularism, communism, nationalism, colonialism and strong feelings of anti-colonialism dominated intellectual debates at the beginning of the twentieth century, by which time the Arabic-language press was also firmly established and western educational systems had been introduced more widely in the Middle East.[14]

All the processes described above had, of course, a strong influence on Muslim debates, and new possibilities, as well as problems and tensions, emerged in society.[15] New ideological and theological movements therefore emerged in order to respond to these developments and counter them. For example, 'The Muslim Brotherhood', *al-Ikhwan Muslimun*, was established by Hasan al-Banna' (1906–1949) in Egypt in 1928, largely as a reaction and response to western influences in the Muslim world and the impact of colonialism and imperialism.[16]

---

12   According to Jakob Skovgaard-Petersen, most of the Middle Eastern cities tripled in size during the 1900–1950 period. Skovgaard-Petersen 2001, p. 9.

13   In Egypt in 1913, over 90 per cent of the value of exports and some 70 per cent of imports were with European states, notably Britain, according to Owen and Pamuk 1998, p. 4.

14   On the transformation of the educational system, see Eickelman 1978.

15   Lindsay Wise and Dale F. Eickelman both argue that 'the spread of mass education, literacy and mass media [increased] the number of "lay preachers" ', a development that indicates that 'the "ulama" were losing their monopoly over religious information and interpretation'. See respectively Wise 2003, p. 33, and Eickelman 1978.

16   On this movement, see, for example, Delanoue 1971 and Mitchell 1993.

Besides the Muslim Brothers, the so-called Salafiyya and *Wahhabi* currents called for reform (*islah*) and changes in society.[17] Irrespective of internal differences, the Muslim Brothers, the Salafiyya and the *Wahhabi* currents could all be presented as reactions and responses to changes in the society. During this period, a vast number of new ideologies were introduced into the Middle East, for example, materialism, secularism, socialism/communism and atheism. Furthermore, during this period it also became clear that Western ideals, such as democracy and parliamentary systems, were only partly introduced in the colonial milieus. Great discontent spread among subaltern subjects in the Middle East when they realised the significant difference between the ideals and theories of the colonial powers and the realities imposed by them.[18]

Contrary to many so-called 'traditional' '*ulama*', that is, those who followed the ideas of *taqlid* (imitation), the 'new Islamic interpreters' who were represented by the followers of the movements above argued strongly that it was necessary for the Muslim community to use *ijtihad* (interpretation independent of the Islamic law schools) to change society.[19] Inspired by these processes, '*ulama*' such as Muhammad 'Abduh (1849–1905) and Muhammad Rashid Rida (1865–1935), whom we also discussed in the chapters on the printing press and on photography, argued that scientific progress and the new technologies were not automatically contrary to Islam. Technological innovations should therefore not be rejected out of hand according to 'Abduh,[20] but should rather be adopted and used for a 'good' Islamic purpose and for the establishment of an Islamic society. In other words, technology as such was not perceived as something contrary to the will of Allah. Whether the technology concerned is *halal* or *haram* is only related to how it is being used and for what purpose (that is, what is the intention of the user).[21] According to Muhammad 'Abduh, technological innovations are not good or bad in themselves – they may be used for either good or bad purposes, and it is the intention of the user that counts, an argument that I will return to several times in this text.[22] From this point of view, they came to the conclusion that the new information and communication technologies should not be rejected, but should rather be appropriated and used to spread the word of Allah (and to do *da'wa*, that is, to call people to Islam). This way of putting the argument is no different from previous examples discussed in this book, and yet again it will be apparent that

---

17　On the Salafiyya movement, see, for example, Shinar 1995.

18　The change from an uncritical appreciation and admiration of the West to a more critical or even hostile attitude is, for example, clearly present in Arabic fiction from the period. See, for example, El-Enany 2006.

19　To grasp the complex relationship and history of the debate over *taqlid* versus *ijtihad* and to differentiate between the two concepts is extremely difficult and would go far beyond the task of this chapter. However, a thoughtful introduction is given in Peters 1980.

20　'Abduh's support for science is clearly illustrated in his *Risalat al-tawhid*.

21　Cf. Rashid Rida 1908 and his discussion of photography and images.

22　A discussion of Muhammad 'Abduh and science can be found in Livingston 1995.

the same arguments are used in legitimising the introduction and use of a new information and communication technology. The intellectual discourse represented by thinkers such as Muhammad 'Abduh paved the way for radio and television broadcasting, making the introduction of the new technologies both possible and acceptable to the theological elite (that is, the '*ulama*'). But this acceptance did not mean that there were no debates and discussions – on the contrary, both radio and television caused debate and controversy among the '*ulama*', and some of these debates are still vibrant and controversial, as illustrated by the book *The Islamic Ruling Concerning Tasweer*, quoted at the start of this chapter.[23]

Radio broadcasting in the Muslim world

When radio was introduced in the Middle East from the 1930s, it almost immediately became a concern for most emerging national states in the region.[24] Hence, to introduce radio broadcasting and to control and monitor it became of great importance in countries such as Egypt, Syria and Iraq, especially after the 1950s, with the establishment of so-called revolutionary regimes in these countries.[25] Developments in Egypt after the 23 July 1952 military coup, the 'July revolution', serve here as an illustration of the political importance that radio broadcasting had on the region. From the quotation below, for example, it is evident that the Egyptian administration had a clear vision of the technology and how it could be used by those in power.

> In the 1970s more than 2,000 program personnel and 2,500 engineering staff, working in 43 studios in the broadcasting building in Cairo put out more than 1,200 radio hours each week in fourteen services, 8 of them for domestic audience. Powerful transmitters made these programs audible all over Egypt and in most of the Arab countries as well, even on medium wave. This system was built essentially after the revolutionary regime came to power in 1950s and decided to stress radio broadcasting as an instrument in support of policy.[26]

From the quotation above, it is clear that radio broadcasting had an important function in the Egyptian political system after the 1950s. Other countries in the region also developed their own radio stations for similar nationalist projects. Besides political purposes, the radio was also used as a tool for educating the

---

23 A strong criticism of radio is found in the pamphlet *The Radio Stations of Shaitaan: Polluting the Month of Ramadhan*, a short text produced and published on the South African Deoband homepage, www.themajlis.net (printed 2008–08–24).

24 See, for example, Rugh 2004, p. 182.

25 Rugh 2004, pp. 182–183.

26 Rugh 2004, p. 184.

masses and for modernising the countries in the region.[27] According to Douglas A. Boyd in his classic study, *Broadcasting in the Arab world: a survey of the electronic media in the Middle East*, radio broadcasts first started in Egypt in the 1920s, but the technology spread quickly to other countries in the region.

An illustration of the transformative and political dynamics associated with the new technologies is the fact that the radio was put to use by, for example, Mustafa Kemal Atatürk in Turkey and Reza Shah Pahlavi in Iran to promote nationalism and build up support for their own political systems.[28] Political use of the radio was especially elaborated and refined in the 1950s by, for example, Gamal Abdel Nasser of Egypt. Via the radio service *Sawt al-'Arab*, the 'Voice of the Arabs', he promoted his vision for Egypt and the whole Arabic-speaking world.[29] But the new technology was soon picked up by other leaders, such as Prime Minister Mohammad Mossadegh in Iran.[30] Although the radio was used to create support for nationalism and pan-Arabism, Douglas A. Boyd demonstrates convincingly that the beginning of radio broadcasting in the Middle East was closely related to the activities of Western entrepreneurs.[31] Although the introduction of broadcasting technology was dependent on western economic support, technology and 'know-how', the early phase of radio broadcasting was predominantly used to spread nationalism and foster national identity and unity in the Middle East. But the radio was also used for other reasons, especially for entertainment, commercial reasons and to spread the word of God (for example, by Ayatollah Abol-Qasem Kashani in Iran).[32] Even though so-called religious programmes constituted an essential part of the offering of early radio (at this point of time, it is difficult to make a sharp distinction between 'religious' and 'non-religious' programmes), it was only after the revolution in Iran in 1978–1979 that radio began to be used as a medium for spreading Islam.[33]

Compared to the introduction of television broadcasting in the Middle East (to be discussed below), the radio set off few theological debates or conflicts in the contemporary material. However, this does not mean that '*ulama*' did not have problems with or opinions about the use of the radio. For example, the Saudi Arabian grand mufti, Shaykh 'Abd al-'Aziz b. Baz (d. 1999), who is a key figure in the modern Wahhabi theological tradition, argues that radio may be a problem

---

27   Cf., for example, Boyd 1975, p. 649.

28   Mowlana 1995b, p. 405.

29   A detailed analysis of the *Sawt al-'Arab* and Nasser's use of the radio to spread pan-Arabism and Egyptian foreign policy is given in Boyd 1975. Cf. also Hammond 2005, p. 47, and James 2006. It should also be stressed that the media are still used as a political tool for creating changes in society. A recent example is the United States, which has, for example, funded the Arabic-speaking Radio Sawa and Farsi-speaking Radio Farda, as well as the al-Hurra TV station in Iraq to counter the impact of al-Jazeera. Roy 2008, pp. 36–37.

30   Boyd 1982, p. 4 and pp. 17–18. Mowlana 1995b, p. 405.

31   Boyd 1982, p. 3–10.

32   Cf. Boyd 1982 and Mowlana 1995b, p. 405.

33   Mowlana 1995b, p. 405. Cf. Wise 2003, p. 47, and Kepel 1985, p. 173.

because it is the most important forum for playing and disseminating illicit music.[34] In his view, most forms of music are forbidden and contrary to the laws of Islam. Muslims should therefore stay away from all forms of music.[35] A second problem is related to the fact that some radio channels and specific programmes use female announcers or presenters to attract a broad audience.[36] In relation to this issue, he writes:

> A woman announcer will exert herself to beautify her voice as much as possible, hoping to have an effect on her listeners. Women should not be announcers; radio should absolve itself from women announcers so as to prevent any form of temptation. There are other vocations more suitable for women, examples being teaching and sewing.[37]

This statement by Shaykh 'Abd al-'Aziz b. Baz could, of course, be read as a criticism of the impact of the radio.[38] However, most '*ulama*' analysed for this chapter seem to argue that the radio poses few if any problems for Muslims. For example, the Deoband Mufti Ebrahim Desai, whom I will return to later on in this chapter, argues that the sale of radio sets should not be forbidden, though the sale of television sets and parabolic antennas should be. He says: 'Radios, on the other hand, are predominantly not used for Haraam.'[39] It is clear that the '*ulama*' discussed in this section are generally more concerned with the negative effects of television.

Television broadcasting in the Middle East

Like the introduction of the radio, television broadcasting in the Middle East is closely related to politics, power and the emergence of new regimes in the region.[40] The first Arab-controlled television system, for example, was started in

---

34 *Fatawa Islamiya*, vol. 8, pp. 197–198.

35 On Islam and music, see, for example, Larsson 2004a, Otterbeck 2004 and Hirschkind 2006, pp. 33–35.

36 Cf. Mühlböck 1988, p. 94.

37 *Fatawa Islamaya*, vol. 8, p. 171.

38 Cf. *The Radio Stations of Shaitaan: Polluting the Month of Ramadhan.*

39 Mufti Ebrahim Desai, 'What is the fatwa regarding selling television sets, dvd players and radios?', Fatwa # 13287, issued on Monday 8 August 2005, retrieved from http://www.askimam.org/fatwa/fatwa.php?askid=c756a2e1156411868f9861410f8870 6b (printed 2008–09–24). This conclusion should be compared with the Deobands of the Mujlisul Ulama of South Africa, see *The Radio Stations of Shaitaan: Polluting the Month of Ramadhan.*

40 The introduction of television broadcasting in the Arabic-speaking world was also the result of non-Arab initiatives. Boyd 1998, p. 182, p. 184 and Abu-Lughod 1997, 2006.

Iraq in May 1956 to focus on entertainment for the Baghdad audience.[41] According to William A. Rugh's outline of television broadcasting in the Middle East, North Africa and the Gulf States, most television stations were set up during the 1960s and 1970s.

In the words of Douglas A. Boyd, television seems to be the 'ideal Arab home entertainment medium'. The reasons for this are on the one hand the hot climate, which prevents people from engaging in outdoor activities, and on the other hand the prevailing cultural preferences. Even though this is a tempting explanation, we should refrain from cultural or climatological explanations. Nonetheless Boyd argues:

> In a region where most entertaining is done in the family centred home, where for much of the year hot weather keeps people of all ages inside for extended periods, where Islam plays a central role in daily life, and where governments are predisposed to control information, television has become a dominant form of entertainment. Television is a reality in all Arab countries – rich and poor alike.[42]

The reference to Islam in the quotation above is not explained or developed by Boyd, but he is most likely referring to the fact that Islam lays down certain rules and regulations for the family, especially relations between the sexes. Since the family plays a central role in Islamic theology and in controlling and limiting interaction between and mixing of the sexes, television is a perfect form of entertainment. For example, television poses little or no threat to the structure of the family and does not lead to or encourage interaction between the sexes outside the control of the family. By staying at home and watching television, opportunities to break the unwritten laws mentioned above are reduced, especially for girls. Other forms of entertainment discussed in this book, such as the cinema or the Internet, are according to the '*ulama*', potentially much more threatening to the family structure and gender laws. By going to the cinema or taking part in online chat groups on the Internet, for example, it becomes very easy for boys and girls to meet members of the opposite sex outside the organised world of the family.[43] Even though most '*ulama*' believed that the cinema and the Internet provide greater opportunities for illicit and immoral behaviour (that is, *zina'*), it is clear that some have problems with radio and television too. For example, according to the book *The Islamic Ruling Concerning Tasweer*, young people are encouraged to commit *zina'* or other immoral acts when they listen to the radio or watch television serials and other programmes.[44]

---

41   Rugh 2004, p. 186.
42   Boyd 1998, p. 183.
43   See, for example, Baune 2005.
44   Cf., for example, *The Islamic Ruling Concerning Tasweer* 1998, p. 232.

According to the '*ulama*' included in this chapter, another problem with television is that it can divert the believer's attention from pious religious activities and obligations to indifference, consumerism and passivity.[45] This development is, for example, obvious during the fast of Ramadan, when several television companies broadcast programmes and serials that challenge the 'original' purpose of that month. Instead of fasting and paying special attention to religion and pious acts, the Muslim who watches these serials is more engaged in consumerism and worldly pleasures according to the '*ulama*'.[46] It is, however, clear that television broadcasting is synchronised with sacred time during Ramadan. According to Walter Armbrust, programmes in Egypt start and end in accordance with the *maghrib*, '*isha*' and *fajr* prayer during the month of Ramadan.[47]

Before I develop the analysis of how the '*ulama*' discusses the new media, however, we must return one more time to the history of television in the Middle East. From the historical records it is clear that Egypt became the centre for both radio and television broadcasting. Compared to other countries dominated by Muslim and Islamic traditions, Egypt had a long history of film production.[48] The 'know-how' learned from the film industry was of great importance for the development of television broadcasting. The film industry could, for example, provide the early broadcasting companies with personnel who had technological competence as well as experienced actors. Many actors from the film industry could therefore be used for making television series. The Egyptian dialect was also of importance because most people in the region were used to film produced in colloquial Egyptian. Because of these advantages, Egypt was almost unchallenged as the leader of television broadcasting in the larger Middle East. This position was first threatened by the rise of satellite television, as discussed in the last sections of this chapter.[49]

---

45   A critical discussion of the negative effects of television is found in Pierre Bourdieu's thought-provoking study *Sur la télévision* (1996; Swedish translation 2006 by Mats Rosengren).

46   On Ramadan television, see, for example, Armbrust 2005 and Möller 2005, pp. 249–252. According to Lila Abu-Lughod (1997), it is also clear that most television serials broadcast in Egypt in the late 1980s were silent over or ignored the alternative political views of the Islamists. However, from a later study (Abu-Lughod 2006), it is clear that Egyptian state television has started paying attention to the Islamists, in many cases by trying to depict them as dangerous or subversive and not to be trusted, see Abu-Lughod 2006.

47   See Armbrust 2005, especially pp. 214–216, dealing with sacred time and television.

48   Cf. the earlier chapter on Islamic opinions about the motion picture in this book.

49   Boyd 1998, pp. 184–185.

Continuity and discontinuity

Both radio and television, but also less advanced or so-called 'small media', such as the cassette, the video recorder (VCR) and the DVD, can be used by both the *'ulama'* and other Muslims to spread Islam.[50] But the technologies could also be used to criticise or even topple regimes and worldly powers.[51] However, in analysing the impact of the new information and communication technologies, it must be stressed that the new media are often used together with 'traditional' media for spreading Islam. The technologies analysed in this book should therefore be studied together with traditional means of communication, for example, sermons, speeches and other forms of educational activities in mosques, *madaris* (sing. *madrasa*) and prayer halls. To be able to understand the new media and their importance for Muslims, the 'traditional' methods of communication should not be forgotten or neglected in the analysis.[52]

For example, most mosques today use public address systems with loudspeakers and microphones to call Muslims to prayer. When delivering his *khutba*, the imam must use a loudspeaker and a microphone to reach the Muslims gathered in the mosque.

In a similar fashion, instruction videos, CDs and Internet sites can, for example, be used in teaching Muslims how to perform the *wudu'* (the minor ablution) or recite the Qur'an (that is, how to perform *tajwid*). Besides these examples, it is also clear that most Muslims have no problems with publishing or for that matter reading printed books. Hence, it is clear that the 'traditional' ways of educating Muslims and transmitting Islamic knowledge have become closely entwined with modern forms of information and communication technologies. This observation should not, of course, be read or interpreted as indicating that the traditional oral forms of transmitting knowledge and authority are being forgotten or abandoned,[53] but it is

---

50   The use of cassettes for doing *da'wa* (calling people to Islam) is strongly encouraged by bin Baz (*Fatawa Islamiyah*, vol. 8, pp. 53–54) and ibn 'Uthaimin (*Fatawa Islamiyah*, vol. 8, p. 62). See also Halldén 2001 and Hirschkind 2006.

51   An analysis of the social and theological importance of audio cassettes and Islamic preachers' use of the new medium in the Middle East, Saudi Arabia and Iran can be found in Halldén 2001; Hirschkind 2006; Naficy 1995; and Srerny-Mohammadi and Mohammadi 1994. A discussion of media and the Qur'an can be found in Hirschkind 2003. On the importance of small media (cassettes, pamphlets, posters, stickers, wall paintings, etc.) for the revolution in Iran, see Sreberny-Mohammadi and Mohammadi 1994, especially pp. 119–123. On the popularity and importance of video-cassettes and video recorders in the Middle East, see Boyd 1998, pp. 185–186.

52   Hamid Mowlana argues: 'One important feature of broadcasting media in the Islamic world is that they are being integrated into a vast and complex system of traditional and oral channels of communication.' Mowlana 1995b, p. 405. See also Allievi 2003, p. 17.

53   The importance of oral transmission over mechanical transmission (via a technology) is, for example, strongly stressed in the pamphlet *The Radio Stations of Shaitaan: Polluting the Month of Ramadhan*.

clear that several information and communication technologies have become part and parcel of the Muslim intellectual heritage. As demonstrated throughout this book, this development has caused new opportunities as well as problems.

The boundaries between 'traditional' and 'new' ways of communication are therefore mixed, blurred and intertwined. For example, many Friday sermons held in mosques today are often reproduced in print, broadcast via radio and television, recorded on cassettes, or posted on the Internet.[54] But what effect does the introduction of new information and communication technologies have on the message? According to Brinckley Messick, using the radio to issue theological opinions (that is, *fatwas*) could here serve as an illustration of both continuity and discontinuity between old and new forms and methods for reaching out to believers.[55] Before the age of mass communication, the *mufti* gave his answer to a theological question in a situation in which two persons met face-to-face. To issue a *fatwa* in a radio programme is therefore associated with new conditions, a fact that provides the Muslim scholar with new opportunities, as well as problems, which can support or alternatively disturb the communication.[56] For example, a broadcast *fatwa* is more likely to address a larger and more general public. The *mufti* who gives an answer over the radio is also separated from his audience in both time and space. The difference between a broadcast and a 'traditional' oral *fatwa* is explained by al-Ghurbani, a Yemeni *mufti* interviewed by Messick:

> Whereas a conventional mufti's fatwa could be read and interpreted by the literate and knowledgeable, for themselves and for others, a fatwa heard over the radio must be immediately and generally clear. He [i.e., al-Gurbani] explained that the radio audience consists of the public at large (the *jumhur*) and therefore includes women and the uninformed. Listeners might hear the broadcast, for example, in a restaurant or while riding in a taxi. As a consequence, the radio mufti has to be relatively expansive, using examples, repetition and reference to related questions to convey his ideas. At the same time, he has to be concise and quickly summarize the issues.[57]

In order to help the audience of the radio program remember his *fatwa*, Muhammad b. 'Ali al-Ghurbani uses more proverbs, poetry, literary references and rhetoric (*balagha*) than he normally does in a so-called traditional setting in which he meets the questioner face to face.[58] Similar mnemonic techniques are used by

---

54　See, for example, Kepel 1985; Skovgaard-Petersen 2004, pp. 163–165; and Wise 2003 on the Egyptian Sheikh Sha'rawi. Cf. also Halldén 2001; 2006a and 2006b.

55　Messick 1996, p. 310.

56　On the art of issuing a *fatwa*, see Masud et al. 1996. Some of the problems with issuing *fatwas* through broadcast media have been highlighted by, for example, Roald 2001, p. 41.

57　Messick 1996, pp. 315–316.

58　Messick 1996, p. 316.

preachers who record and spread their sermons on cassettes or via the Internet.[59] Al-Ghurbani, discussed above, could serve here as an example of a scholar who directly or indirectly adjusts his way of preaching (or for that matter, of spreading Islam) because of the impact of the radio. The new media are thus changing and developing both Islamic discourse and the practice of spreading Islam. Even though most '*ulama*' today accept radio and television, the question remains of how so-called pious Muslims should use these media in a correct and approved Islamic way (that is, according to the interpretation supported and upheld by the specific law school or group of '*ulama*'). Although it is impossible to find a unanimous answer to this question, the impact of new information and communication technologies is debated in both printed collections of *fatwas* (dating from the beginning of the twentieth century) and contemporary debates taking place on, for example, the Internet, or in broadcast radio and television shows.

The introduction of the new technologies did not only have an effect on the theological debates and ways of disseminating the word of Allah. As noted already in, for example, the earlier chapters on the cinema or photography in this book, the new media have had a profound effect on the organisation of public and private life in modern cities in creating new patterns of social relations within both society and the family. From the big picture, it is clear that the introduction of the media discussed in this chapter created new opportunities as well as problems. For example, should the broadcast media be seen as a threat to the established order and the legacy of the past, or have they provided new opportunities that have opened up novel ways of being a citizen in the Middle East? For the anthropologist Lila Abu-Lughod, it is necessary to remember that the new information and communication technologies are not only a threat to the established order of society. This is also the conclusion of Douglas A. Boyd, who writes:

> The Arab culture is traditionally an oral culture and with few competing forms
> of information and entertainment, radio listening was, and in some places still is,
> a major leisure-time activity.[60]

Still, it is necessary to examine specifically whether the broadcast media actually have a so-called pacifying effect on their audiences.[61] According to Abu-Lughod's experience of doing fieldwork in Egypt, the introduction of new media such as the cassette recorder, the radio and the television set has created mobility and new opportunities for preserving and developing various cultural expressions. Instead of forgetting about 'their' culture, as is often predicted by both local inhabitants

---

59   Cf. Halldén 2001, 2006a and 2006b.

60   Boyd 1998, p. 183.

61   Instead of arguing that radio and television have led to local people ceasing to produce their own culture and that those who make use of the new media are reduced to passive consumers, it is necessary to situate these developments in a much broader context. For this kind of criticism in the West, see, for example, Bourdieu 2000 and Williams 2001.

and social anthropologists, the media have helped, for example, the Bedouins in Awlad 'Ali on the border of Egypt and Libya to commemorate their traditional odes and to create new markets for Bedouin songs.[62] Nonetheless the introduction of the television set is likely to change traditional hierarchies within the household. From this point of view the new media embodies a transformative power capable of having an effect on so-called 'traditional' societies. This transformation is illustrated by the fact that the television set itself makes the whole family watch what is being broadcast together as a leisure activity, with men, women and children all being engaged in watching television. To be able to watch television, it is necessary for the family to get together, regardless of gender or age.[63] This is a simple but illustrative example of the potentially transformative effect of new forms of information and communication technology.

However, the transformative effect of cassettes and television, briefly discussed above, cannot be compared with that of the cinema. Going to the movies is a public and open activity that is beyond the control of either parents or the '*ulama*'. When the light is turned off in a cinema, it is no longer possible for parents or the '*ulama*' to be sure that the audience is upholding the laws of Islam and behaving in a 'correct' manner in the darkness. Compared to going to the movies, watching television programmes is in most cases an activity that takes place in either the home or a coffee house, that is, in a setting that is controlled and monitored by parents, relatives or others sharing the public space in, for example, a coffee house. Television therefore does not have the same potential to cross gender boundaries and break the rules laid down by parents or the '*ulama*'. Because of this potential, the cinema was perceived as a more alarming threat to religious and cultural norms, rules and values, and as a result it is still prohibited in Saudi Arabia.[64] This distinction is clearly illustrated by one of Abu-Lughod's informants, who insisted strongly that it is more immoral to go to the cinema than to watch television.[65] According to this informant, most if not all movies contain scenes that are contrary to what she believes are the teachings of Islam. At the same time, this young Cairo schoolgirl openly admitted to Abu-Lughod that she watched *Dallas*, the American soap opera (a programme also associated with what most '*ulama*' would label as un-Islamic habits, such as greed, drinking alcohol, sex and adultery). The informant sympathised with the Dallas family in the soap opera, 'but found J.R. objectionable because of his illicit love affairs. Bobby, on the other hand, was a good person whose conduct was close to Islamic behaviour'.[66] From this point of view, it is even possible to argue that the character Bobby could be seen as an

---

62   Abu-Lughod 1989.

63   Abu-Lughod 1989, p. 8.

64   According to Boyd's analysis, this difference may be one of the reasons why television is an accepted phenomenon in 'more' Islamic countries, such as Saudi Arabia and the Gulf States. Boyd, 1982, p. 7, and Boyd 1998, p. 184.

65   Abu-Lughod 1989, p. 10.

66   Abu-Lughod 1989, p. 8.

edifying example for Muslims watching *Dallas*, an American soap opera. This is not the right place to develop the discussion about Islam and popular culture, but it is clear that some '*ulama*' are concerned about Western popular culture.[67] Even though the representatives of the '*ulama*' are critical and negative, it is also clear that 'ordinary' Muslims may actually embrace and make use of popular culture to strengthen their religious identity. The tension between what the '*ulama*' say and what the 'ordinary' Muslim thinks and does is, for example, clearly illustrated in the discussion and reception of J.K. Rowling's books and the films about Harry Potter. For example, in the online discussion group, *Muslim Message: The Online Muslim Community*, a debate was started on the subject of Harry Potter. Although the discussion was soon turned into a debate about Salman Rushdie and not about Rowling's books, a female participant eagerly defended the idea that it was possible to be a 'good' Muslim and a lover of fantasy literature at the same time. She admitted openly in the discussion forum that she is a great fan of *The Lord of the Rings* and *The Chronicles of Narnia*. According to her these stories convey the same message as one finds in the story about David and Goliath, that is, the struggle between good and evil.

> The message of Good versus Evil, the wonderful feeling of a small odd being magnified and carried to succeed despite all doubts. A small and hopeful child, person overcoming something scary fearful, terrifying and shakes them to the core yet overcomes it and cures the world from it.[68]

According to the reader quoted above, Harry Potter is basically a story about the struggle between good and evil, and from this point of view, Rowling's books can be an inspiration for Muslims to conduct good deeds and fight against all forms of evil, no matter how powerful they are. The Harry Potter books could even be described as a form of edification.[69]

Although it is my impression that television is perceived as a minor problem compared to, for example, the cinema or the Internet, it is clear that several '*ulama*' still have problems with it. Those who have been influenced by or trained in the Wahhabi or Deoband traditions are in general very sceptical and critical of

---

67 Examples   include   Mohamed   El-Moctar   El-Shinqiti,   *Watching   and Reading   'Harry   Potter':   Permissible?*,   retrieved   from   http://www.islamonline. net/servlet/Satellite?pagename=IslamOnline-English-Ask_Scholar/FatwaE/ FatwaEandcid=1119503548670 (printed 2008–08–20); and Yusuf al-Qaradawi, *Pokemon Games*, retrieved from http://www.islamonline.net/servlet/Satellite?pagename=IslamOnline-English-Ask_Scholar/FatwaE/FatwaEandcid=1119503543930 (printed 2008–08–20).

68 Re: Harry Potter, Reply #1, see http://www.muslimmessage.net/discussion/index. php?PHPSESSID=c2515a37555e9c6181258c79ee8554a1andtopic=439.0   (printed   and retrieved by 2005–09–05).

69 A more detailed discussion of Islamic opinions about Harry Potter can be found in Larsson (in press).

television.[70] Although the criticism can be formulated in many different ways, the critical *'ulama'* assembled from the material analysed for this chapter argue that television is a problem because:

- Television is based on picture-making.
- Music is part and parcel of television.[71]
- The female voice is part and parcel of television broadcasting.
- Most television series encourage illicit behaviour, immorality and sin.
- Television is an agent of *zina'* (fornication).[72]
- Television encourages criminality, violence and destruction.
- Television brainwashes Muslims.
- Television has an addictive influence upon Muslims.
- Television diverts man's attention from the remembrance of Allah.
- Watching television is a waste of time (that is, an unnecessary activity).
- Television has a bad effect on health, while it pacifies the audience.[73]

From this list, it is clear that these *'ulama'* regard television as mainly harbouring negative culture and bad behaviour. Watching television is bad for both one's physical and mental health and is time-consuming and indeed a waste of time.

In spite of the criticism above, it is easy to argue that the introduction of radio and television broadcasting played a more important and influential role than the printing press in the eighteenth and nineteenth centuries. Due to low levels of literacy among the general public in the Middle East, broadcast media had a strong advantage over print media, which required an education and the ability to read modern standard Arabic (MSA).[74] The broadcast media therefore had an advantage

---

70   Cf., for example, the *fatwas* issued by the homepage *Ask-the-Imam*, or published in the printed collection *Fatawa Islamiya* analysed for this chapter. The criticism voiced by these *'ulama'* may, however, be shared and supported by other *'ulama'* who are not followers of either the Wahhabi or Deoband traditions. Cf. Abu-Lughod 1997, p. 315.

71   Regarding criticisms of music in television programmes, it is important to remember that a Muslim scholar may have a negative opinion about music, but still support television. For example, Yusuf al-Qaradawi is very critical of music, and his views on this subject do not differ very much from those we find among the Deoband and Wahhabi *'ulama'* I have discussed in this chapter. At the same time, al-Qaradawi is an outspoken supporter of television as a means of calling people to Islam. Cf. al-Qaradawi 2001, pp. 296–300.

72   On the concept of *zina'*, see, for example, Peters 2002 and Schacht 1995b.

73   This list is based on information taken from the book *The Islamic Ruling Concerning Tasweer*, pp. 226–241, but similar arguments are also found in the *fatwas* issued by Saudi Arabian *'ulama'* who are informed by the Wahhabi school of thought or *'ulama'* who belong to the Deoband traditions.

74   The current low levels of literacy are mainly due to the diglossia caused by the difference between *fusha* – which is used for 'high functions', formal prayers, speeches and

because they were oral and could reach educated and uneducated audiences alike.[75] This benefit was soon realised by leaders such as Gamal Abdel Nasser, who made extensive use of the radio in spreading his political ideals of pan-Arabism and in building up modern Egypt.[76] For example, when asked by the UN Secretary General, Dag Hammarskjöld, to 'disarm the radio' and use it less aggressively in support of pan-Arabism and Egyptian foreign interests, Nasser replied:

> How can I reach my power base? My power lies with the Arab masses. The only way I can reach my people is by radio. If you ask me for radio disarmament, it means that you are asking me for complete disarmament.[77]

Although Nasser's response is a clear illustration of the power attributed to radio in the Middle East, it should be remembered and stressed that the benefits of the radio could also turn into problems for political leaders. For example, in Saudi Arabia it disturbed the regime to realise that Egyptian radio was very popular among its citizens, and from this point of view it posed a threat. At this time, most Egyptian radio programmes were used to express strong anti-Saudi rhetoric. To curb this development, setting up a Saudi Arabian radio system to counter Nasser's Pan-Arabism had a high priority for the establishment and the political elite in Saudi Arabia.[78] The media could, in other words, also be used by foreign nations or groups who wanted to challenge the authorities and call for a different political or religious order in society.[79] Because of the political potential of the new media, the press, radio and television broadcasting companies were soon placed under strict state control. Most countries in the Middle East also imposed heavy censorship on the press and the broadcasting media.[80] However, with the development of satellite broadcasting and the Internet during the last decade, political monopolies and state control have been challenged and criticised by numerous political and religious leaders, both within the Middle East and by Muslims in the Diaspora, a subject we will return to below.

---

lectures – and the colloquial dialects of Arabic used for 'low' functions (e.g. in the home, in the streets or with friends). Maamouri 2008, p. 76.

75   Cf., for example, Boyd 1975, pp. 645–646; Rugh 2004, p. 181.

76   Boyd 1975 and 1982, p. 18.

77   Quoted in Boyd 1975, p. 651.

78   On this question, see Boyd 1998, p. 184. Cf. Mühlböck 1988, p. 165.

79   Foreign powers used and still frequently use radio to interfere in the internal affairs of the region during both the Cold War and present-day wars. See, for example, Boyd 1975; Boyd 1991 and Morad, p. 212. Cf. Boyd 1998 and Roy 2008, pp. 36–37.

80   Cf., for example, Ayalon 1995; Boyd 1982; Eickelman 2003; Rugh 2004; Wise 2003, pp. 43–44.

Watching television: an Islamic issue?

From a secular point of view, religion is often analysed and understood as a phenomenon that is separate or distinct from the rest of society and its citizen's activities.[81] The separation between religion and worldly affairs is often explained as an outcome of complex processes, such as the enlightenment, secularisation, modernity and more recently globalisation.[82] For certain Muslims (especially for so-called Islamists), the distinction between religion and worldly affairs is often seen as something problematic, defective and difficult that the West is imposing on the Muslim community.[83] Even though it is an idealised picture, or a cliché, to use Olivie Roy's choice of words, that Muslims never make a distinction between religion and worldly affairs, many Muslims argue strongly that Islam is an all-encompassing theological system embracing all human activities (cf., for example, the followers of *al-Ikhwan al-Muslimun* discussed at the beginning of this chapter, or Muhammad 'Abduh's book *Risalat at-tawhid*, or for that matter the Egyptian Yusuf al-Qaradawi).[84] For many so-called Islamists or neo-fundamentalists, it is not possible to make a distinction or separation between religious and worldly affairs, since all areas are included in Islam. It is argued that Islam is both *din* (faith) and *dawla* (state). To act 'correctly' is therefore as important as it is to have the 'right' belief, according to, for example, Tariq Ramadan.[85] Islam is consequently presented as a religion that shows believers the 'straight path' (*sirat al-mustaqim*), a path that will guide and help them to find the right track leading them to paradise and God.[86]

The '*ulama*' argue that, to be able to act in accordance with Islam and to follow the will of Allah, believers must show *adab*, courtesy or good manners and piety, in all human areas.[87] Accordingly, questions such as table manners, how to dress or what to eat are therefore essential and important aspects that believers should consider if they want to consider themselves Muslims. Consequently, it should come as no surprise that the '*ulama*' also argue that believers must show *adab* when they discuss how one should make use of the new information and communication

---

81   This conclusion naturally depends on our definition of religion. Thus it is essential to remember that religion can be broadly defined either according to substance (i.e. 'defining religion by what it is, not by what it does') or function (i.e. the function and role of religion in society, for the individual, for the group).

82   Cf., for example, Beyer 2006.

83   On Islam and secularism, see Larsson 2010.

84   On this movement, see Delanoue 1971 (especially p. 1069) and Mitchell 1993. See also Schleifer 2004. Cf. also Roy 2004, p. 4.

85   Tariq Ramadan's *To Be A European Muslim: A Study of Islamic Sources in the European Context* is filled with numerous examples and illustrations showing that Islam does not make a separation between thought and action. Cf., for example, Ramadan 2002, p. 20.

86   Cf., for example, Al-Fatiha (Q 1) in the Qur'an.

87   The importance of *adab* is, for example, emphasised in al-Kaysi 1989. See also Bray 2006, pp. 13–14, and Metcalf 1984 for several examples.

technologies. In this section I will take a close look at some Muslims who ask questions that are related, directly or indirectly, to television broadcasting and the watching of television. The analysis is based on an in-depth reading of theological answers from three different so-called *fatwa* services, namely *IslamOnline. net* from Egypt/Qatar, *Ask-Imam.com* from South Africa, and the printed Saudi Arabian collection of judicial answers called *Fatawa Islamiya*, consisting mainly of answers given by Shaykh 'Abd al-'Aziz b. Baz.[88] The opinions of the three so-called *fatwa* services on television are summarised in Table 4.1.

The table illustrates clearly that it is not possible to find any *one* Islamic opinion about the permissibility of television broadcasting or the watching of television. But although the *'ulama'* are partly divided on this topic, it is my impression that the opinions articulated by the theological institutions mentioned above are illustrative and representative of a large majority of Muslims. The table shows well the tensions within Islamic discourses on television. The *fatwa* services selected for my analysis are also some of the most important institutions for issuing authoritative judicial and theological answers to Islamic questions in the contemporary Muslim world, especially for Muslims using the Internet. Even though it is very difficult to estimate or grasp the importance and impact of a homepage that issues theological answers, both *IslamOnline.net* and *Ask-Imam. com* seem to be among the most visited Muslim websites at the time of writing.[89] But the number of visitors should not automatically be seen as some kind of marker of quality, and it is necessary to be cautious in analysing online sources.[90]

Even though all *'ulama'* are more or less sceptical about the new information and communication technologies and their potential for transforming society, the answers given by the *'ulama'* contain substantial differences in the conclusions and solutions provided. For example, in an answer from *IslamOnline.net*, issued on 25 August 2000, an unknown *mufti* (his name is not given in the text) says the following about watching television:

---

88   For information about the *Dar al-Ifta'* in Egypt, see http://www.haneen.com.eg/ fatwa/Search_Fatwa.aspx. For information about *fatwas* taken from Ask-Imam.com, see, http://islam.tc/ask-imam/index.php. For information about *fatwas* taken from Islam-Online. net, see http://www.islam-online.net/English/index.shtml.

89   *Ask-Imam.com* was set up by a single scholar, Mufti Ebrahim Desai, and the site is located in South Africa. A description of the webpage is given by Bunt 2003, pp. 167–168. A general description of media, religion, democracy and equal rights in South Africa is found in Hackett 2006. The homepage for IslamOnline.net is registered in Doha, Qatar, but it is staffed by a hundred people based in Cairo. Even though a large number of muftis are linked to this homepage, the key scholar is the Qatar-based Yusuf al-Qaradawi. The majority of the staff in Cairo are students or graduates of al-Azhar University. Cf. Bunt 2003, p. 147; Gräf 2007, 2008.

90   To determine how these homepages are being used and to what extent they are influencing Muslim debates in the West, it would be necessary to conduct field research and interview Muslims. This does not apply to this study.

Table 4.1   Opinions on television

Institution	Islam.Online.net	Fatawa Islamiya	Ask-Imam.com
Television is halal or haram	Halal	Halal	Haram
Conditions for accepting or prohibiting television	Television is not good or bad in itself. It is the content and the intention of the user that matters.	Television is not good or bad in itself. It is the content and the intention of the user that matters.	All images (photos, films, etc.) are forbidden according to Islam.
Acceptable television programmes	Educational and Islamic programmes are acceptable.	Educational and Islamic programmes are acceptable.	No programmes are acceptable (not even Islamic programmes).[91]
Problems associated with television		Music and singing is promoted by television.	Watching television programmes is a waste of time.[92]
Prohibitions		(non-Islamic) Television series and parabolic antennas are forbidden.[93]	The selling of television sets is forbidden.

Source: Islam.Online.net; Fatawa Islamiya; askimam.org

---

91   See Moulana Suhail Tar Mohammed 'I understand the Hadeeth …', Fatwa # 14717 (15 November 2006), retrieved from http://www.askimam.org/fatwa/fatwa.php?askid=982ba80d1caa45fb72c78fa817895a44 (printed 2008–09–24).

92   According to Mufti Ebrahim Desai of the askiman.org homepage, watching television is always a waste of time. In contrast to his opinion, the '*ulama*' associated with, for example, IslamOnline.net seem to argue that it is the content and the reason for watching television that matters. For example, they argue that it is not automatically forbidden for Muslims to watch football matches on television. Dr Jamal Ad-Din 'Atiyya, a member of the Islamic Fiqh Academy affiliated to the Organization of the Islamic Conference (OIC), states in a *fatwa* issued for the *IslamOnline.net* that: 'There is no harm in watching football matches or other sporting matches, on condition that we do not waste most of our time in watching. Watching such matches will not benefit us; the benefit will be for the one who practices sports.' Faysal Mawlawi and Jamal Ad-Din 'Atiyya, 'Watching Football and Playing Professionally', 1 June 2006, retrieved from http://www. islamonline.net/servlet/Satellite?pagename=IslamOnline-English-Ask_Scholar/FatwaE/FatwaE&cid=1148980352168 (printed 2008–09–24). The popular Egyptian preacher and television star, Amr Khaled, also stresses that sport is not contrary to the spirit of Islam – 'on the contrary, he is such a fervent fan (he used to play on the junior national team as a teenager) that he not only invites football players to guest star on his show, but also ends his Saturday afternoon mosque sermons early if there is a match scheduled, so he and his audience do not have to miss any game time'. Wise 2003, p. 42.

93   *Fatawa Islamiya*, vol. 8, pp. 178, 181.

> Television is a tool. In general, it is filled with a lot of impurities and poisonous stuff. It contaminates everyone's deen and ethics. You can hardly get any benefit in watching TV. I don't like to put it in the category of halal and haram. I, as a Muslim, am convinced that we should have an alternative in investing our time.[94]

Even though this *fatwa* does not contain an explicit prohibition against watching television, it is clear that the *mufti* concerned does not regard this as an 'Islamic activity'. However, in the same institution it is also possible to find answers modifying the reply given above. In an answer issued on 28 April 2002, it is not the medium, but the message that is seen as a problem for Muslims:

> In fact, watching television is exactly like getting involved in any sort of reading books. Whatever affects ethics and religion negatively is Islamically unhealthy, and what is supportive to them is Islamically recommended.[95]

Unlike the first answer, this *fatwa* does not contain a direct criticism of the medium as such. In this case it is the content and the intention of the user of the technology that may be the problem.[96] Thus, it is argued, if the broadcast message is not indecent, but beneficial, educational and informative for Muslims, it is good and there are no reasons to ban the information.[97]

From a critical point of view, it should come as no surprise that *IslamOnline. net* provides theological answers in support of Muslims being allowed to watch television programmes. For example, Yusuf al-Qaradawi, who at the time of the issuing of the *fatwa* above was without a doubt the most prominent scholar associated with *IslamOnline.net*, is also a talk-show host for the programme *Sharia and Life* (*al-shari'a wa-al-hayat*) on the satellite television channel al-Jazeera.[98] By appearing on this television programme, he is among other things demonstrating that it is not the broadcasting technology that is the problem, but the content of the medium and the intention of its user that matters. He says:

---

94   Fatwa 25 August 2000 (IslamOnline.net, printed 2003–12–17).

95   Fatwa 28 April 2002 (IslamOnline.net, printed 2003–12–17).

96   This opinion is, for example, more or less shared by the *Dar al-Ifta'* in Egypt in a *fatwa* on the watching of television. See, 'Watching TV: Answer 2' (Dar al-iftaa al-Massriah, printed in 2003–12–15).

97   Fatwa 28 April 2002 (IslamOnline.net, printed 2003–12–17). A similar argument is also used by Yusuf al-Qaradawi in a *fatwa* of 14 January 2004, 'Watching TV: Permissible?', retrieved from http://www.islamonline.net/servlet/Satellite?pagename=IslamOnline-English-Ask_Scholar/FatwaE/FatwaEandcid=1119503544868 (printed 2008–09–24). A similar conclusion is reached by Sheikh Jad-al-Haq of al-Azhar University; see Abu-Lughod 1997, p. 315.

98   On Yusuf al-Qaradawi and satellite television, see, for example, Gräf 2008; Gräf and Skovgaard-Petersen 2009; Mariani 2006, and Skovgaard-Petersen 2004.

I have never ever hesitated to use television. From the day it was invented, many would ask me about it, and I would say that it is simply a tool, and a tool used for Islam will be judged by the intent with which it is employed. The television by itself is not to be judged either way; it is like, say, a rifle: is that forbidden or allowable? In the hands of a *mujahid*, it is a tool for striving in the way of Allah and of defending truth; in the hands of a bandit, it is an implement of crime. Similarly, some people may use the television for things unseemly to religion, morals, or traditional values; but when we use it for calling people to Allah, to increase their awareness of the truth, even simply to give them correct information or considered opinion, then the television is an instrument of good.[99]

The quotation above illustrates clearly how some '*ulama*' argue that the technology as such is not good or evil, it is the content and the purpose for which the media are being used that matter.[100] The quotation is also an example of how the '*ulama*' put the new information and communication technologies to use in spreading Islam to a global audience. The importance of the new media is clearly understood by Yusuf al-Qaradawi:

It has its adherents everywhere, and the benefit of al Jazeera is that it has increased the size and breadth of my audience wherever they are. If there were two hundred thousand attending my lecture in Algeria, or if my books were published in runs of ten or twenty thousand each edition, and they went into numerous reprints – for example, *al-Halal wal-Haram* was reprinted sixty or seventy times, and it was translated into more languages than I can count, even local dialects, all over the world – all of this is limited. But Al Jazeera has provided me with millions of viewers; where my audience was once numbered in the thousands or tens of thousands, they are now in the millions. I never go to a country now where people do not know me through Al Jazeera. Once they know me by name; now they know my face. My name was known, or perhaps my thought was known, and some people recognized the name as well. Well, now they put a face to the name. All of this is the effect of *al-Sharia wal-Hayat* and Al Jazeera, Allah be praised![101]

Thus, by using the Internet and satellite broadcasting, al-Qaradawi has truly become a global 'media mufti', that is, a Muslim scholar who uses the latest information and communication technologies to spread his views on Islam to a global audience

---

99   Quotation taken from Schleifer 2004.

100   As we have seen in this chapter, Yusuf al-Qaradawi is not alone in expressing this opinion about information and communication technologies. A similar argument, for example, is clearly seen in Ahmad Kutty, 'Women Working in Media', 11 August 2005, retrieved from http://www.islamonline.net/servlet/Satellite?pagename=IslamOnline-English-Ask_Scholar/FatwaE/FatwaEandcid=1119503547148 (printed 2008–09–24).

101   Quotation taken from Schleifer 2004.

that resides far beyond his local context.[102] According to Bettina Gräf, however, it would be more accurate to describe al-Qaradawi as a translocal theologian who makes use of the latest information and communication technologies.[103] Regardless of how we define Yusuf al-Qaradawi, it is clear that *IslamOnline.net* (together with his personal homepage, www.qaradawi.net) and the television show, 'Sharia and Life', are powerful instruments that attract a global Muslim audience in the Middle East, Europe and the United States.[104]

Even when television is not marked by the '*ulama*' as something inherently evil, it can still become a problem for Muslims. For example, if watching television becomes more important than performing the obligatory Islamic rituals or taking care of one's family (which is also part of being a 'good' Muslim), it will be necessary to restrict, or even prohibit the individual from watching television.[105] This opinion is, for example, articulated by '*ulama*' associated with both the *IslamOnline.net* and the *Dar al-Ifta'* in Cairo.[106] Compared to Yusuf al-Qaradawi, it is clear that the online service called askimam.org is much more negative and critical of television. It states openly in a *fatwa* that 'Television will remain prohibited irrespective of who employs it as a tool of dissemination'.[107] For example, Moulana Suahil Tar Mohammed, who is associated with the *Ask-the-Imam* site, stresses that many '*ulama*' have a false understanding of television. He writes:

> Unfortunately some scholars have erred in this regard and have permitted using television to combat the media based on necessity. We are compelled to state that the Deen of Allah is not in need of such filth to be promoted. Had the Deen of Allah been in need to be promoted via television, Nabi Sallallahu Alaihi Wa Sallam would not have prohibited picture making or mentioned such stern warnings regarding it, as whatever Nabi Sallallahu Alaihi Wa Sallam said or

102   On this development, see, for example, Mandaville 2001; Mariani 2006; Skovgaard-Petersen 2004; and Wise 2003, p. 26.

103   Gräf 2007, pp. 418–419.

104   Anne-Sofie Roald's research on the distribution and use of Arabic satellite channels among Arabic-speaking immigrants in Scandinavia shows, for example, that more than 91 per cent of the respondents in her survey watched the TV channel al-Jazeera on a daily basis. See Roald 2003, pp. 47–48.

105   Cf. *The Islamic Ruling Concerning Tasweer* 1998, pp. 236–237. A similar concern for time is found in Yusuf al-Qaradawi's pamphlet *Time in the Life of the Muslim*.

106   Fatwa 28 April 2002 (IslamOnline.net, printed 2003–12–17) and the Fatwa, 'Watching TV: Answer 1' (http://163.121.12.9/fatwa/fatwa_result. aspx?imgpath=fanswers/a_fatwa130.gif, printed 2003–12–18).

107   Fatwa/Can you answer queries about television and video? (http://www.islam. tc/ask-imam/view.php?q=6930, printed 2003–12–18). Cf. *The Islamic Ruling Concerning Tasweer* 1998, pp. 233–235. This answer was given in response to the point that satellite television channels such as al-Jazeera exist even though Muslims should know that watching television is *haram*. See, for example, Steger 2003, pp. 2–7.

did was actually from the side of Allah and Allah's knowledge encompasses everything from creation till Doomsday and beyond that.[108]

According to this scholar, television does not foster good ideals and religious values, but only negative feelings, violence and immorality. In one of his answers, Mufti Ebrahim Desai quotes a teacher to demonstrate his case and to show the negative side effects of watching television. According to him, television broadcasting bears a great responsibility for negative developments in society. The following example is a clear illustration of this trend:

> I [the female teacher] asked one of the boys in my class: 'Who is the most powerful, Allah or the Power Rangers?' Without batting an eye, he exclaimed with childish certainty: 'The Power Rangers!' When I told him that Allah was the Most Powerful and that the Power Rangers were weak in sight of Muslims, the boy was greatly disappointed.[109]

According to Desai, watching television encourages children to become sexually active and to have sex before they are ready, that is, before they have been married according to the laws of Islam.[110] He stresses, contrary to the belief of many parents, that a television set is not a good and innocent baby sitter. By referring to facts issued by the Television Centre at the City University of New York, Desai says that, 'By the time he [that is, the consumer] is 17, the average child sees 200,000 to

---

108　Moulana Suhail Tar Mohammed, 'I understand the Hadeeth ...', Fatwā # 14717 (15 November 2006), retrieved from http://www.askimam.org/fatwa/fatwa.php?askid=9 82ba80d1caa45fb72c78fa817895a44 (printed 2008–09–24). Even though most Deoband '*ulama*' are convinced that the television is mainly harmful for the Muslim community, it should be stressed that not all theologians equate television with pictures. Muhammad ibn Adam of the *Darul Iftaa* in Leicester, UK, argues on the basis of the Pakistani scholar Taqi Usmani that television is something different from pictures. He writes: 'Shaykh Mufti Taqi Usmani (may Allah preserve him) and many other scholars have declared that live broadcastings of images do not fall within the ambit of picture-making (taswir). A picture is something that is permanent and static, whilst the image broadcasted live is not permanent hence cannot be termed a picture. A live broadcast is in reality a reflection of the actual image, similar to seeing an image in a mirror.' He continues, however, by saying: 'Note that the above discussion does not in any way relate to watching Television. Watching TV and keeping it at home is another matter altogether, for which a separate answer is needed. The many harms and evils of keeping a TV at home are known to all. This answer only relates to the permissibility of viewing a Halal image through a live broadcast or a videotape/DVD.' Muhammad ibn Adam, Photographs: Please Clarify Your Position. Retrieved from http:// www.daruliftaa.com/question.asp?txt_QuestionID=q-16155977 (printed 2008–08–15).

109　Fatwa/Television (http://www.islam.tc/ask-imam/view.php?q=2538, print 2003–12–18).

110　He argues that most, if not all, television series and films promote *zina'* (adultery and fornication).

400,000 sex acts on TV, 100,000 to 200,000 acts of violence and 17,000 to 33,000 murders.'[111] Furthermore, watching television not only threatens the morality of the society, it can also lead to serious health problems, such as heart disease and stress. These side effects are causing some of the most serious health problems in the world, according to Desai. And to be able to resist this 'poison', it is necessary for Muslims to abstain from watching television.

This is, however, not the only example of how Deoband *'ulama'* have forbidden Muslims from watching television or warned them against doing so. For example, in 2004 the *Dar ul-'Ulum* at Deoband in India issued a *fatwa* declaring the watching of television an impermissible act that contradicts the laws of Islam. Mahmud al-Hasan Bulandshari, the *mufti* who issued the *fatwa*, declared every form of television forbidden to Muslims. Television is 'a means for [frivolous] entertainment'. However, as clearly illustrated by Yoginder Sikand of the Centre for Nehruvian studies in New Delhi, India, the followers of the Deoband tradition were divided on the issue. Even though the majority of *'ulama'* who follow this school were sceptical of most television programmes, other argued that the broadcast media could be used to counter 'anti-Islamic propaganda and for inviting people to Islam'.[112]

Satellite television, global and translocal muftis

With the development and introduction of transnational satellite broadcasting in the 1990s, the media landscape in the Middle East changed dramatically. However, since the impact of satellite television has been covered and analysed in a large number of articles, books and conferences, my discussion in this section will be limited to the so-called Islamic television channels (or specific programmes that deal with Islam and Muslim issues).[113] But since this is also a large subject, my discussion will primarily be focused on the opinions of the *'ulama'* already covered in this chapter. Because the Deoband and Wahhabi *'ulama'* are sceptical of television broadcasting in general, they are excluded from this analysis. Besides Yusuf al-Qaradawi, who uses the new technology extensively, I have also included a comparison with the Egyptian popular preacher Amr Khaled.[114] Important questions here are: what kind of *'ulama'* use satellite television to preach about

---

111   Fatwa/Television. Wife insists ... (http://www.islam.tc/ask-imam/view.php? q=2538, printed 200 (printed 2003–12–15).

112   Sikand 2006, pp. 48–49.

113   For example, on the development of the satellite channel al-Jazeera, see Zayani 2005; El-Nawawy and Iskandar 2002; on transnational satellite broadcasting in the Middle East, see, for example, Sakr 2001. Besides the significance of satellite television, it is also important to stress that several Muslim groups have started their own local TV stations in the West. On this development, see, for example, Bentzin 2003; Jonker 2000; and Landman 1997.

114   On Amr Khaled, see Wise 2003, 2004, and Mariani 2006.

and call people to Islam? And why do they use satellite television? But before we answer these questions, it is necessary to determine whether the '*ulama*' associated with the three *fatwa* services analysed in this chapter have any specific opinions about the introduction of satellite broadcasting and the use of parabolic antennas as compared to their views on terrestrial television, that is, does satellite broadcasting raise new questions?

Although the general audience in the Middle East seems to be very happy with the fact that state monopoly and control over the media have been challenged, even broken, with the introduction of satellite broadcasting, it is clear that some '*ulama*' (together with many politicians and state leaders) are sceptical, even critical, of this development.[115] The Saudi Arabian theologian Shaykh 'Abd al-'Aziz b. Baz can serve as an example of a theologian who is critical of the impact of satellite broadcasting:

> In recent years, what has come to be known as a 'dish' has pervaded our society, bringing into every home all kinds of falsehood, disbelief, images of partially or fully naked women, scenes of drinking and debauchery, and other forms of evil. As it has come to my knowledge that most people here now own these devices and that they are made and sold here in our country, I must warn you of the inherent dangers involved and of the necessity of fighting these dangers, first by not bringing these devices into our homes and then by warning and preventing others from doing so. The production and sale of these devices must be made forbidden because of the tremendous evils they facilitate, causing the people to help each other in sin and transgression, spreading disbelief and corruption among the Muslims.[116]

Furthermore, it is also clear that Shaykh 'Abd al-'Aziz b. Baz is calling for greater censorship and control over the media. His argument is that, if the new information and communication technologies are to be used to call people to Islam, they should only present a 'true' and 'sound' interpretation of Islam (that is, an interpretation acceptable to himself). According to my understanding, the call for more censorship and greater restrictions should primarily be viewed here as an illustration of the fact that many '*ulama*' perceive, directly or indirectly, correctly or incorrectly, that their authority and positions as religious leaders and interpreters of Islam have been undermined because more Muslim voices can be heard since the introduction of satellite broadcasting and the Internet. To retain control and preserve his position as the main interpreter of Islam in Saudi Arabia, Shaykh 'Abd al-'Aziz b. Baz was therefore reluctant to accept the principle of freedom of opinion in the media.[117] To quote Dale F. Eickelman, the media (especially the

---

115   An illustrative example is found in Teitelbaum (2002) on the Internet in Saudi Arabia.

116   *Fatawa Islamiya*, vol. 8, p. 178.

117   Cf. *Fatawa Islamiya*, vol. 8, p. 169.

Internet) 'has eroded the ability of authorities to censor and repress'.[118] Moreover, the so-called new media have opened the door not only to novel discussions, but also to innovative interpreters who claim to have an equal right to take part in the debate and formulation of an Islamic theology in the public sphere.[119] Compared to Yusuf al-Qaradawi, whom we have discussed extensively in this and other chapters in this book, the Islamic television channel *Dream Teve* and later *Iqra'* promotes, for example, Amr Khaled as an alternative voice.[120] One of the most interesting things about the Egyptian Amr Khaled is that he has no formal theological training and has not received any diploma from an institution of Islamic learning (for example, al-Azhar University in Cairo or the Islamic University of Medina, Saudi Arabia). Because of his lack of formal training he does not issue any *fatwas*, his prime goal being to emphasise emotions and positive feelings among Muslims who are split between local traditions and the temptations of a modern, Western way of life.[121] For this target group, Amr Khaled's message is appealing. He says:

> A good preacher should be more compassionate than disciplinary. My main concern is to make you people love religion instead of fearing it.[122]

Although he has no theological training, or rather because he issues no theological answers, he is very popular with Muslims who belong to a certain upper-class social milieu in Egypt.[123] With the help of satellite television programmes, small media (for example, cassettes, videos, DVDs) and a functional homepage in Arabic and several other languages, Amr Khaled has rapidly become a superstar in contemporary global discussions of Islam and Muslims in the Middle East, Europe and the United States. Without bending the argument too much, he is an important example and to some extent a personification of how the new information and communication technologies can be used to spread alternative interpretations

---

118   Eickelman 2003, p. 33. Cf. also Wise 2003, p. 11.

119   An illustrative example of how new media can open up debates about society, Islam and gender roles is the publication of the novel *Banat al-Riyad* ('The Girls from Riyadh') by Raja' 'Abd Allah al-Sani'. This so-called chick-litt novel was originally distributed and published as an e-letter before it was printed. According to Gail Ramsey, the book addresses '(1) the problem of the lack of female power, (2) the problem of feeling and (3) writing on the Internet as action'. Ramsey 2007, p. 188.

120   The television channel *Iqra'* was first launched in 1996 as part of the ART media organization, but it started with a transmission from Rome in 1998. According to Mohammad Hammam, executive manager of *Iqra'*, the channel has two aims: 'to correct the superficial and misrepresented image of Islam for world audience, as well as to mend Muslims' misunderstanding of their religion'. See Shahba 2005 and Tash 2004.

121   Cf. Wise 2003, p. 5 and p. 28.

122   Quotation taken from an interview with *Al-Ahram weekly Online*, 28 Nov–4 Dec 2002 ('Preaching with a passion'), retrieved from http://weekly.ahram.org.eg/2002/614/fe2.htm (printed 2008–09–24).

123   Wise 2003, p. 17.

of Islam, that is, interpretations that are beyond the control of the so-called 'establishment Islam' (that is, the educated '*ulama*') and the state. Furthermore, he does not fit into the stereotypical image of 'the government's attempt to categorize Islamists as poor, ignorant, uncouth, fringe extremists'.[124] According to Lindsay Wise, this is the main reason why Amr Khaled is such a controversial preacher in Egypt today.[125] His way of putting an argument does not oppose the state, and he does not issue any *fatwas* that could be considered a threat to the social order in Egypt. It is therefore problematic or even impossible for the Egyptian state to label him a radical Islamic preacher whom they could ban. The controversy involving Amr Khaled is therefore 'not so much because of what he says, but how he says it, and to whom he says it'.[126] His way of presenting Islam is an alternative to the secular state and the more conservative interpretation offered by al-Azhar University. Wise writes:

> His relatively youthful good looks and snappy clothes, intangible charisma, easy charm and unaffected air of friendly, open intimacy seems to appeal strongly, particularly to his target audience of elite 'Westernised' youth and women, many of whom are looking for ways to build closer and more meaningful ties with their culture and religion, but do not necessarily identify with the more traditional Azharite or 'fundamentalist' preachers, who some perceive either as out-of-touch disciplinarians or rabid extremists, marginal to society, uncouth, and dangerously ignorant.[127]

Amr Khaled's dress code and way of talking and interacting with his audience differ greatly from how more traditional '*ulama*' approach their audiences. His pedagogy is also different from how other so-called media '*ulama*', such as Yusuf al-Qaradawi, address their followers. Compared to the theological elite, Amr Khaled is simply a *rijal al-din* (that is, a man of religion) and is primarily seen as a *da'iya*, a person who invites people to Islam.[128]

Conclusions

The introduction of media based on sound and images rather than on text was of great importance in most regions with low literacy and an unequal distribution of education. The political leaders of the Middle East, such as the Egyptian leader Gamal Abdel Nasser, understood the political power and importance of the development of radio broadcasting. Because of its ability to reach out to the whole

---

124 Wise 2004.
125 For example, in 2002 he had to leave Egypt and move to London. Wise 2003, 2004.
126 Wise 2003, p. 18.
127 Wise 2003, p. 39.
128 Wise 2003, pp. 28–29.

population, the radio soon became a political instrument which it was important for the political elite to monopolise and control. From a theological point of view, radio caused few problems and discussions – at least if we compare it to media such as photography, film or television. However, some *'ulama'* were concerned with the fact that women's voices could be heard on the radio. A more serious problem was the fact that the radio is used for playing music, a topic that has been debated by the *'ulama'* for a long time. The radio and later the ability to record cassettes became a tool for opposition to and criticism of the state. According to Charles Hirschkind, for example, the distribution of cassettes containing Islamic preaching is therefore very important for opening up debates and public notions of Islamic ethics. This medium, that is, the cassette, also seems to have made theological discussions more democratic and open to contradictory opinions.[129]

With the introduction of television broadcasting in the Middle East, the *'ulama'* were faced with new opportunities as well as problems. According to the *'ulama'* discussed in this chapter, television posed a much more serious problem for Muslims, since television programmes are filled with music, singing and various forms of immorality. Hence it became necessary for the *'ulama'* to develop strategies for how to handle the new media. For some *'ulama'* it was better to ban television as an un-Islamic media. However, this strategy was not satisfactory to other *'ulama'*, for whom it was better to find other possibilities. As with earlier discussions in this book, some *'ulama'* argued that the media as such are not the problem, and that it is the content and the intentions of the producers and the audience that determine whether the media are good or bad. With the rise of satellite television, it is also evident that some *'ulama'* – in particular the Egyptian Yusuf al-Qaradawi and the popular preacher Amr Khaled – have made extensive use of television in spreading their interpretations of Islam. By using satellite television, it has become much easier to reach a global audience and target new groups. As with Charles Hirschkind's analysis of the place of cassettes, using television to transmit religious programmes has opened up discussions about religion and democratised them. Several examples in this chapter and in other studies have demonstrated that the new media have the potential to open up the debate and involve more people in discussions of how to interpret and apply Islamic ethics and rulings.

---

129   Cf. Hirschkind 2006.

Chapter 5

'The Invisible Caller':
Islamic Opinions on the Use of the Telephone

So the King [that is, Ibn Sa'ud] gathered the rebel theologians and told them
to divide themselves into two groups, one to remain with him at the capital of
Riyadh, and the other to go to Mecca, four hundred miles away. At the appointed
hour, some days later, the King made one of the mosque Imams read a chapter of
the Qur'an at Riyadh into the transmitter, and one of the Mecca group then read it
back, with the text attested as audible at both ends by many witnesses. What does
this test prove, except your guilt? asked the critics. The King replied read your
Qur'an. Does it not say that the devil and his cohorts cannot pronounce even one
word of our Holy Book? This miracle therefore is not of the devil but of nature.[1]

This quotation is taken from the story of the Saudi Arabian king, 'Abdul 'Aziz al
Sa'ud (1876–1953), and his debate with a group of 'ulama' who were critical of
the introduction of the wireless telephone. By a creative use of the holy revelation,
however, it was possible for the king to convince the critics that the transmission of
sound from place A to place B was not the result of some kind of evil intervention
produced by Shaytan (Satan) or a jinni. By referring to the uniquely divine quality
of the Qur'an, the king was able to persuade the members of the 'ulama' who
were sceptical of the introduction of the communication device. Even though no
'ulama' today are convinced that the telephone embodies some kind of evil force,
it is clear that the media still cause debates among Muslims.

But before I develop and outline some of the questions raised by the 'ulama',
it is important to remember that the introduction of the telephone also gave rise
to debates in the West.[2] In his book *Understanding Media*, for example, the
Canadian media and communication researcher Marshall McLuhan recalls that
the telephone was surrounded by a mystique, and the belief of the 'ulama' in
Saudi Arabia quoted in the introduction could therefore easily be compared to
stories about the telephone in the West. To support his argument, McLuhan recalls
a practical joke. In the early days of the telephone, it was common for one person
to call another and asked them to cover their telephone with a blanket. The reason
given was that the telephone company was going to clean the wires, and owners
were therefore advised to cover their telephones in order to protect their homes

---

1   This story is recorded in Eddy 1963, p. 258.
2   See Briggs and Burke 2002, pp. 146–148 (especially the illustration depicting
'Weavers of Speech' on p. 146).

from the pollution and grease that would be coming out of the wire as a result of this procedure. According to McLuhan, it seems that those on whom this practical joke was inflicted expected the wires to hiss and growl, and that some kind of pollution would come out of them. This is an important reminder that in the West too, the early history of the telephone was perceived as a communication tool surrounded by a mystical aura as in the Saudi Arabian story above.[3] Regardless of geographical or cultural difference, it seems that both the '*ulama*' in Saudi Arabia and the people in the West could have similar negative perceptions about the introduction of the telephone.

The mystique that surrounds the telephone is, moreover, also manifest in the Arabic language. A telephone is known as a *hatif* in Arabic, a word that carries several meanings, for example, 'shouting, calling loudly', but also 'invisible caller, voice'.[4] Without developing the etymology further, it is clear that the word *hatif* is associated with the mysterious transmission of sounds and messages. Despite the intriguing etymology and the place of the telephone in Muslim societies, there is hardly any information about the reception and introduction of this particular technology in Middle Eastern studies.[5]

Judging from the large number of *fatwas* that deal, directly or indirectly, with questions relating to how Muslims should use the telephone, it is quite surprising that the debate over the place of the telephone in Islamic jurisprudence has, to the best of my knowledge, not been the subject of any academic studies.[6] Yet even though I have been unable to find Islamic books or pamphlets that specifically deal with the telephone and its place in Islamic law, it is evident that a large number of *fatwas* actually address questions that have a bearing on its use. For example, does the telephone break the rules of *khalwa* (privacy), or are men and women free to use the phone without any restrictions, no matter whether they are married or related to each other? Is it possible to divorce one's wife via email or cell-phone text messages? Could the beginning of the fasting period depend on telephone reports from Muslim countries?[7] What should Muslims do if they receive a telephone call while praying? Are Muslims allowed to use cell phones during the Friday *khutba*? What about the possibility to use recordings of recitations from the Qur'an or Islamic ring tones in your cell phone?

---

3   McLuhan 1964, p. 308.

4   Wehr 1976, p. 1018. The *hatif* was also associated with a 'voice coming from an idol' and is 'an audible voice without possessing a visible body'; see Fahd 1971, p. 273.

5   One important exception is Campbell 2007.

6   That said, it is also important to stress that it is in general difficult to find studies focusing on how religious groups or congregations have debated about or used the telephone. Besides Campbell 2007, it is also important to mention Umble 1994 and Åberg 2003, p. 187.

7   This is the same problem that Jacob Skovgaard-Petersen analysed and discussed in relation to the telegraph; see Skovgaard-Petersen 1997a, pp. 80–99.

The analysis of Islamic views on how to use the telephone is important for several reasons. First of all, the telephone is one of the most widely distributed and widely used technologies for modern communication all around the world. Secondly, the discussion of how to use the telephone is also closely related to the debate about online chatting and the use of the Internet, which I will analyse in the next chapter. Thirdly, with the development of the cell phone and its applications (for example, SMS, MMS chat, and so on), using the telephone has entered the public sphere in a very direct manner. The debate about the cell phone is also closely related to the current debate about Islamic morals and ethics, especially among Muslims who pay close attention to the necessity of living in accordance with the laws of Islam.[8] For the Muslims discussed in this study, the question of how to use the telephone is therefore an unavoidable aspect of being a Muslim. How individuals with a Muslim cultural background actually use the telephone is, according to the theologians, a revealing and relevant example of their belief in Islam.[9]

The law of *khalwa*

In a cultural or a religious context that strives to uphold a strict separation between the sexes, the telephone could become a problem because it is a technology that can easily help its users come into contact with the opposite sex, no matter what the physical distance, or to break established norms.[10] With the development of the telephone technology (and even more so the cell phone), it has become both possible and very easy to contact individuals with whom you have no relationship (that is, people to whom you are not related by blood or family ties).[11] Hence, by using the telephone, it is simple to break or test the boundaries of the law of *khalwa* (privacy).[12] This fundamental principle in Islamic theology stipulates that those who are outside the *mahram* relationship – that is, 'a relationship either by marriage or by close blood ties' – should have no or only restricted contact with each other.[13]

---

8   On this movement, see Hirschkind 2006. That said, it is also important to stress that the introduction of the telephone also caused discussions about the ethics of telephoning. One discussion, for example, concerned whether swearing on the telephone should be viewed as an offence. According to the critics, it was also believed that the new technology and its anonymity could encourage people to tell lies. The lack of face-to-face contact could consequently be seen as an incitement for lying. Briggs and Burke 2000, p. 150.

9   A similar way of putting the argument is provided by the Ultra-Orthodox Jewish information in Campbell 2007.

10   Similar problems are also discussed within the Amish and Mennonite community according to Umble 1994.

11   This 'problem' is also highlighted by the Ultra-Orthodox Jewish community in Israel; see Campbell 2007.

12   Netton 1997, p. 144.

13   On the Islamic definition of *mahram* (unmarriageable kin), see, for example, the Deoband fatwa by Muhammad ibn Adam, 'Who is a Mahram?', retrieved from http://www.

This law is, for example, essential in Islamic discussions about how and why the sexes should be separated.[14] In the following discussion, however, it will become clear that the separation prescribed by the '*ulama*' is not limited to physical contact. With the development of information and communication technologies, such as the telephone, the cell phone or the Internet (email, chat forums, and so on), it has also become important to restrict non-physical or virtual contacts. Even though these technologies have made it much easier to question or break this principle, it is evident from the discussion that the debate is not a new one. The '*ulama*' discussed in this section are, for example, also concerned with written contact (for example, through love letters). According to Yusuf al-Qaradawi, the reason for this separation is 'not a lack of trust in one or both of them; it is rather to protect them from wrong thoughts and sexual feelings which naturally arise within a man and a women when they are alone together without the fear or intrusion by a third person'.[15] From his point of view, the law of *khalwa* includes telephone calls, and the use of this particular technology should be limited to unavoidable telephone calls.[16] Hence, al-Qaradawi accepts telephone calls that are categorised as necessary (for example, business calls or contacts with schools or health centres), for which it is not necessary to restrict the conversation to married couples or relatives, though it is essential to ensure that they are 'free from any sort of evil'.[17]

From the *fatwas* I have analysed, however, it is clear that the '*ulama*' may have different approaches to the telephone. For example, Muhammad ibn Adam from the *Darul Iftaa*, a Deoband site located in the UK, who most likely agrees with al-Qaradawi regarding his definition of *khalwa*, does not make any references to telephone calls in his *fatwa* on 'Being Alone with Someone of the Opposite Sex in a Work Situation'. This is striking, since in his question the questioner informs the *mufti* that he has been talking to non-*mahram* women on the telephone at work. This is an illustration of the fact that the telephone can be seen either as a technology that breaks the laws of *khalwa* or as one to which the '*ulama*' are more or less indifferent.[18] The answer can, however, also be seen as indicating

---

daruliftaa.com/question.asp?txt_QuestionID=q-19424987 (printed 2008–09–09).

14   Sonbol 2002, p. 121 demonstrates that the policy of gender separation is legitimated by the *hadith* literature. However, Islam is not the only religion that emphasises the necessity of separating men and women. On gender segregation in Judaism, see, for example, Gal Berner 2002, especially p. 36.

15   al-Qaradawi 2001, p. 147.

16   The Amish community studied by Umble 1994, p. 105, for example, also shares this opinion. They argue that the telephone should only be used for emergency calls (such as calling a doctor, the fire brigade or a veterinarian).

17   Sheikh ibn Jibreen (1986b), 'Speaking to women on the phone', and Sheikh Ahmed Kutty (2005), 'Talking Intimately With the Opposite Sex', retrieved from http://www.islamonline.net/servlet/Satellite?pagename=IslamOnline-English-Ask_Scholar/FatwaE/FatwaEandcid=1119503549134 (printed 2006–05–26).

18   Muhammad ibn Adam, 'Being Alone with Someone of the Opposite Sex in a Work Situation', retrieved from http://www.daruliftaa.com/question.asp?txt_

that the *'ulama'* have no problems with telephone calls that are restricted to work situations. If this interpretation is correct, Muhammad ibn Adam's answer does not say much about his views on the more general use of the telephone.

What about telephone sex?

Even though a *mufti* may be indifferent to telephone technology, it is essential and basic for the *'ulama'* to stress that Muslims should be careful when talking to the opposite sex. According to the *'ulama'* I have examined for this chapter, it is clear that the Muslims of today are facing new attitudes, problems, forms of behaviour and an increasing number of worldly temptations that have made it more difficult to follow the principles of Islam. The *'ulama'* argue that the world has, for example, become more tempting thanks to Western influences, materialism, secularism and consumerism. As compared with earlier periods, it is therefore more difficult to avoid sin and un-Islamic forms of behaviour. The Saudi Arabian Sheikh Muhammad Salih al-Munajjid can serve here as an example of this opinion. He writes:

> Nowadays, all the doors of immorality have been opened, and Satan and his supporters have made it very easy for people to commit sin. This has been followed by the spread of *tabarruj* (wanton display) and unveiling among women, people allowing their gazes to wander to things they should not look at, an increase in mixing between the sexes, the popularity of immoral magazines and lewd films, increased travel to corrupt countries and the establishment of a market for prostitution, an increase in the violation of honour and an increase in the number of illegitimate births and abortions.[19]

Even though many *'ulama'* argue that modern society has made it much more difficult to uphold the virtues of an Islamic life, it is clear that indecent conversations between non-*mahram* are far from being a new phenomenon. For example, the Qur'an warns believers and urges them to avoid all kinds of *zina'* (that is, fornication or adultery):[20]

> And do not commit adultery – for, behold, it is an abomination and an evil way. (Q 17:32)

QuestionID=q-15275576 (printed 2008–09–09).

19   Al-Munajjid 2004, pp. 50–51. He also runs and supervises the homepage http://www.islam-qa.com/en.

20   Joseph Schacht defines Zina' as 'fornication, i.e. sexual intercourse between persons who are not in a state of legal matrimony or concubinage and cannot claim a shubha (i.e. the "resemblance"of the criminal action to a permitted one from which the bona fides of the offender is presumed)'. Schacht 1995b, pp. 658–659.

According to Sheikh Ahmed Kutty, the Prophet Muhammad is also reported to
have said:

> Eyes commit adultery, ears commit adultery, hands commit adultery, and feet
> commit adultery, and the private part either consummates it or repudiates it.

Against this background, it is quite obvious and should come as no surprise that
Sheikh Ahmed Kutty is not happy with a question on telephone sex raised by a
Muslim. He continues and replies as follows:

> Although you are certainly allowed to speak to your fiancée, your conversations
> at all times must be governed strictly by the Islamic ethics of interaction between
> males and females. The fact that you are considering marriage with someone or
> that you are engaged to a person does not imply any license to break the law,
> for the person you are proposing to or are engaged to still remains a stranger to
> you as far as intimate relationship is concerned. So take care not to get carried
> away by your chats into overstepping the limits of *halal* and *haram*. If, as you
> have stated, your conversations involve sexual matters, then I am afraid you
> are overstepping the permissible boundaries. So I advise both of you to repent
> sincerely to Allah and cut out such conversations cold turkey.[21]

The *mufti* Muhammad ibn Adam, whom we discussed earlier, has also received
a question about telephone sex. As in Sheikh Ahmed Kutty's answer, he is also
sceptical and negative regarding indecent and 'sexy' conversations, but he argues
that the problem is not intimate discussions between a married man and women; it is
the masturbation that is sinful. He explains that mutual masturbation (that is, a kind of
masturbation that includes physical contact that involves both partners) is accepted,
but individual masturbation is wrong. Hence, he comes to the conclusion that:

> If during a phone conversation, the objective is not to masturbate, rather the
> spouses are merely intimate, then this would be permitted. It would be permitted
> to have an erotic and sexual conversation with one's spouse, provided one does
> not fear falling into masturbation or any other unlawful act.[22]

---

21   Sheikh Ahmed Kutty (2005) 'Talking Intimately with the Opposite Sex', retrieved
from   http://www.islamonline.net/servlet/Satellite?pagename=IslamOnline-English-Ask_
Scholar/FatwaE/FatwaEandcid=1119503549134 (printed 2006–05–26). Muzammil Siddiqi
also takes a strong position against all kinds of so-called cyber *zina'* (that is, phone sex
or online sex). See Siddiqi (2004) 'Cyber Sex and Zina', retrieved from http://www.
islamonline.net/servlet/Satellite?pagename=IslamOnline-English-Ask_Scholar/FatwaE/
FatwaEandcid=1119503544546 (printed 2006–05–26).
22   Muhammad ibn Adam, 'Is it Permissible to have Phone Sex with One's Wife?',
retrieved   from   http://www.daruliftaa.com/question.asp?txt_QuestionID=q-18481892
(printed 2008–08–15).

The necessity of maintaining a strict separation between the sexes is also discussed by, for example, Muzammil Siddiqi, former President of the Islamic Society of North America, in relation to online chatting. In his *fatwa* on Internet chats between males and females, Siddiqi makes a comparison between letters, telephone conversations and online chatting:

> Internet chat is very similar to writing letters or talking to someone on the phone. Actually it is a combination of both. Muslims have to observe the same rules as they observe in writing letters or making telephone calls. Islam does not permit love letters or intimate conversations between males and females who are not married to each other.[23]

The *fatwas* issued by Muhammad ibn Adam, Sheikh Ahmed Kutty and lastly Muzammil Siddiqi illustrate clearly that the '*ulama*' are concerned about the impact of the new information and communication technologies. The discussion and answers given by the '*ulama*' can all serve as illustrations of how the new technologies can be perceived as a threat. According to the '*ulama*' discussed in this chapter, unnecessary and indecent conversations have been promoted and facilitated by the development of the telephone, which from this point of view can be seen as a technology capable of violating the moral order, as well as religious norms and values. As we shall see from the following examples, however, this is not the only side effect of telephone technology.

The telephone and the mosque

Besides moral issues, the '*ulama*' analysed for this chapter are worried about how the technology might influence the devotional and daily life of Muslims.[24] For example, how should a Muslim behave if he or she receives a telephone call while praying? The problem is that it is improper to answer a call while praying, but also it is rude not to respond to a call. In a *fatwa* posted on the webpage of

---

23   Siddiqi, Muzammil (2005) 'Internet Chats between Males and Females', retrieved from   http://www.islamonline.net/servlet/Satellite?cid=1119503543228&pagename=Isl amOnline-English-Ask_Scholar%2FFatwaE%2FFatwaE (printed 2006–05–26). Sheikh Ahmed Kutty gives a similar argument in another *fatwa* on online chatting. See Sheikh Ahmed Kutty (2005), 'Online Chatting in the Eyes of Shari'ah', retrieved from http://www. islamonline.net/servlet/Satellite?cid=1119503547082&pagename=IslamOnline-English-Ask_Scholar%2FFatwaE%2FFatwaE (printed 2006–05–26). Muhammad ibn Adam also stresses the similarity between telephone sex and cyber sex. He writes: 'Phone sex is very similar to cyber sex, although the latter is typically free of charge. Cyber sex is the logical continuation of phone sex on modern computer networks.' See Muhammad ibn Adam, 'Is it Permissible to have Phone Sex with One's Wife?', retrieved from http://www.daruliftaa. com/question.asp?txt_QuestionID=q-18481892 (printed 2008–08–15).

24   Cf. Campbell 2007.

IslamOnline.net in 2002, for example, it is stressed that all believers must prepare themselves both physically (that is, make the correct ablutions) and mentally (to adopt the right intentions) before they start to pray. For example, if you pray at home, you must turn off the TV and switch off the phone to prevent all possible distractions.[25] But if some of these precautions are forgotten, the believer should follow tradition and the example set by the Prophet Muhammad. In his time there were, for obvious reasons, no telephones or TV broadcasts to disturb one's prayers, but believers could still be distracted and interrupted while praying. For example, 'Whoever notices something alarming whilst praying, the men should say "Subhanna Allah" and women should clap their hands'.[26] With the help of analogical reasoning (*qiyas*), it is therefore possible for the *mufti* to find a solution for the question about improper telephone calls during prayers. In response to the question regarding receiving a call while praying, for example, the Saudi House of Fatwa outlines the Islamic point of view by saying:

> If a person is in the position you describe [i.e., in the question] and the phone starts ringing, it is permissible for him to lift the receiver, even if he has to move a little way forward or backward, or to the right or left, on the condition that he keeps facing the *Qiblah* and says 'Subhaan Allah' so that the person on the line will know that he is praying.[27]

This is a good example of how a 'modern' problem is solved with the help of analogical reasoning. By applying the answer given in the *fatwa* above, believers will be emulating the *sunna* of the Prophet Muhammad and the early Muslim community. For believers this is an illustration of the fact that Islam can be interpreted to fit all situations, regardless of time or place.

------

25   According to Muhammad ibn Adam at the *Dar ul-Ifaa*, Leicester, UK, it is totally unacceptable to use a cell phone in a mosque. He writes: 'It is not appropriate to use cell phones in Masjids, unless absolutely necessary, for it entails disturbing those who are engaged in worship (ibadah). To harm and disturb another individual is a sin in itself, let alone when one is engaged in an Ibadah, such as offering Salat.' Muhammad ibn Adam, *Mobile/Cell Phones During Hajj in Mosques*, retrieved from http://www.daruliftaa.com/ question.asp?txt_QuestionID=q-13413991 (printed 2008–09–09).

26   The recommendation and the *hadith* quoted above are taken from The Saudi House of Fatwa, 'Receiving a call while praying', retrieved from http://www.islamonline. net/servlet/Satellite?pagename=IslamOnline-English-Ask_Scholar/FatwaE/FatwaE   *Dar ul-Ifaa* cid=1119503545614 (printed 2006–05–26).

27   The Saudi House of Fatwa, 'Receiving a call while praying', retrieved from http://www.islamonline.net/servlet/Satellite?pagename=IslamOnline-English-Ask_ Scholar/FatwaE/FatwaE&cid=1119503545614 (printed 2006–05–26). This *fatwa* is also reproduced by Sheikh Muhammad al-Munajjid, 'Answering the telephone whilst praying', retrieved from http://www.islam-qa.com/en/ref/8647/telephone (printed 2008–09–09). According to al-Munajjid, the *fatwa* originates from *al-Lajnah al-Daa'imah li'l-Buhooth al-'Ilmiyyah wa'l-Iftaa'*, 7/32.

The ability to have music or other kinds of improper messages such as ring tones on your cell phone is another problem that the '*ulama*' discuss in relation to the cell phone. The fact that visitors to the mosque forget or neglect to turn off their cell phones while praying is a real problem, according to many '*ulama*'. Even more problematic is the fact that the new technology has made it possible to use recordings of recitations from the Qur'an as ring tones. This use is problematic first of all because it can be seen as a proliferation of the holy message, and secondly it can be used wrongly. For example, is it correct to interrupt the recitation by picking up the phone? And what happens when the recitation is sounded (that is, when the phone rings) in an improper place? Should the individual who is using the recitation of the Qur'an always be in a state of ritual purity? While these questions touch upon essential aspects of Islamic devotion, the use of so-called Islamic ring tones was banned by the Islamic Jurisprudence Council in Saudi Arabia in November 2007.[28] Although this could be seen as an attempt to prevent the use of Islamic ring tones for cell phones, it is evident that ring tones (both Islamic and non-Islamic) continue to be a problem in many mosques. This problem was, for example, addressed by a Swedish online discussion group in summer 2008. The discussion, which among other things included a debate over the improper use of musical ring tones inside the mosques, extended over a couple of days. Even though this is an isolated and local example, it illustrates how the cell phone is being discussed by Muslims. From this point of view, the debate about ring tones is an example of how the cell phone can conflict with Islamic rules and regulations and be perceived as a threat for those who want be 'good' Muslims. The development of Islamic ring tones is also an example of how the message of the Qur'an is now being mass-produced, a topic that I will return to in the last chapter, which deals with information and communication technologies and the Qur'an.

From the questions posted on the Internet, it is also clear that it is not only the 'ordinary' lay Muslims who are affected by the new information and communication technologies. In a question to IslamOnline.net, for example, a Muslim asks whether it is allowed to use a cell phone while attending the *salat al-jum'a* (the Friday Prayer). His question is based on the fact that several 'brothers keep them on and receive paging and calls in the mosque. Sometimes, even the *imam* interrupts his *khutba* (sermon) to answer a call from work'.[29] Again, it is Sheikh Ahmed Kutty who replies to the question posted on the Internet. In an upset tone, he replies:

---

28   'Quranic Ringtones Haram', *Arab News*, Friday 9 November 2007 (28 Shawwal 1428), retrieved on http://www.arabnews.com/?page=1&section=0&article=103380&d=9 &m=11&y=2007 (printed 2008–08–15).

29   Sheikh Ahmed Kutty (2003) 'Using Cell Phone during Friday *Khutbah*', retrieved from   http://www.islamonline.net/servlet/Satellite?pagename=IslamOnline-English-Ask_ Scholar/FatwaE/FatwaE&cid=1119503546460 (printed 2006–05–26).

It should be common knowledge for every Muslim that during the Friday Prayer we must observe silence; we are not allowed to disrupt the *khutbah* or Prayer by engaging in any activity. The Prophet (peace and blessings be upon him) is reported to have said: 'Whoever indulges in idle talks or deeds during the *khutbah*, his Jum'ah is invalid.' Therefore, the use of cell phones during the *khutbah* by the imam or the followers is totally unacceptable. It is a sign of disrespect for this important symbol of Islam.[30]

The fact that an *imam* could be disturbed by 'idle talk' (*lahw*)[31] is, however, neither a modern phenomenon nor a problem that springs from the new information and communication technologies alone.[32] During the medieval period too, the *muhtasib* or market inspector – as demonstrated in sources from al-Andalus – was expected to ensure that all Muslims were present at the Friday sermon. Besides the obligation to attend the prayer, the congregation should not be engaged in any kind of commercial activity, whether inside or outside the mosque.[33] Like the '*ulama*' discussed in this volume, the *muhtasib* had to 'promote good and forbid evil'.[34] The very basis of this endeavour was to help, convince or even force believers to focus on the important things in life (that is, on religious affairs). From this point of view, the occupation of *muhtasib* in medieval al-Andalus does not differ much from the work and efforts made by present-day '*ulama*' at IslamOnline.net. Although we should not bend the argument too much, I suggest that this illustration reminds us that the new information and communication technologies do not automatically cause new problems or possibilities. The difficulties as well as the promises are more or less the same, regardless of time or place. The differences with the new technologies have more to do with degree than kind.

---

30   Sheikh Ahmed Kutty (2003), 'Using Cell Phone during Friday *Khutbah*', retrieved from   http://www.islamonline.net/servlet/Satellite?pagename=IslamOnline-English-Ask_ Scholar/FatwaE/FatwaE&cid=1119503546460 (printed 2006–05–26).

31   *Lahw* is also associated with 'insult, abuse, invective, vilification, defamation'; see Wehr 1976, p. 862.

32   It should also be stressed that Muslims are discussing how to behave in the mosque. This kind of debate cannot be related to idle talk (*lahw*), but it is an example of how Muslim '*ulama*' debate how to behave according to Islamic rulings. Not even the mosque is spared from these kinds of discussions, and it is essential for Muslim '*ulama*' to outline how to behave there. One example of this kind is found in Muhammad bin Adam, 'Discourses in Masjids and Disturbing Others', http://www.daruliftaa.com/question. asp?txt_QuestionID=q-18304717 (printed 2008–08–15).

33   Wickens 1956, pp. 120–121.

34   Cf. Cahen and Talbi 1971.

Marriage and divorce

The ability to connect people and to establish contact, regardless of time or place, is a specific characteristic of the telephone. This is a great possibility, but according to the *'ulama'* this potential can also raise new questions and problems. For example, can the technology be used to arrange marriages and divorces? If so, the telephone becomes something that should be addressed by the *'ulama'*, and the technology itself has to be situated in relation to Islamic law. In this section, I will examine more closely some *fatwas* that show how the *'ulama'* have been discussing marriage and divorce in relation to the telephone, and more recently in connection with the ability to send text messages (SMS).

It is no exaggeration to state that all *'ulama'* emphasise the importance and relevance of marriage and the fact that Islam does not promote celibacy. To have children and raise a family are basic aspects of Islam. The family is perceived as the source of the happiness, security and foundation of society. Furthermore, the family helps men and women preserve their faith and focus on the important things in life. Sheikh Yusuf al-Qaradawi explains:

> Marriage consummates one's faith, spares one looking at other women, enables one to preserve his chastity and offers one a lawful means to satisfy his sexual desire.

And he continues:

> Marriage is the sole means of establishing a family, the nucleus of society. No respectable human society could ever exist if not based on the family. Shaded by the close relations of motherhood, fatherhood as well as parent-child and sibling relations, warm feelings of love, altruism, mercy, care and cooperation are instilled in a Muslim.[35]

From the quotation above, it is clear that marriage between a man and a woman is a central component according to al-Qaradawi. Contrary to most contemporary 'Western' marriages, an Islamic marriage more usually includes the families of the two spouses. Consequently, it is important that they come to an agreement on the marriage. Hence, it is the families that must approve of the marriage, and it is not automatically up to the spouses to decide whether their love is sufficient for them to marry. To settle or arrange a marriage between two families is, however, far from being a new phenomenon. Prior to the arrival of modern information and communication technologies, wedding arrangements were generally settled by visiting the other family or by sending a delegate to negotiate the conditions

---

35   al-Qaradawi, 'The Philosophy of Marriage in Islam', retrieved from http://www.islamonline.net/servlet/Satellite?pagename=IslamOnline-English-Ask_Scholar/FatwaE/FatwaE&cid=1119503543574 (printed 2008–09–09).

for the marriage. This is the theoretical or ideal way of arranging a marriage, but it is likely that Muslims have always had love affairs that challenged the theory and circumvented the laws of Islam. This question is beyond the scope of this study, but it is nonetheless relevant to stress that the new technologies have made it much easier to break the religious rules and start a relationship, date or flirt without the involvement or consent of one's family. It has also become easier to become involved in love affairs and to be unfaithful to one's wife or husband.[36] One example relating to this is the following question raised by a young girl. In her request for a *fatwa*, she explains her situation as follows:

> I'm in an online relationship with a guy. It's been three years since I came to know him. We haven't seen each other at all. The only way we contact each other is via emails, phone calls, or chat. I'm 16 years old and he is a few years older than me.[37]

In his answer, Sheikh Ahmad Kutty explains that the girl is too young for marriage and that the boy should know better. Consequently she is advised to end the relationship. Still it is important to underline that the Internet is flooded with so-called online services for dating and matrimony. IslamOnline.net and a vast number of other sites on the Internet provide this service, for example. Even though these services may well have been set up with the aim of bringing people together for marriage, it is obvious that they also can be used for flirtation or short-term relationships between boys and girls.[38] But with the development of the Internet, it has even become possible to arrange a marriage over the Net. This practice is, however, condemned by the former President of the Islamic Society of North America, Dr Muzammil H. Siddiqi, who explains that:

> According to Muslim jurists, it is not permissible to marry someone by mail or phone. The same thing can be said about the e-mail. Marriage in Islam is a formal legal contract. It should be very clear who is marrying whom. The Shari'ah emphasizes the announcement of marriage and does not allow any ambiguity in this matter. It is for this reason that witnesses for *Nikah* are necessary. If the parties who want to get married are not present, they can appoint a *wakil* (representative). The person who is getting married has to appoint his/her *wakil*. It is permissible to appoint a *wakil* through telephone, fax or email. The *wakil* then should do the *ijab* (proposal) or *qubul* (acceptance), in person, on behalf

---

36   See, Ahmad Kutty, 'Communicating With Non-*Mahram* Behind Husband's Back', retrieved from http://www.islamonline.net/servlet/Satellite?pagename=IslamOnline-English-Ask_Scholar/FatwaE/FatwaE&cid=1119503549546 (printed 2008–09–02).

37   Ahmad Kutty, *Having an Online Relationship*, retrieved from http://www.islamonline.net/servlet/Satellite?pagename=IslamOnline-English-Ask_Scholar/FatwaE/FatwaE&cid=1203759014332 (printed 2008–09–09).

38   See, for example, Baune 2005.

of the person who appointed him. Two witnesses who also personally know the party that is not present are necessary for the contract of marriage.[39]

Despite his criticism and aversion to online marriages, it is likely that some Muslims practise this method, not least to try and obtain visas and green cards for travel to the West.[40] Even though it is impossible to know how many marriages have been settled or arranged with the help of emails or telephone calls, the question raised in the *fatwa* shows that some Muslims are engaged in something that the *'ulama'* do not approve of. This is a reminder of the difference between theory and practice and that lay Muslims do not always follow or listen to the *'ulama'* and their opinions.[41] A similar 'problem' is also discussed in relation to the possibility of obtaining a divorce.

Even though Islamic traditions and law strongly support marriage, it is still possible for both men and women to obtain a divorce under the right conditions. It is generally easier for the husband to do this, but the ability to annul a wedding is also available to women.[42] The condition for obtaining a divorce could, however, change over time, and several scholars have noted differences between theory and practice. A divorce is fulfilled when the husband (or the wife) says the word *talaq* ('I divorce you') three times before witnesses. It is, however, debated whether the three *talaq*s can be said at one time or if they should be uttered over a longer period (for example, over three cycles of menstruation).[43] Without going into any details about the conditions for obtaining a divorce, it is clear that the new technologies could be used to annul a marriage contract.

Even though the *'ulama'* at IslamOnline are concerned by the fact that the telephone and especially the sending of an SMS via cell phone can be used improperly for divorcing one's spouse, they are convinced that a text message would also count as a legal text. To put it differently, writing *talaq* three times and sending it by SMS provides legal grounds for divorce. Sheikh Hamed al-Ali, an instructor in Islamic Heritage at the Faculty of Education, Kuwait, and *imam* of *Dahiat As-Sabahiyya Mosque*, explains and clarifies his Islamic view on the possibility of divorce via email or SMS. He says:

> The most correct view is that written divorce does count whether the writing is on paper, a text message via cellular phone, or other methods. However, we

---

39   http://www.zawaj.com/is-marriage-through-email-allowed-in-islam/ (printed 2011–06–28).

40   This issue is, for example, clearly addressed in Baune 2005.

41   Cf. Olivier Roy, who stresses that ' "Real" Muslims act and live without waiting eagerly for the *ulama*'s point of view'. Roy 2004, p. 110.

42   Cf. Doumato 1995, p. 51.

43   An example of this debate is found in a *fatwa* issued for IslamOnline.net. See, A group of Muftis, 'Ruling on Triple Divorce', retrieved from http://www.islamonline.net/servlet/ Satellite?pagename=IslamOnline-English-Ask_Scholar/FatwaE/FatwaE&cid=1119503543664 (printed 2008–09–09). See also Pearl 1987, pp. 100–102 on the various forms of *talaq*.

have to make sure that the husband is the one who wrote the words of divorce. If he admits that he wrote the divorce, then it counts and is considered as a valid divorce. Otherwise, there must be two just witnesses to prove that he is the one who wrote the divorce, because it might be someone else who wrote the divorce.[44]

This is an example of how the *'ulama'* apply *qiyas* (analogical reasoning). The fact that it is possible to send a text message via a computer or as an SMS does not differ from a text written on a piece of paper. It is the intention (*niyya*) and the validity of the message that counts: the media used for the transmission of the message is of little or no importance. This way of putting the argument is also clearly a way of saying that the technology is neither good nor bad in itself. It is only the intention and action that count, and the traditional ways of solving a theological problem should apply to the new technologies as well.

The sighting of the new moon

Another problem related to the debate over the telephone concerns the sighting of the new moon. This issue is linked to the discussion about when to begin and end fasting during the month of Ramadan. In the *hadith* literature, it is reported:

> Start your fast at the sight of the new moon and break your fast at the sight of the new moon (of the next month). If (at the end of) the month (the sky) is overcast count off thirty (days).[45]

This *hadith* does not, however, clarify whether it is necessary for believers to observe the new moon with their own eyes, or whether it is sufficient to receive the information second hand transmitted via, for example, the telephone, the television, the radio or the Internet. Although most Muslims agree that it is not necessary to observe the new moon with your own eyes, it is stressed that the report must be delivered by trustworthy witnesses.[46] Still, it is evident that this issue is causing anxiety, confusion and even disagreement among Muslims. This debate is pursued not least on the Internet and in Muslim online discussion forums. An illustration of the debate is found in the following question posted to the *'ulama'* at IslamOnline. net:

---

44   Sheikh Hamed Al-Ali, 'Divorcing One's Wife via E-mail or Cell Phone Text Message', retrieved   from   http://www.islamonline.net/servlet/Satellite?pagename=IslamOnline-English-Ask_Scholar/FatwaE/FatwaE&cid=1119503545280 (printed 2008–09–09).

45   This *hadith* is quoted in Juynboll 2007, p. 555

46   See Ahmed Kutty, 'New Moon: Sighting or Calculating?', retrieved from http://www.islamonline.net/servlet/Satellite?pagename=IslamOnline-English-Ask_Scholar/FatwaE/FatwaE&cid=1157962457023 (printed 2008–09–09).

Dear scholars, As-Salamu 'alaykum. As you know, there is no centrally recognized authority for determining the beginning of the lunar month, especially Ramadan. Muslim minorities depend mostly on the reports coming from Muslim countries with Muslim majorities either by telephone or telegraph. Can Muslim minorities start fasting depending on the news of the new moon reported by telegraphs or telephones or any other electronic machines? Jazakum Allahu khayran.[47]

In his answer, Sheikh Ahmad Kutty stresses that both the beginning and the end of Ramadan, as well as the actual fasting, represents a collective enterprise. It is therefore paramount that the community follows a collective decision taken by the *imam*, rather than following individual recommendations. Even though it is possible to find different answers regarding when to begin and end the fasting period, 'the decision [regarding] which of the options must be followed must be taken by the community as a collective body and not by individuals tuning on to radios or receiving emails'.[48]

The debate over the observation of the moon and Ramadan is, however, not a new problem but goes way back in Muslim history. Jacob Skovgaard-Petersen, for example, has analysed this debate in relation to the introduction of the telegraph in the Muslim world.[49] From this point of view and in this case, the telephone is not giving rise to any new problem. Consequently it should be analysed, debated and used in similar ways to the earlier forms of information and communication technologies.

Dial-a-Fatwa

Even though the discussion over the use of the telephone depends on earlier debates and methods for solving theological problems (that is, *qiyas*), it is clear that the technology also can be used in the service of Islam. For example, the telephone has made it much easier for an individual Muslim to contact a *mufti* or a specific sheikh.[50] The ability to eliminate physical distance is of special importance for Muslims living in areas and countries not dominated by Muslim or Islamic traditions (for example, in Europe or the United States), or by converts to Islam. Today, for example, it is possible to call a large number of different Islamic telephone services that have been set up to help Muslims with practical problems, family issues and theological queries. Even though we lack studies of

---

47   Ahmed Kutty, *Fasting Depending on Phone Reports From Muslim Countries*, retrieved   from   http://www.islamonline.net/servlet/Satellite?pagename=IslamOnline-English-Ask_Scholar/FatwaE/FatwaE&cid=1119503549152 (printed 2008–10–10).

48   Ahmed Kutty, *Fasting Depending on Phone Reports From Muslim Countries*.

49   Cf. Skovgaard-Petersen 1997a, pp. 80–99.

50   Cf. Larsson 2006b.

these services or statistical estimates of those using them, it seems that Islamic counselling via Islamic telephone services is growing.[51]

One example is the *al-Hatif al-Islami* (The Islamic Phone) service set up in Saudi Arabia to help those who are unable to attend a mosque (for example, the sick, elderly or women). This service is, however, not free of charge, and callers have to pay a small amount of money in order to obtain a *fatwa*.[52] As discussed earlier in this volume, paying for a religious service is a controversial issue in itself, and consequently the establishment of the Dial-a-Fatwa service has been criticised. In his response to this criticism, Sheikh Abdul-Aal, an imam at a mosque in Jeddah's Safa district, stresses that the poor will be given the service for free and that:

> The money paid for fatwa consultation will be utilized in helping poor families in the district and the same neighbourhood; for purchasing religious books in addition to being spent on those working at the mosque.[53]

Nonetheless it is clear that levying a fee for religious services is a hot topic, and many '*ulama*' seem to be arguing that this is contrary to the laws of Islam.

The ability to call in with a question is, however, something positive according to Sheikh Abdel-Moeti Bayyoumi, Dean of the Faculty of Religion Fundamentals in Cairo, who answers questions concerning '*aqida* (Islamic doctrine) on the Egyptian telephone service Islamic Line:

> Asking via the telephone is less embarrassing. People can disclose details of their personal lives that they would not reveal in an office ...[54]

This is an example of how the anonymous and private aspects of the new information and communication technologies can be used to raise problematic or even embarrassing questions. But Sheikh Abdel-Moeti Bayyoumi does not address the possibility that the telephone service, or for that matter an online service, can also be used to ask provocative, insulting or blasphemous questions. In another interview, Sheikh Khalid El-Guindi, one of the founders of the Egyptian telephone

---

51   See Caroline Hawley, 'Egypt dials up for spiritual help', *BBC News*, Friday 1 September 2000, retrieved from http://news.bbc.co.uk/1/hi/world/middle_east/906262. stm (printed 2008–09–09). Similar telephone services are also provided by other religious groups, Cf. Åberg 2003, p. 187.

52   ' "Ring-a-Fatwa": Hot Line for Religious Questions', *Arab News*, Sunday 15 October 2006 (22 Ramadan 1427). Retrieved from http://www.arabnews.com/?page=1&se ction=0&article=88221&d=15&m=10&y=2006 (printed 2008–09–09).

53   ' "Ring-a-Fatwa": Hot Line for Religious Questions', *Arab News*, Sunday 15 October 2006.

54   Quoted from Nadia Abou El-Magd, 'Dial-a-fatwa', *Al-Ahram Weekly*, 31 August–6 September 2000, Issue No. 497. Retrieved from http://weekly.ahram.org.eg/2000/497/eg8. htm (printed 2008–09–24).

service Islam Line, illustrated this side of the technology by admitting that: 'Nearly 80 per cent of the questions so far have either been about masturbation or the veil – when to wear it and how important it is as a religious obligation.' As with the Saudi initiative, the Egyptian telephone line also charges its callers a small fee (approximately 50 US cents per minute).[55] Islam Line promises to answer all questions in 24 hours, that is, the caller leaves a message, and one of the four especially appointed theologians calls him or her back as soon as they have found an answer to the specific question. Without bending the argument too much, this development supports Gregory Starrett's conclusions that mass production (and in particular the new information and communication technologies) has the potential to turn Islamic texts, artefacts and services into products that can be viewed as religious commodities. This shows the potential of technological developments to push theological discussions in new directions and make '*ulama*' identify the problems and opportunities associated with them. As with the other media discussed in this volume, the telephone is a tool that can be used to promote individualised and independent interpretations that may be at odds with those of the '*ulama*'. From the point of view of the latter, these technologies have to be adjusted to fit the norms of the religious community.[56]

Conclusions

Even though the '*ulama*' discussed in this chapter often have strong opinions about the introduction and use of the telephone, it is clear that they lack the power to ban the technology. In fact, it is far from likely that they would be prepared to prohibit use of the telephone. Nonetheless it is clear that some of the '*ulama*' are arguing in ways which resemble, for example, the Amish and Mennonite theologians studied by Diane Zimmerman Umble. In the first decade of the twentieth century, the telephone also caused splits and conflicts among the Amish and Mennonite communities in the United States. Like the '*ulama*', they argued that the telephone was having a negative effect on morals, and that the new information and communication technologies were 'blurring the boundaries between the community and the outside world'. The telephone 'provided temptations to gossip', and it was not possible for members of the community to monitor conversations over the phone. According to Umble, the Amish and Mennonite leaders saw telephone communication as 'individualistic' and felt that members could establish private lines with the outside world (that is, the non-Amish and non-Mennonite community).[57]

---

55   Caroline Hawley, 'Egypt dials up for spiritual help', *BBC News*, Friday 1 September, 2000. Retrieved from http://news.bbc.co.uk/1/hi/world/middle_east/906262. stm (printed 2008–09–09).

56   Cf. Campbell 2007 and Umble 1994.

57   Umble 1994, p. 104.

Even though the '*ulama*' included in this study do not use the same line of argument as the Amish and Mennonites studied by Umble, it is clear that they could also see the telephone as being associated with theological and practical problems. Regardless of theological differences or geographical distance, the '*ulama*' are to a high degree unanimous in their conclusions and ways of putting the argument. The discussion about the telephone is, for example, generally based on analogical reasoning (*qiyas*), and the telephone is compared with earlier forms of communication, especially with writing letters. These '*ulama*' therefore argue that the telephone should be studied in the light of earlier discussions about other information and communication technologies. The debate about the telephone also shows how the '*ulama*' try to develop methods or strategies for solving new questions. The use of analogical reasoning is, of course, not new or unique to this debate, but the cases discussed in this chapter could all serve as examples of how the '*ulama*' develop strategies for handling questions about new information and communication technologies and how they are engaged in the 'social shaping of technology'. Like Heidi Campbell's analysis of the 'Kosher' cell phone, which was developed to meet the demands of the Ultra-Orthodox Jewish community in Israel, the '*ulama*' discussed in this chapter are eager to stress that the telephone should not prevent Muslims from living a religious life. In Campbell's words, 'when the technology challenges the moral life of the community something about the technology must change'.[58] Judging, however, from the discussions and examples in this chapter, it is evident that the '*ulama*' have not been able to push the market into producing a *halal* cell phone resembling the Jewish example, but instead have had to focus on ethical guidelines for how to use the telephone. From this point of view, the discussion about the telephone is a preparation for the discussion that will follow on debates about the Internet, the topic of the next chapter.

---

58   Campbell 2007, p. 201.

Chapter 6

'Do Not Engage in Unnecessary Chatting':
Fatwas on Internet Etiquette for Muslims

Although the distribution of and access to the Internet is much lower in the Middle East and the Third World in general – at least compared with Europe, the United States and other parts of Asia[1] – from the earliest stages of the Internet, Muslims have been very active in cyberspace.[2] Although it is difficult to find support for any one explanation for this, it seems that many exchange students from the Middle East to the West were active at the beginning of the history of the Internet (especially in the United States).[3] Although the academic study of religion on the Internet – or for that matter online religion, to use Christopher Helland's categories for differentiating between various forms of religiosity on the Internet – is a fairly new subject, an extensive number of publications have already focused on Muslim activities in cyberspace and on Islam on the Internet.[4] However, to the best of my knowledge, few if any studies have concentrated on how various *'ulama'* actually debate, view and judge the new technologies.

The aim of this chapter is therefore to analyse a limited selection of contemporary Sunni Muslim judicial opinions on the use of the Internet. The *fatwas* analysed in the chapter try in various ways to answer the question of whether Muslims are allowed to use the Internet or not. If the answer is yes, what kinds of restrictions are the *'ulama'* calling for, and what are the benefits and problems involved in using the new technology? Another key question is whether the improved communication technologies (email and chatting) are in tune with Islamic shari'a.

All the *fatwas* analysed in this section have been issued by the *'ulama'* associated with the Egyptian/Qatari homepage IslamOnline.net, an Internet portal I have also used extensively for the discussion of Islamic opinions on other topics

---

1   According to the United Nations Development Programme and its *Arab Human Development Report 2003: Building a Knowledge Society*, 'There are less than 18 computers per 1,000 persons in the region, compared to the global average of 78.3 computers per 1,000 persons' (p. 64). On the introduction of the Internet in the Middle East see, for example, Gonzalez-Quijano 2003 on Lebanon, Teitelbaum 2002 on Saudi Arabia and Cunningham 2002 on Jordan and Wheeler 2004.

2   See, for example, Anderson 2005.

3   Cf. Anderson 2005, p. 255.

4   See, for example, Anderson 2003, 2005; Bunt 2000, 2003, 2004; Gräf 2007, 2008; Larsson 2005, 2006b, 2007; Lohlker 2000; Mandaville 2001.

in earlier chapters in this book. As already noted in the introduction to this book, IslamOnline.net has gone through considerable changes over the last year, and at the time of writing this section there seems to be a struggle over power and control of the webpage at the time of writing this section. However, all the texts analysed in this chapter date to the period when the webpage contained both Arabic and English texts.

During my visit to the homepage's translation office in Cairo in the summer of 2004, I was informed that approximately 60 Muslim scholars were associated with the homepage, and that they were consulted as experts and in issuing judicial opinions (that is, *fatwas*). As a result, they provide Muslims all around the world with guidelines for how to live their lives in accordance with Islam. In 2004 IslamOnline.net answered on a daily basis approximately 250 questions, and during my visit to Cairo the so-called *fatwa* database linked to the homepage contained roughly 12,000 answers in Arabic and 3,000 in English translation. According to Bettina Gräf, who has studied the webpage, IslamOnline.net employed some 150 staff in Cairo and Doha, Qatar. The quotation below from Gräf summarises the history and current status of this Islamic portal:

> The body behind IslamOnline (IOL) is the Al-Balagh Cultural Society in Qatar, which was established in 1997 on the initiative of Qatari IT specialist Maryam Hasan al-Hajari and Dr. Hamid al-Ansari, a scholar at the Shari'a Faculty of the University of Qatar. In its early stages the project was supported by the University of Qatar, especially by Yusuf al-Qaradawi, the 1926-born, Azhar-educated Egyptian scholar theorist of the Islamic Awakening movement who still chairs the Al-Balagh Society today. The headquarters and IT development of IOL are based in Doha, while most of the content is produced by more than 150 employees at the IOL offices in Cairo. IOL is mainly financed by donations and by selling its technical know-how to other Islamic institutions around the world. In promotional material for the site, Yusuf al-Qaradawi defined the site's mission this way: 'This project is neither nationalistic nor one aiming at a grouping or a group of people; it is a project for the entire Islamic community. It is the jihad of our era.'[5]

To meet the demands of the global Muslim audience, but also in order to harmonise with the new technologies and their limitations, it was emphasised by the staff at IslamOnline.net that all answers provided by the homepage should be of a general nature rather than specific or individualised. This principle was based on the fact that a *fatwa* posted on the Internet can be read by several individuals who are situated in different local contexts. As a result, it is neither possible nor important to give a specific answer adjusted to fit a unique individual and his or her context. This awareness of the transformative effect of

---

5   Gräf 2008, p. 1.

the new technologies for the issuing of theological answers was also emphasised in relation to the translation process from Arabic into English, in which the guiding principle for the staff at IslamOnline.net was to be clear by attempting to give general answers that several individuals could follow, regardless of local differences. Although it is difficult to evaluate the answers given by the staff at IslamOnline.net, the personnel in the translation office in Cairo were well aware of the impact and importance of the new information and communication technologies. For example, with the introduction of the Internet the relationship between the questioner and the mufti has been fundamentally changed, since it is not possible to provide answers face to face, as in the traditional setting of a local mosque.[6] Furthermore, because an answer posted on the Internet can be read and used by a large number of users, it is not wise to give specific answers designed for a particular person, but only general answers that can be used by as many Muslims as possible, regardless of context or theological orientation.[7] However, according to Gräf, it should be stressed that Yusuf al-Qaradawi, 'does not discuss the qualitative difference between a *fatwa* given face-to-face and an online *fatwa*, or the implications of these different channels for questions of authority, scope and validity'.[8]

Even though the Sheikh does not discuss this issue, the development from the specific or individual to the general is also stimulated and supported by the use of the Internet. Furthermore, the growing importance of the new information and communication technologies for issuing *fatwas* is an example of what Olivier Roy considers the 'deterritorialisation' of Islam. Migration, globalisation and the growing importance of the new media have made Islam 'less and less ascribed to a specific territory and civilisational area'.[9] Roy says that:

> The Muslim ummah (or community) no longer has anything to do with a territorial entity. It has to be thought of in abstract or imaginary terms.[10]

As Roy indicates, the introduction of the new information and communication technologies, together with patterns of migration and globalisation processes, has raised questions concerning the transmission of religious knowledge and the establishment of religious authority. All of these questions are also related to the essential question of authority. How is authority preserved and guaranteed on the Internet? To put it in Peter Mandeville's words:

---

6   Cf. Mandaville 2001, p. 183.
7   Cf. Larsson 2004b.
8   Gräf 2007, p. 414.
9   Roy 2004, p. 18.
10   Roy 2004, p. 19.

one can [...] never be sure whether the authoritative advice received via these services is coming from a classically-trained religious scholar or a hydraulic engineer moonlighting as an amateur *'alim*.[11]

The quotation above is an example of how the Internet can be seen as an instrument or a technology that relativises religious authority and questions the traditional ways of guaranteeing a proper and sound transmission of knowledge. This is one of the major reasons why the *'ulama'* are concerned about the Internet. At the same time, most of them are willing to overlook, or neglect, this problem as long as they can use the technology themselves to disseminate their views of how Islam can and should be interpreted. Furthermore, it is very difficult to determine whether this outcome is a result of the introduction of the new information and communication technologies or one of the transformations brought about by processes of secularisation, westernisation and 'modernisation'. Even though this study is focused on the discussion and impact of the Internet, it is wise to consider the technological, social, intellectual and economic development of the world in a broad perspective. Despite my focus on technological developments, it is not my ambition to offer a monocausal explanation. It is necessary to combine and consider several aspects if we want to grasp the complexity of the discussion about the new information and communication technologies and Islam. Furthermore, it is also essential to analyse Islamic web milieus in relation to their off-line context. The interplay between what people actually think, say and do online should always be analysed in connection to what they think, say and do off-line.

A general background

The capacity to enhance communication and to facilitate contact between humans, regardless of time and space, is one of the greatest benefits of the Internet. With the development of the World Wide Web and the Internet, it has become easier, safer and cheaper to communicate with people all over the globe. With the help of an email, or via chat groups or news groups, the possibility to interact and exchange ideas has increased for many people all over the world.[12] The transformative power of the Internet is clearly highlighted by Manuel Castells in the following quotation:

> The Internet is a communication medium that allows, for the first time, the communication of many to many, in chosen time, on a global scale. As the diffusion of the printing press in the West created what MacLuhan named the 'Gutenberg Galaxy', we have now entered a new world of communication: the Internet Galaxy.[13]

---

11   Mandaville 2001, p. 183.
12   Anderson 2003, p. 47.
13   Castells 2001, pp. 2–3.

However, the potential of the Internet described by Manuel Castells generates new possibilities to explore and learn more about unknown world-views and alternative lifestyles, as well as new problems and challenges. For the optimist, this is a unique opportunity to learn more about the world. However, this same development could also pose problems. For many religious groups, the Internet is both a challenge and a promise that can either erode authority or sustain the established power structure. With the help of the technology, it is, for example, possible, and quite easy, for the so-called lay believer to question religious authorities and establish his or her own world views. As demonstrated in the earlier chapter on broadcasting media, the Egyptian popular preacher Amr Khaled is an illustration of how a Muslim preacher who lacks a formal Islamic theological education can use the Internet and other media to make his voice heard. On his satellite television shows, homepage and via other media, he provides an alternative interpretation of the sacred traditions and in doing so challenges the authority of the *'ulama'*.[14] From this point of view, the Internet could be described as a resource or a tool either for questioning religious authority or for challenging the established power structure.[15] According to Olivier Roy, the sociological and technological developments that follow the new technologies have made room for a new kind of Muslim intellectual:

> The new intellectual has an autodidactic relation to knowledge. Knowledge is acquired in a fragmented (manuals, excerpts, popular brochures), encyclopaedic, and immediate manner: everything is discussed without the mediation of an apprenticeship, a method, or a professor. Popularisation implies direct access to material that has become dogmatic through the obfuscation of the procedures by which it emerged. The new media, such as radio, television, cassettes, and inexpensive offset brochures, make snatches of this content available. The new intellectual is a tinkerer; he creates a montage, as his personal itinerary guides him, of segments of knowledge, using methods that come from a different conceptual universe than the segments he recombines, creating a totality that is more imaginary than theoretical.[16]

The fragmenting of knowledge described by Roy in the quotation above is, of course, also stimulated and fostered by the rise of the Internet.[17] On the other hand, the new information and communication technologies could also be used for maintaining, upholding and extending religious traditions and for preserving cultural norms and values.[18] This trend is, for example, illustrated by the Sunna

---

14   Cf., for example, Mariani 2006.

15   Cf. Anderson 2003; Baune 2005 and Hammond 2005, p. 272. But this development is also fostered by smaller forms of media, such as cassettes, pamphlets, booklets and brochures. Cf. Eickelman 2003 and Starrett 1996, p. 135.

16   Roy 1994, pp. 96–97.

17   Mandaville 2001.

18   Cf. Anderson 2005, p. 262.

Project, initiated by the Thesaurus Islamicus Foundation, or by the homepage *al-tafsir.com*.[19] With the new technology it has, for example, become easier to preserve and increase our knowledge of the *hadith* literature or the interpretation of the Qur'an. With the help of computer technology:

> It has become possible to process enormous quantities of data in a matter of seconds, and software supporting an almost infinite variety of search methods may open up whole new horizons for the researcher. The hadith, previously consulted only by a fairly narrow category of specialists, has now become accessible to people with an interest in virtually any aspect of Islamic studies, who can make use of them without the need to acquire a detailed familiarity with the format and peculiarities of each text.[20]

Although this development makes it easier for 'ordinary' Muslims to learn more about Islam, the same development could also create division and instil relativism.[21] Having access to Islamic sources is not the same as having knowledge about how to use or interpret them according to, for example, the Muslim Student Association in the United States. On their homepage, which among other things contains a large section of translations from the *hadith* tradition, a warning is posted to all Muslims that they should not confuse information with knowledge.

Warning (especially for Muslims)

There are many early hadith scholars and teachers to whom we are indebted for introducing the critical science of collecting and evaluating ahadeeth. These teachers each collected many different ahadeeth. They did not allow students to quote from their collections until the students had actually come to them and learnt from them directly.

Today, the situation is different. The collections of ahadeeth have for the most part stabilized, and with the advent of the printing press, the collections are easily mass-produced. There is a blessing in all this of course, but there is a real danger that Muslims will fall under the impression that owning a book or having a database is equivalent to being a scholar of ahadeeth. This is a great fallacy. Therefore, we would like to warn you that this database is merely a *tool*, and not a substitute for learning, much less scholarship in Islam.[22]

---

19   The fact that it is possible for Muslims to store large quantities of information (for example, religious texts) on a computer is discussed in Mandaville 2001, pp. 178–179; also Sardar 2003.

20   The Sunna Project: Encyclopaedia of Hadith: The Ihsan Network (no date), p. 4.

21   Cf. Roy 2004.

22   http://www.usc.edu/dept/MSA/reference/searchhadith.html (retrieved and printed 2005–09–19).

Even though the growing impact of computers and new technologies harbours problems, at least according to some of the *'ulama'*, the improved ability to communicate with other Muslims is also of great importance for Muslims, especially for those who live in a context that is not dominated by Islamic values and expressions.[23] No matter how the technology is used, it is evident that a theologian who wants to retain his mandate must evaluate both the problems and the advantages that the new technologies might give rise to. Hence, it is necessary to present himself and his interpretation online. This awareness was, for example, clearly manifest in an interview I conducted with the Swedish Sheikh Muhammad Muslim, who is, among other things, the theological leader of a Swedish-based, sufi-inspired group called *Sidrat al-Muntaha*. Apart from buying flight tickets and checking email, he did not use the Internet very much. Still, he laughingly remarked: 'If you do not exist on the Internet, you do not exist at all.'[24]

Moving into cyberspace

Although the *'ulama'* may have different opinions about the new information and communication technologies – as illustrated in the previous chapters – the judicial answers given by the *'ulama'* who are attached to IslamOnline.net are more or less joined in their defence of the Internet. For example, a group of Islamic researchers clearly articulates this opinion in a *fatwa* on 'Islamic Etiquette for using online messengers'.

> The Internet is a blessing that Allah Almighty has bestowed on us, and we should thank Him for it. We should express our gratitude to Him by making good use of it. It is an act of ingratitude to misuse the Internet in the ways we know to be indecent.[25]

Accordingly, the Internet can be seen as a blessing that exists only because of God's goodness. The new technology is therefore part of his plan. To use an Islamic vocabulary, the technology could even be seen as a manifestation or *aya*, a sign from God, which confirms the existence of God and his divine plan.[26] For example, like the earth, for which all Muslims are responsible according to the Qur'an (cf. Q 38:26),[27] the Internet is also a gift that comes with responsible behaviour and correct belief. Consequently, the *'ulama'* emphasise that the Internet can be used

---

23 Cf., for example, Mandaville 2001, Roy 2004.

24 Larsson 2006b, p. 97.

25 'Islamic etiquette for using online messengers', retrieved from http://www. islamonline.net/servlet/Satellite?pagename=IslamOnline-English-Ask_Scholar/FatwaE/ FatwaEandcid=1119503547366 (printed 2005–08–23).

26 Cf. Jeffery 1960.

27 On nature as a sign of God's existence and his plan, see Netton 2003.

for both 'good' or 'bad' purposes, 'correct' or 'wrong' objectives. Yet again, it is the responsibility and the intention (*niyya*) of the user that decides whether the technology brings harvest or sorrow.[28] However, since mankind is in general weak according to the Qur'an (cf. Q 33:72; 80:17 and 70:19–23), it is essential and obligatory to develop guidelines, rules and regulations for how to use the Internet in accordance with Islamic laws. Sheikh Ahmad Kutty, a senior lecturer and Islamic scholar at the Islamic Institute of Toronto, Ontario, Canada, says:

> Thanks to the sophisticated means of modern communication, everyone finds himself tempted to try everything new in technology. Thus, it's very important for each Muslim to know where he stands and to always keep in mind that, as he is given full right to make use of any opportunity offered by modern technology, he is also required not to forget the duty he owes to Almighty Allah Who subjects to him all such avenues of comfort and prosperity. He must not deviate, whatsoever, from the teachings of his religion, in order to preserve his noble identity.[29]

Although this answer should be analysed carefully, it is interesting to note that similar arguments are also used for solving other questions that could be related to the pursuit of a modern lifestyle. For example, if we turn to the classical debate on music, it is common for most '*ulama*' to take a stance against most forms of it.[30] However, today it is quite common to hear Muslims – but not necessarily educated '*ulama*' – argue that Muslims can listen to music (including Western music) if they first perform their duties to God, their family and the Muslim community.[31] Some Muslims, such as Yusuf Islam (formally known as Cat Stevens), argue, for example, that certain forms of music can function as a way or method of calling people to Islam (that is, for doing *da'wa*).[32] Music is therefore only a problem when it makes people turn away from God. If the believer has performed the five obligatory prayers, he or she is free to use the rest of the day according to his or her own will. But even though Sheikh Yusuf al-Qaradawi stresses that it is necessary for all Muslims

---

28   Here I am using *niyya* to refer to intention in its broad and general meaning. In a classical meaning, it is as follows: 'The acts prescribed by the Islamic *Shari'a*, obligatory or not, require to be preceded by a declaration by the performer, that he intends to perform such an act. This declaration, pronounced audibly or mentally, is called *niyya*. Without it, the act would be *batil* [invalid]'. See Wensinck 1995, p. 66.

29   'Online chatting in the eyes of the Shariah', retrieved from http://www. islamonline.net/servlet/Satellite?pagename=IslamOnline-English-Ask_Scholar/FatwaE/ FatwaE&cid=1119503547082 (printed 2005–08–23). This answer was originally published on the homepage of the Islamic Institute of Toronto; see http://www.islam.ca/answers. php?id=417 (printed 2005–08–24).

30   Cf., for example, Otterbeck 2004 and earlier discussions on music in this book.

31   Larsson 2004a, p. 88 and Ramadan 2002, p. 203.

32   On Yusuf Islam and music, see Yusuf Islam, 'Music a Question of Faith or Da'wah', retrieved http://www.mountainoflight.co.uk/. Cf. Gardell 1995, pp. 250–257.

to have some free time for recreation, play and relaxation, time is associated with rules and regulations.[33] Time is a framework for how to behave at specific hours (for example, during prayers or the period of fasting).[34] Since time is perceived as a gift from God, the believer is responsible for his or her activities as well as for inactivity. Consequently both al-Qaradawi and Tariq Ramadan argue that Muslims must evaluate topics such as music, or for that matter new information and communication technologies, compare the pros and cons, and ask if they are in tune with Islamic law.[35] This reservation may be seen as an illustration of the possibility that Muslims will become more individualised and less collective than former generations, since they are not automatically following the advice and answers given by the *'ulama'* without investigating the question on their own. Even though this conclusion must be substantiated with more empirical data, I am inclined to agree with Roger Allen and Steven Vertovec, who argue that this development will give rise to new modes of interpretation, especially among young Muslims who have been born and raised in the West:[36]

> Among many Muslim European youth there has arisen a desire to analyse religious scriptures for themselves. This embodies reclaiming the concept of *ijtihad* ('interpretation' or 'independent judgement'), which in turn involves both a rejection of authority (of their parents and of the ulema or body of Islamic scholars) and a revitalisation of belief and practice.[37]

Although this development is not only caused by the introduction of the new information and communication technologies – the Internet was, for example, preceded by the spread of mass education in the Middle East[38] – these technological developments are still enhancing and supporting this trend.[39] The debate over, for example, online chatting is therefore an illustration in its own right of the fact that the *'ulama'* are receiving questions that have been formulated and moulded by the rise of modern society. For example, Ines Baune and Deborah L. Wheeler have demonstrated that chatting on the Internet (especially with the opposite sex) is one of the most popular activities among young people in the Middle East,

---

33   Gräf 2007, p. 412.
34   al-Qaradawi 2001, pp. 287–288.
35   Cf. al-Qaradawi 2001, pp. 287–288, and Ramadan 2002, p. 203.
36   Cf. also Mandaville 2001.
37   Vertovec and Rogers 1998, p. 11.
38   Cf. Eickelman 1992.
39   See Mandaville 2001, pp. 169–170. Cf. The *hadith* database set up by MSA in the United States, see http://www.usc.edu/dept/MSA/reference/searchhadith.html (printed and retrieved 2005-10-10).

North Africa and the Gulf region.[40] According to Baune's findings, the Internet is especially attractive to young people because it facilitates and creates new possibilities for its users. From her field notes from Morocco, Baune concludes that the Internet is very popular among the young generation:

> Chatting with the opposite sex, flirting, making friendships, or simply to be amused; to get to know people from all over the world, learning about foreign cultures and mentalities, finding somebody to marry, or trying to find somebody to take them out of Morocco …[41]

A similar conclusion is made by a female informant interviewed for Deborah L. Wheeler in her study of female Internet users in the Arabic-speaking world:

> I hear stories about girls who go online to find a husband … there are a lot of covered girls [*mutahajibat*] who go to the cybercafes for this reason … they chat and chat and chat … I think it's great …[42]

All in all, it is not only the questions that have been coloured by the modern ways of life – the answers given by the '*ulama*' are also closely related to this development. The *fatwa* collections and the answers given by the '*ulama*' are also theological manuals that are coloured directly or indirectly by the prevailing attitudes and norms that have been formulated by contemporary societies. Therefore, the prime task of the '*ulama*' is to help Muslims uphold their faith and stick to what they believe is the essence of Islam, as well as to take part in everyday activities without losing their faith. From this point of view, the question and answer formula (that is, the *ifta*' institution and the issuing of legal advice) are vital, especially for Muslims living in non-Muslim contexts, such as Europe or the United States. In these milieus it is more demanding and more difficult to perceive and uphold Islamic rulings and in general much more difficult to be a practising Muslim.[43]

Islamic etiquette for online communication

To make the best use of the Internet, the '*ulama*' argues that Muslims must follow certain guidelines in order to avoid the disadvantages of the new technologies. For example, in the *fatwa* bank of IslamOnline.net it is possible to find several questions and answers that are occupied with discussing and outlining the problems and

---

40   Baune 2005 and Wheeler 2004. An illustrative example of this trend is the Saudi Arabian novel *Girls of Riyadh* (*Banat al-Riyad*) by Raja' 'Abd Allah al-Sani'. This book is written as an open e-letter to an online discussion list on the Internet; see Ramsey 2007.
41   Baune 2005, pp. 131–132.
42   Quotation taken from Wheeler 2004, p. 151.
43   Cf. for example Mandaville 2001.

possibilities attached to the new information and communication technologies. The answers given by the *'ulama'* in this specific theological milieu contain practical information, as well as theological analysis of the Internet. Generally, the answers could all be seen as an attempt to formulate an Islamic etiquette for online communication. For example, the *'ulama'* associated with IslamOnline.net emphasise that all Muslims should be aware that most individuals in contemporary society are busy and consequently are reluctant to answer unnecessary questions posted on the Internet. Time is valuable and precious for all Muslims, and believers should therefore always consider whether surfing on the Internet or participating in a chat group becomes more time-consuming than rewarding.[44] Here the concern with time is related to the Islamic view that our earthly lives are limited and that we should always remember that we have to answer for our deeds, thoughts and actions in the afterlife according to the Qur'an. All human activities should therefore be focused on those things that are best according to God:

> We know that there are people whose time is extremely valuable and others who do not care about how they use time. Muslims should not waste their time. They should realize how valuable time is and how important it is to use it in doing what will benefit them in both this world and the Hereafter.[45]

The above *fatwa* issued by 'A Group of Islamic Researchers' is also an indirect reference to the Qur'an and the discussion about time. However, the answer also places great emphasis on the fact that 'true' Muslims should avoid idle talk (*lahw*).[46] In line with this argument, Sheikh Ahmad Bin Hamad al-Khalili, the grand mufti of Oman, concludes that 'A true Muslim, as the infallible Prophet (peace and blessings be upon him) said, can never be a slanderer, a curser, an indecent, or an abusive person'.[47] According to him it is not possible for a 'true' Muslim to be a slanderer on the Internet. This idealistic opinion of al-Khalili's shows that the Qur'an and the *hadith* traditions can be used by certain *'ulama'* to explain and outline a so-called Islamic ethics for how to use the new information and communication technologies.

---

44   The question of time in the life of Muslims is thoroughly analysed and discussed by Yusuf al-Qaradawi in the book *Time in the Life of the Muslim*.

45   'Islamic etiquette for using online messengers', retrieved from http://www. islamonline.net/servlet/Satellite?pagename=IslamOnline-English-Ask_Scholar/FatwaE/ FatwaEandcid=1119503547366 (printed 2005–08–23).

46   Cf., for example, Q 31:6 or 28:55.

47   'Electronic Insults: A Grave Sin?', retrieved from http://www.islamonline. net/servlet/Satellite?pagename=IslamOnline-English-Ask_Scholar/FatwaE/ FatwaEandcid=1119503548938 (printed 2005–08–24). But *lahw* could also be linked to singing and the playing of instruments, i.e. any activity that is considered morally questionable. See Otterbeck 2004, pp. 13–14.

However, the fact that abuse, indecent behaviour and insults are discussed in relation to online activities shows that the Internet can give rise to negative and un-Islamic behaviour, according to the '*ulama*' discussed above.[48] However, this is a general problem for online communication according to, for example, Susan Herring, a development that is not unique to Muslims.[49] As has been clearly demonstrated by the Danish sociologist Morten Thomsen Højsgaard, Muslims can also encounter a very harsh and negative climate of discussion on the Internet.[50] It is therefore clear that the Internet can be used as a very powerful tool for spreading anti-Muslim and anti-Islamic opinions.[51]

In a communication setting that is dominated by anonymity and few offline contacts (that is, participants seldom meet face to face outside the Internet), it seems to be much easier to use harsh and aggressive language than in an offline setting. Instead of being polite, patient and tolerant – this is also an essential part of Islamic ethics according to the '*ulama*' I have discussed in this chapter – Muslims are also affected and corrupted by the so-called un-Islamic behaviour that frequently prevails in many online discussions and on the Internet in general. From this point of view, online behaviour and electronic communication have become matters of vital concern for Islamic ethics and an important aspect of them, especially for Muslim parents who want to raise their children according to Islamic law. Sheikh 'Abdul-Majeed Subh, who earned his degree from the al-Azhar in Egypt and who is affiliated with the IslamOnline.net site, states:

> We must instil in our children some kind of conscious immunity against the negative effects of the media rather than exclusively prohibiting it. In other words, children will have the ability to consciously discern the right from the wrong from within themselves and subsequently not fall into what is forbidden. This is opposed to external forces (like constant parental censorship) that induce children to avoid the forbidden but in an involuntary manner. The former helps our children recognize what is *haram* (unlawful) and enables them to willingly abstain from the negative messages the media carry.[52]

Although the connection between technological developments and the behaviour of participants in an online communication should be analysed carefully, this is an indication that information and communication technologies can give rise to new forms of behaviour.[53] However, it is difficult to determine whether this

---

48   See 'Electronic Insults: A Grave Sin?'
49   Cf., for example, Herring 1996 and Thomsen Højsgaard 2006.
50   Thomsen Højsgaard 2006.
51   One example is the Internet portal called WikiIslam; see Larsson 2007.
52   Sheikh 'Abdul-Majeed Subh, 'Protecting Our Children from the Evils of Media', retrieved from http://www.islamonline.net/servlet/Satellite?pagename=IslamOnline-English-Ask_Scholar/FatwaE/FatwaE&cid=1119503544136 (printed 2008–09–24).
53   See Helland 2005.

change is due to technological developments or to more general changes in human communication (especially among young people). From this point of view, the question of push and pull is a so-called chicken-and-egg question, that is, which comes first, the technological development, or the general change in the mentality of the users? No matter how we answer this question, this is an issue that concerns many of the *'ulama'*.

The Internet and analogical reasoning

When discussing online chatting, the *'ulama'* in this study also use analogical reasoning (that is, *qiyas* in Arabic). This method is an essential part of Islamic law, and most *'ulama'* view *qiyas* to be a sound method for discussing and deciding whether an act or a new issue is legal or illegal according to the *shari'a*.[54] However, according to the critics of *qiyas*, it is only God who can decide between right and wrong, and all answers are in the Qur'an, that is, one cannot use one's own personal opinion (*ra'y*) to make a decision.[55] Both Sheikh Ahmad Kutty and Dr Muzammil H. Siddiqi use *qiyas* in stressing that online chatting is similar to writing letters or talking to someone on the telephone.[56] The art of writing letters, talking on the telephone and chatting are not discussed in the Qur'an, nor for that matter in the *hadith* literature, but according to the *'ulama'* it is still necessary to draw up guidelines for how Muslims should behave when they do these things. This is an illustration of how analogical reasoning can be used to solve new problems and possibilities. According to Siddiqi, 'Islam does not permit love letters or intimate conversations between males and females who are not married to each other'. He says:

> In all our correspondence and conversations we must observe *haya'* or modesty. Boys and girls should not chat with each other just for socialization or passing time. It is *haram* (unlawful) for a *non-mahram* Muslim male and female to indulge in long conversations with each other unless it is necessary for education or business. All conversation must be decent. The Qur'an reminds us again and

---

54   A discussion about *qiyas* can be found in Hashim Kamali 1987, pp. 128—129.

55   Cf. Q 16:89: 'We have sent to you the Book as an explanation for everything'; and Q 42:10: 'In whatever you differ, the verdict therein belongs to God'. A thorough introduction to the theological debate about tradition and rationalism (i.e. independent reasoning) in Islam can be found in Abrahamov 1998.

56   Cf. Sheikh Ahmad Kutty, 'Online chatting ...'. For a discussion about communication between the sexes on the telephone, see Sheikh ibn Jibreen, 'Speaking to Women on the Phone', and for letter writing, see Sheikh ibn Jibreen, 'Correspondence between Young Men and Women is not allowed'.

again that all our words are recorded and we shall be held accountable for our words as well as our deeds on the Day of Judgment?[57]

The quotation from Dr Siddiqi's *fatwa* shows that it is necessary and important to uphold a strict division between boys and girls in both real life and cyberspace. For most '*ulama*', a separation of the sexes is essential and a prerequisite for the preservation of Islamic ethics. From this point of view, the Internet, especially the possibility to chat anonymously online, represents a serious problem. Irrespective of Dr Siddiqi's recommendations, however, it is evident that practising Muslims too are using the Internet to talk to the opposite sex.[58] Judging from the large number of *fatwas* that discuss this issue, it seems that both Muslim parents and the '*ulama*' are concerned and troubled by the fact that the Internet has created new possibilities and ways of communication, especially between the sexes. This form of interaction is often beyond the control of parents and the '*ulama*' and the rules and regulations they have laid down. From this point of view, the Internet is an arena dominated and controlled by its users. With the help of the new technology, it is easy to break the law of *khalwa* (privacy), that is, that boys and girls who are not married, relatives or business partners should avoid all forms of contact and intimate conversation. This rule is imposed for the protection of both the man and the woman, while the separation of the sexes should help them avoid 'wrong thoughts and sexual feelings', according to al-Qaradawi.[59] *Khalwa* applied traditionally only when a male and a female were alone in person, but with the development of writing, this 'law' was also applied to letters and other forms of written communication. With the rise of technology, the law of *khalwa* now also applies to online chatting and talking to someone on the telephone according to Siddiqi.[60] To avoid this problem, it is always necessary to ask what the purpose of the communication is. Siddiqi also says that all Muslims should abide by the following guidelines:

> [C]ommunication between a man and a woman should be of a goal that complies with enjoying what is good and preventing what is bad. Any communication of chatting between a man and a woman if not for a good cause, it will be a possibility for the cause of *Shaytan* (Satan). One should always ask him/herself why do I want to write to that man/woman or talk to him/her? The answer will be

---

57 'Internet Chats Between Males and Females' retrieved from http://www. islamonline.net/servlet/Satellite?pagename=IslamOnline-English-Ask_Scholar/FatwaE/ FatwaEandcid=1119503543228 (printed 2008–09–24). This *fatwa* was originally published on the homepage of Pakistani Newspaper, *pakistanlink.com*, retrieved from http://www. pakistanlink.com/religion/08202004.html (printed 2005–08–29).

58 Cf. Baune 2005, especially p. 135. See also Wheeler 2004.

59 al-Qaradawi 2001, p. 147.

60 Cf. 'Internet Chats …'.

helpful to take action. Keep far away from desire as Satan has very complicated approaches to insinuate you to deviate from righteousness.[61]

For young Muslims who engage in chatting online but who want to stay Muslim, at least according to Siddiqi, one must therefore ask an older and more experienced person to guide and moderate the discussion.[62] From my personal observations, this method, or recommendation, is rarely if ever applied in Muslim cyber milieus.

Looking for a future spouse on the Internet

Online dating is likely to be one of the most popular activities on the Internet.[63] Although as a Muslim one should uphold and protect one's privacy – at least according to the '*ulama*' discussed above – it is evident from the large number of *fatwas* that discuss this topic that Muslims also engage in dating and love affairs on the Internet.[64] A large number of Muslim homepages provide Muslims too with the possibility of looking for a future spouse on the Internet.[65] The existence of so-called marriage databases should be analysed carefully, but it seems that the Internet can be used as an efficient tool for finding a 'proper' Muslim wife or husband, especially for Muslims living in countries or regions not dominated by Islamic and Muslim traditions. For example, in Europe and the United States it is often difficult to find an 'appropriate' Muslim wife.[66] For this target group, the Internet is potentially a tool of use in finding a future spouse. But as I will show below, the new technology can also be used for indecent flirtations or for other forms of illicit behaviour, at least according to the '*ulama*' discussed in this chapter. In other regions, such as the Middle East and the Gulf states, where it is often of great importance to control or minimise contact between the sexes, the Internet provides its users with a new way of exploring and breaking established cultural norms and adopting new forms of behaviour.[67] However, this is not a new problem, since similar discussions were already in full swing when the '*ulama*' discussed the phenomenon of Muslims visiting cinemas (see the earlier chapter on cinema in this book).

---

61   Cf. 'Internet Chats ...'.

62   See also Barak 2005 and Baune 2005.

63   Cf. Wheeler 2004.

64   Cf. Baune 2005.

65   See, for example, Qiran.com (http://www.qiran.com/index.asp), Singlemuslim. com (http://www.singlemuslim.com/) or Zaway.com (http://www.zawaj.com/), retrieved and printed on 2005–08–30.

66   This aspect is, for example, emphasised on the Swedish Muslim homepage, Islamiska informationsföreningen, Göteborg, retrieved from http://home.swipnet. se/~w-67715/ (printed 2005–09–08). See also Froman 2006, pp. 92–104.

67   Cf. Wheeler 2004.

Hence, to grasp the opportunities provided by the Internet, the '*ulama*' argues that it is necessary to uphold and follow the rules and regulations stipulated by the *shari'a*. Although the laws of marriage are also appropriate and valid for the Internet, it is evident that the information and communication technologies have fashioned new possibilities as well as nuisances for the 'faithful' Muslim. As noted in the previous section, the Internet has made it easier to communicate and interact with other individuals who also have access to the Internet. For example, with the help of a computer, it is possible to flirt online and fix dates without involving one's parents or relatives.[68] This possibility is of great importance in cultures and communities that maintain strict boundaries between the sexes. It is also possible to send out and post pictures to get dates on the Internet, but this habit is strongly criticised and even condemned by some of the '*ulama*' included in this study.[69] On this issue, Sheikh Hamed al-Ali, who is Instructor of Islamic Heritage at the Faculty of Education, Kuwait, and *imam* of *Dahiat As-Sabahiyya Mosque*, says:

> This may cause troubles and lead to evil. It is not allowed to put the pictures of Muslim ladies on the Internet for marriage seekers, and it's also unfathomable to publish the pictures of Muslim ladies and expose their PRIVATE emails for everyone to see. Though it's allowed for the suitor to look at the lady he's proposing to, this can't be taken as a proof to legitimize the case at hand, because publishing the pictures online will make the pictures sighting general, for the suitor and others.[70]

For Sheikh Hamed al-Ali, pictures of women posted on the Internet should only be allowed if they are sent directly to the future husband. If they are published in an open and public forum, it is *haram* (forbidden). This recommendation follows the basic rules and regulations for how a marriage should be arranged as valid according to Islamic law.[71] Thus, it is only the husband who is allowed to set eyes on his future wife, that is, after all the details have been settled between the family of the man and the wife. Although this is more or less a classical opinion on how a marriage should be conducted in order to be in compliance with Islamic law, Sheikh Hamed al-Ali is not against the taking of pictures as such (cf. the earlier chapter on photography in

---

68   Cf. Baune 2005 and Wheeler 2004.

69   See Sheikh Faysal Mawlawi, 'Guidelines for Publishing Photos via the Internet', retrieved   from   http://www.islamonline.net/servlet/Satellite?pagename=IslamOnline-English-Ask_Scholar/FatwaE/FatwaE&cid=1119503545478 (printed 2005–09–05).

70   'Marriage through the Internet: Is it Permissible?', retrieved from http://www. islamonline.net/servlet/Satellite?pagename=IslamOnline-English-Ask_Scholar/FatwaE/ FatwaE&cid=1119503545044 (printed 2005–08–30). Arabic text retrieved from http:// www.islamonline.net/servlet/Satellite?pagename=IslamOnline-Arabic-Ask_Scholar/ FatwaA/FatwaA&cid=1122528617652 (printed 2005–08–30).

71   On Islamic law and marriage, see Schacht 1995a, pp. 26—28.

this book). Although his opinion on this matter is not general or true for all *'ulama'*, his *fatwa* is a clear illustration that the *'ulama'* can accommodate themselves to the fact that photography is part and parcel of everyday life. His answer could therefore be seen as an illustration of how the *'ulama'* discussed in this book have adjusted their theology to the contemporary situation. For Sheikh Hamed al-Ali, photography is not a problem: rather, it is how and why the technology is being used that is important for Muslims to discuss and understand.

In a virtual world of sex and 'ibadat

All Muslims who log on to the Internet are exposed to an unlimited number of possible and impossible world views. As noted earlier in this chapter, for the believer who is eager to keep his or her faith, the Internet can give guidance and help, but it can also lead one into temptation and sin, at least according to most of the *'ulama'* discussed in this book. The great possibility of the new technology is that the user can explore alternative world views that open up new ways of understanding his or her position in society.[72] Although this is something positive for some people, the same development could be a problem according to others. In the last section of this chapter, a number of possibilities as well as problems are discussed and compared with a selection of *fatwas* that directly or indirectly address questions concerning sexuality, faith and the Internet. We start with the problems and then move on to the possibilities of the information and communication technologies according to the *'ulama'* addressed in this chapter.

According to the *'ulama'*, one disturbing possibility with the new technology, which I have already discussed extensively in this and other chapters in this book, is that it can be used to break down the essential and basic separation between the sexes according to Islamic law. But even more disturbing for the *'ulama'* is the fact that the technology can be used for looking at pornography or for committing *zina'* (adultery and fornication), that is, for example, intercourse between a man and woman who are not married.[73] Here the *'ulama'* are talking about virtual forms of *zina'*, that is, when the Internet user is engaged in so-called 'cybersex', for example, virtual intercourse, but also 'telephone sex'.[74] Islamic law strictly forbids all these activities, and it is argued that devoted Muslims should not distinguish between real forms of *zina'* and virtual forms of improper behaviour that are facilitated by

---

72   However, it should be remembered that the academic study of the impact of the new information and communication technologies could be divided into two ideal positions. On the one hand, there are scholars like Jon W. Anderson and Dale F. Eickelman, who argue that the new technologies have a positive potential to open up and democratise the Middle East and other parts of the world. On the other hand we find, for example, Jürgen Habermas and Pierre Bourdieu, who argue that the new media are destructive, although pacifying their audiences.

73   Peters 2002, p. 509.

74   On phone sex, see earlier chapter.

the new technologies. According to Dr Muzammil H. Siddiqi, a virtual form of *zina'* is comparable to an 'ordinary' form of *zina'* committed in the 'real' world outside the Net.[75] There is no difference between carnal sins and illusory sins.

In the virtual world of the Internet, Muslims are also likely to come across unlawful forms of gambling (online poker, various forms of betting, etc.).[76] According to most '*ulama*', gambling is either linked to unnecessary amusement (that is, is a waste of time), or betting and other illicit ways of earning money (cf. Q 2:219 and 5:90–91).[77] The general condition for permitting games and play is that they 'educate' or are 'good' for Muslims. Hence, it is argued that gambling (or the game) should not prevent Muslims from fulfilling their duties towards God, society and the family. Furthermore, being engaged in games and play is often seen as a childish activity that adults should avoid. Although the rules for gambling are quite clear, the material analysed for this chapter indicates differences among the '*ulama*' on how to view gambling. The boundaries between what is lawful and unlawful are therefore an open question, and it is easy to find contradictory opinions on this subject. The diversity of opinions involved can be illustrated by Muslim discussions about chess. According to some '*ulama*', chess is *halal* (lawful), but to others it is *makruh* (not suitable), and for yet others it is *haram* (forbidden).[78] For Yusuf al-Qaradawi, the playing of chess is lawful and does not constitute a problem as long as Muslims follow three conditions:

- One should not get so absorbed in it that he delays his prayer; chess is well-known to be a stealer of time.
- There should be no gambling involved.
- The player should not utter obscenities or vulgarities.[79]

If the conditions stipulated by al-Qaradawi are met, there should be no problem in playing chess on, for example, the Internet, but this by no means nullifies the unlawfulness of other forms of gambling based on betting or chance – on the contrary.

But even Muslims who try to avoid all virtual sins that are present on the Internet could easily end up in trouble when using a computer to seek knowledge about God and Islam.[80] Because of the construction of the Internet, a 'sound' interpretation

---

75   'Is Cybersex or phone sex considered to be 'Zina'', retrieved from http://www.pakistanlink.com/religion/2001/0413.html (printed 2005–08–30).

76   On gambling and the Internet, see Dr Monzer Kahf, 'Ruling on New Forms of Lottery', retrieved from http://www.islamonline.net/servlet/Satellite?pagename=IslamOnline-English-Ask_Scholar/FatwaE/FatwaEandcid=1119503545142 (printed 2005–09–19).

77   See Karic 2002, p. 281. Cf. Rosenthal 1986 and al-Qaradawi 2001, pp. 300–302.

78   al-Qaradawi 2001, pp. 295–296.

79   al- Qaradawi 2001, p. 296.

80   See Sheikh Muhammad Iqbal Nadvi, 'Protecting our Children from Internet Abuse', retrieved from http://www.islamonline.net/servlet/Satellite?pagename=IslamOnline-English-

found on a specific webpage is only a mouse click away from an 'unsound' or even a so-called heretical interpretation of Islam. The hypertextuality of the Internet, provided and upheld by the linked collections, makes it extremely difficult, if not impossible, for a single user to see when he or she is entering into a new Islamic discourse (for example, a webpage dominated by another law school or run by a certain Muslim scholar who belongs to a specific or even 'sectarian' group). On the Internet, a certain webpage may provide references to a number of different and conflicting opinions on Islamic theology, and it is up to the user to find the so-called correct interpretation. This trend seems to go along with the fact that Muslims have also become more privatised and individualised in their interpretations of their religion and that the new technologies foster a spirit that questions traditional authorities and established ways of transmitting religious knowledge.[81] But the technology can also give rise to other kinds of problems. This dilemma could, for example, be illustrated by a question from a Muslim in Indonesia who is afraid of erasing downloaded files containing recitations from the Qur'an:

> Sometimes, I download Islamic audio materials from the Internet to listen to lectures. When I am done with the audio, I want to delete it so that I can have some space on my computer, but I am hesitant because sometimes the lectures contain Qur'anic verses being recited. Is it okay for me to delete the audio files even though they contain Qur'anic verses?[82]

The answer to this question is that it is not a sin to erase audio files containing verses from the Qur'an as long as the individual does not intend to undermine the Glorious Qur'an.[83]

Besides all the problems addressed in this chapter, the Internet also has new possibilities for *da'wa* (calling people to Islam). This function of the Internet is clearly addressed and emphasised by an IT student, Maryam al-Hajari, one of the founders of IslamOnline.net.[84] The Internet can, for example, easily be used to collect money for beneficial and good deeds (for example, collecting *zakat*). In her interview with Bettina Gräf, for example, Maryam al-Hajari stresses that Yusuf al-Qaradawi has described the Internet, and especially Islamic websites, as 'the jihad of our time'.[85]

Ask_Scholar/FatwaE/FatwaE&cid=1119503548020 (printed 2005–10–10).

81   Cf., for example, Anderson 2003.

82   Dr Sano Koutoub Moustapha, 'Deleting Audio Files Containing Qur'anic Verses', retrieved from http://www.islamonline.net/servlet/Satellite?pagename=IslamOnline-English-Ask_Scholar/FatwaE/FatwaE&cid=1119503547794 (printed 2005–09–19).

83   This opinion is given by Dr Sano Koutoub Moustapha, Professor of Jurisprudence and its principles at the International Islamic University, Malaysia; see Dr Sano Koutoub Moustapha, 'Deleting Audio Files ...'.

84   Gräf 2008, p. 3.

85   Quoted in Gräf 2008, p. 10.

For some *'ulama'*, it is even possible to embrace Islam by saying the Muslim creed or *shahada* on the Internet.[86] Although this is a controversial opinion not shared by all Muslims (for the critics it is not possible to have two persons who can witness and confirm that the person had the right intention when embracing Islam via Internet), it illustrates how the new technology is influencing contemporary Muslim debates on Islamic theology. Less controversial is the idea that a computer could help Muslims calculate the correct prayer times, convert dates between *hijri* and other calendar systems, or give the exact times for the beginning and ending of the fasting day during the month of Ramadan.[87]

The new possibilities provided by the Internet can, however, also cause controversy and conflict among Muslims. Like the introduction of the telegraph as discussed by, for example, Jacob Skovgaard-Petersen, the fact that a computer can calculate the time for the prayers or the beginning of Ramadan could also be a controversial topic for some Muslim groups.[88] For the critics it is necessary that believers see the changes of the moon with their own eyes. However, this is not a practical solution for most Muslims living in Europe or the United States, who, like all Muslims outside the Arab world, have to rely on information provided by the *'ulama'* in, for example, Saudi Arabia in making such calculations.

Conclusions

The introduction of the Internet in the Middle East and the wider Muslim world have caused both new problems and possibilities. On the one hand, the Internet has been viewed as an important tool for establishing democracy and opening up political and theological discussion. The fact that more people can be engaged in such debates and even challenge the political and religious order is presented as a prerequisite for establishing democracy. On the other hand, it is evident that both politicians and the *'ulama'* may perceive this development as a difficult and even dangerous phenomenon that should be countered. Even though authoritarian regimes might have different reasons for hindering the new media, *'ulama'* too may feel threatened by the possibility that they might lose control of their authority to interpret the religious tradition. The *'ulama'* discussed and analysed in this chapter give different responses to this development. While some *'ulama'* are very critical of the Internet, others are more positive and open to the potential of the technology. A larger number of *'ulama'* discussed here, for example, are using the Internet to issue and distribute their theological opinions and answers. This development is most clearly illustrated by the large number of so-called

---

86   See Group of Muftis, 'Giving the Shahadah Through the Internet', retrieved from   http://www.islamonline.net/servlet/Satellite?pagename=IslamOnline-English-Ask_ Scholar/FatwaE/FatwaE&cid=1119503545282 (printed 2005–10–10).

87   Cf. Anderson 2003, p. 48, and Mandaville 2001, p. 179.

88   See Skovgaard-Petersen 1997a, pp. 80–99.

online *fatwa* services found on the Internet today. Still, it is evident that Muslim parents and the *'ulama'* are both concerned by the fact that the Internet is being flooded with what is perceived as negative and destructive information, and that the technology is mainly being used for un-Islamic and immoral purposes.

From a sociological point of view, however, it is interesting to note that Muslim parents in, for example, Morocco seem to be less concerned by the fact that their children go to cybercafes to explore the Internet than by the fact that they go to the cinema. Although we should abstain from making general conclusions on the basis of Ines Braune's studies from North Africa, we may speculate why the Moroccan parents included in her study perceive the Internet or cyberspace as a less 'dangerous' place than the movie theatre. One plausible explanation could be that the Internet is 'only' a virtual meeting place and not a physical space. The contact that children are able to make on the Internet is virtual, contrary to the interaction in, for example, a cinema. When the lights are turned off and the movies start, it is possible for boys and girls to be physical and to engage in carnal sins, that is, real physical contact.

Nonetheless it is clear that most *'ulama'* have mixed feelings about the introduction and use of the Internet. From the *fatwas* analysed in this chapter, for example, it is clear that the *'ulama'* associated with the Islamic portal IslamOnline. net are positive about the technology. On the basis of the table below, however, it is possible to see that the Internet is associated with 'good' as well as 'bad' qualities.

Table 6.1　　'Negative' and 'positive' effects of the Internet

'Negative effect'	'Positive effect'
Time-consuming.	No problem if used for a good purpose.
The anonymity of the Internet fosters slander and backbiting.	It is possible to find a future spouse on the Internet (under the condition that Islamic law regarding marriages is upheld).
It has become easier to break and challenge gender boundaries stipulated by Islamic law.	
The Internet is filled with pornography and fosters illicit behaviour (*zina'*).	It has become easier to spread 'correct' information about Islam. It has also become easier to do *da'wa* and to collect *zakat* via the Internet.
Online gambling and betting are serious problems.	
The very structure of the Internet (the hypertextuality) is a serious challenge to the authority of Muslim theologians. The Internet is bringing about the relativisation and privatisation of the Islamic faith.	The new technology can help Muslims calculate the times for prayers and for the beginning and end of Ramadan.
It can be controversial to erase downloads with recitations from the Qur'an.	
The Internet erodes traditional methods for calculating the beginning and end of Ramadan.	

Regardless of how the '*ulama*' analysed for this chapter view the Internet, it is clear that Muslim parents and '*ulama*' are both calling for the development of an Islamic ethics of the Internet. But even though several '*ulama*' are concerned by the new information and communication technologies, they do not hesitate to use the Internet for disseminating their own opinions and interpretations of Islam. From this point of view, it is clear that the Internet is one of the forms of media that most contemporary '*ulama*' are using. This is most likely explained by the low cost and simplicity of using the new technology for spreading specific interpretations of Islam. This will most likely open up the debate about how to interpret Islam. Today the Internet is filled with self-proclaimed 'experts on Islam' who have little or no training according to the classical standards of the Islamic tradition. This shows how the Internet can be used as a tool for questioning established religious authority. The Internet is therefore a virtual battlefield on which a large number of the '*ulama*', lay preachers and experts fight over how to interpret Islam in a 'proper' and 'sound' way.

Chapter 7

The Ultimate Test:
The Qur'an and Information and
Communication Technologies

For a long time she would allow her eyes to rest on the two open pages before her. The letters in green ink from right to left, row beneath row, each shape mysteriously captivating, each dot above or below a letter an epitome of the entire scripture, each assembly of letters a group of dervishes raising their hands in zikr [remembrance], each gap between two enigmatic shapes a leap from this world into the next, and each ending the adventure of the day of Resurrection. [...] After spending much time in just looking at the open book, she would then, with strange light glowing on her face, lift her right hand and with the right finger start touching the letter of each line, then another line, to the end of the page. [...] At that moment she had passed into a state of total identity with the word of God. Her inability to read the scripture was her ability to hear once again: Read! Read, in the name of thy Lord.[1]

The quotation above is taken from Neal Robinson's *Discovering the* Qur'an: *A Contemporary Approach to a Veiled Text*, and the original passage comes from the Indian/Pakistani critic and writer Muhammad Hasan Askari (1919–1978). Besides the poetic beauty of the text, the poem is an illustrative example of the special position that the Qur'an occupies among Muslims. Even though the woman in the text is unable to read from the revelation, she feels a special sense of belonging to the founding text of Islam. Askari's text is also an example of how the Qur'an is able to remain holy even though it has been mass-produced with the aid of printing.

The aim of this last chapter is to analyse Muslim debates about information and communication technologies that can be linked specifically to the Qur'an. We have already touched upon some of the technologies and the problems associated with them, but compared to former discussions, this chapter is mostly focused on the Qur'an itself. My text includes a discussion and analysis of how the reproduction and mass production of the Qur'an through printing, recording and digitalisation (DVDs and other electronic media) has been debated by Muslims. As in the other chapters, my main concern and focus is again on the '*ulama*' debating the Qur'an and the new media. For example, what happens when the Qur'an is printed, recorded and mass-produced? Do the media have an effect on the sacred text?

---

1   Robinson 2003, p. 24.

Do the printing, recording and digitalisation of the Qur'an represent the ultimate test for the '*ulama*'? More important questions are: what might have happened to the holy revelation when it was mass-produced? Could the printers guarantee that the Qur'an had been handled with the respect and dignity it deserved when it was printed, recorded, or, even more particularly, put on the Internet? Hence, the aim of this final chapter is to focus on some of the debates that followed the earliest print and sound recordings of the Qur'an, as well as to analyse the impact of the digitalisation and computerisation of the Qur'an and other Islamic texts. What kind of questions, problems and possibilities do the '*ulama*' included in the chapter identify in relation to the introduction of the phonograph, the radio and the Internet? What kinds of opinions and debates is it possible to identify and connect with the mass production of the Qur'an?

As demonstrated in earlier chapters, the introduction of the printing press and the possibility to mass-produce the Qur'an have been much debated issues among the '*ulama*' from the eighteenth century until today.[2] My analysis includes examples from remote places, such as Java and Egypt, but also contemporary Europe and the United States. Even though the chapter attempts to cover a wide range of places and discussions over a long period of time, all my examples are focused on the relationship and interplay between information and communication technologies and the Qur'an. The '*ulama*' discussed in the text belong to and follow different law schools, and they may have different attitudes towards the new media and modernity. Nonetheless they are all interconnected, since they all discuss the impact and use of the new media and are also concerned with the impact that information and communication technologies will have on how Muslims perceive Islam and religious authority.

New media, new forms of behaviour?

An important aspect of the introduction of information and communication technologies in the Islamic discourse is that they present new opportunities as well as problems. The potential to record and store large quantities of information (for example, religious texts) will have an effect not only on theological discussions, but also on the everyday practice of 'ordinary Muslims'. For example, when a computer can hoard the entire Qur'an, the incentive to learn the whole text by heart can be diminished.[3] Furthermore, a recording of a recitation of the Qur'an can, for example, easily end up in places that are not so sacred. An Internet user can without difficulty visit a webpage that contains Islamic texts and thereafter move on to a more questionable homepage (for example, a site containing pornography). A piece of paper that has Allah's name written on it can easily be thrown away as

---

2   According to Labib al-Sa'id, for example, the printing press has been wrongly used in Africa to print a distorted version of the Qur'an. See Labib al-Sa'id 1975, pp. 121–122.

3   Cf., for example, Sardar 2003.

garbage. It could also be placed in an improper place or touched by people who are not ritually pure.[4]

With the introduction of the printing press, the phonograph, radio and television broadcasting, and finally the Internet, it is even possible to argue that the Qur'an has become a commodity like any other. In pointing this out, I am not saying that the Qur'an has lost its religious function or position – on the contrary – but the text is nowadays displayed in novel ways thanks to the new information and communication technologies. For example, given present-day possibilities to mass-produce and print cheap paper copies of any text (including holy texts), the whole text of the Qur'an or parts of it can easily be reproduced. Selected quotations from the revelation can, for example, be attached to posters and other forms of display, such as stickers, key rings, picture frames and posters. The use and display of 'religious kitsch' is therefore a topic that needs to be analysed and documented more, and few academics have focused on these religious artefacts.

Today the Qur'an is sold by street vendors in, for example, Cairo and Damascus, together with T-shirts, plastic toys, soft drinks and packets of Kleenex.[5] Commercial and religious commodities are therefore mixed and sold side by side with little or no hesitation. Cheap printing and desktop publishing technologies have all contributed to making the word of God ubiquitous. Consequently, it is possible to argue that the Islamic revelation is being exposed in a new fashion ranging from graffiti on brick walls to posters, picture frames and stickers in taxis and private homes, to homepages on the Internet. On the one hand, this development can be analysed and seen as a process that empowers and places the individual in the centre.[6] The commercialisation and increasing display of the Qur'an that have taken place in the twentieth and twenty-first centuries can also been seen as a sign of a growing religious awareness among Muslims.[7] On the other hand, however, for many '*ulama*', especially those trained according to the so-called classical norms of the established institutions of learning such as the al-Azhar University in Egypt or in Mecca and Medina, this development can also be seen as something negative and destructive, and as threatening the customary order and the sacred tradition.[8] One clear illustration of this development is the debate over Islamic ringtones for mobile phones, which I have referred to in the earlier chapter on the telephone. At the risk of repetition, it is important to highlight a report in *The Arab News* November 2007 that the Islamic Jurisprudence Council in Mecca, Saudi Arabia, under the chairmanship of Grand Mufti Abdul Aziz al-Asheikh, had banned use of the verses of the Qur'an as ringtones for mobile phones. The meeting came to the following conclusion:

---

4   On this topic, see ibn 'Uthaimin, Throwing Away Paper that Has Allah's Name Written on it, *Fatawa Islamiyah*, vol. 8, p. 367.

5   See Starrett 1995 and Hirschkind 2006, p. 36.

6   Cf. Hirschkind 2006, p. 35.

7   Hirschkind 2003, p. 347.

8   Cf. Roy 2004, p. 34.

It is demeaning and degrading to the verses of the Holy Book to stop abruptly at the middle of a recitation or neglecting the recitation, as happens when they are used as ringtones in mobile phones. On the other hand, recording the verses from the Holy Qur'an in phone sets with the intention of recitation and listening is a virtuous act.[9]

For the critics, technological developments have among other things made it easier to use the Qur'an in a 'wrong' way. The ability to manufacture and distribute cheap, mass-produced copies of the Qur'an either in Arabic or in translation is therefore not automatically a positive development. This is an illustration and an important reminder of the potential of information and communication technologies to cause anxiety and mixed feelings among the '*ulama*'.

As illustrated in the earlier chapters for this book, the debate over the new technologies should also be related to a number of important changes in social and educational structures in the Middle East. With growing literacy and mass higher education, the number of people who can read and discuss the contents of the Islamic revelation has also increased in the modern period, a fact that has led to a novel debate with the established religious order. This development has often produced conflicts over authority and interpretation.[10] Furthermore, the mass production of the Qur'an can also mean that people stop treating the text with the respect and dignity it deserves and requires, an issue I shall return to shortly.

'None but the purified shall touch'

The discussion that followed the recording and broadcasting of the recitation of the Qur'an is, in its complexity, an illustration of the significance of the material qualities of the different media technologies.[11] For example, the mass production and transmission of the Qur'an via recordings or hypertexts, which I discuss in this chapter, have all placed the question of ritual purity in a new context. The importance of ritual purity is, for example, emphasised and prescribed when touching the Qur'an:

> Behold, it is a truly noble discourse, [conveyed unto man] in a well-guarded divine writ which none but the pure [of heart] can touch: a revelation from the Sustainer of all the worlds! (Q 56:77–80)

---

9   'Qur'anic Ringtones Haram', *Arab News*, Friday 9 November 2007 (28 Shawwal 1428), retrieved from http://www.arabnews.com/?page=1&section=0&article=103380a&d =9&m=11&y=2007 (printed 2008–08–15).

10   Hirschkind 2003, p. 347. On literacy in the Arabic-speaking world, see *Arab Human Development Report 2003: Building a Knowledge Society*, and Maamouri 2008.

11   Cf. Hirschkind 2003, p. 341.

When the Qur'an (or the recitation of the text) is transferred to a digital format or recorded, the question of ritual purity is highlighted in a new way. Although this problem is solved in different ways, Sano Koutoub Moustapha, professor of *fiqh* and its principles at the International Islamic University, Malaysia, advocates abandoning the old principles of ritual purity (*wudu'*) when the Qur'an is being transmitted via a new medium. In his *fatwa* on this topic he writes:

> It is recommended to have wudu' when you listen to the Qur'an. A Muslim should always try to be in wudu'. However, it is not prohibited to listen to the Qur'an without being in a state of purification. In other words, wudu' is not a prerequisite for listening to the Qur'an.[12]

Although it is possible to analyse and understand Sano Koutoub Moustapha's answer in many different ways, his opinion on this particular subject represents a clear break with, for example, the views of Imam Malik ibn Anas, the scholar who lent his name to the Maliki school of law, who among other things stresses the importance of *wudu'* when listening to the Qur'an.[13] It is therefore possible to argue that Abdulkader Tayob is right when he claims that the Islamic perception of purity has been affected by modern technological developments. He writes:

> Modern technological developments have had an impact on the conception and practice of Islamic purification. Advances in plumbing, sanitation, and the 'sparkling clean' culture of advertising have intruded into the Islamic debate on purification. Traditional texts that deal at length with clean pools and wells have become obsolete for most Muslims living in towns and cities. Even the invention of the toothbrush has affected the way Muslims practice Islamic purification.[14]

If we agree with Tayob, it is understandable why Sano Koutoub Moustapha holds a different opinion on purity compared to Imam Malik ibn Anas: he is a child of his own time. For Imam Malik ibn Anas and other medieval *'ulama'*, it was unthinkable that one should only try to be in a state of *wudu'*. According to these authorities, the believer was either in a state of ritual purity or not: there is no intermediate position according to Imam Malik ibn Anas! However, this conclusion is supported and shared by the great majority of contemporary *'ulama'* as well.

However, before we analyse the discussions that took place among certain *'ulama'* in the late nineteenth and early twentieth centuries, it is necessary to say something briefly about the epistemology and ontology of the Qur'an.

---

12 'Is Wudu' Necessary to Listen to Qur'an?', retrieved from http://www.islamonline.net/fatwa/english/FatwaDisplay.asp?hFatwaID=116620 (printed 2008–10–10).

13 Cf. Imam Malik ibn Anas, *Al-Muwatta'*, p. 76.

14 Tayob 1995, p. 372.

How to use the Qur'an

The 'proper' and 'improper' use of the Qur'an is a very seriously debated issue among both medieval and contemporary '*ulama*'. For example, the practice of using verses from the Qur'an set in amulets and talismans to cure illnesses and hold back the evil eye is much debated. This practice is, for example, condemned by ibn Taymiyya (1263–1328) and many other medieval and later '*ulama*'.[15] But it should also be stressed that other '*ulama*' have few if any problems with the use of amulets and talismans. This shows that it is generally problematic to make a clear separation between 'popular' and 'educated' interpretations of Islam. Making too strong a separation between so-called high and low Islam is questionable, and the boundary between the Islam of the religiously educated elite and the beliefs of the wider masses are often thin and theoretically constructed. For example, followers of various Sufi groups are often presented as being part of popular belief, but also Sufi sheikhs can be highly educated in accordance with classical traditions and rituals. Hence, the boundary between the educated '*ulama*' and the sufi sheikhs is often thin and open to debate.

If we return to the discussion about amulets and talismans, it is clear that these artefacts also can be seen as commercial reproductions of the Qur'an. The mass production of the text is, however, no new phenomenon. Verses from the Qur'an have, for example, been inscribed on religious buildings, inside mosques, on coins and other religious objects since the very beginning of the history of Islam. Inscriptions and engravings could be reproduced for their artistic value, the beauty of the Arabic of the Qur'an, educational purposes or to connote power and authority.[16] No matter how we interpret Qur'anic inscriptions, they were clearly produced with the aim of being consumed by a large audience. This conclusion is, for example, supported by Karl Schaefer and his analysis of the importance of block-printed amulets. He writes:

> Handwritten Arab amulets are quite common and it was customary in mediaeval times for a person faced with a potential danger to request such a charm from a *Sufi* (Muslim mystic), who would compose a text to protect against one or more specifically identified dangers. Block-printed amulets were, presumably, mass-produced, perhaps to meet heavy demand for such protections.[17]

---

15 One extreme form of amulet is, for example, the garments used by medieval soldiers for protection that were covered with quotations from the Qur'an. Freed Leemhuis reports that the two last suras of the Qur'an (Q 113, 114) are popular as protectors of this sort, often being referred to as *al-mu'awwidhatan* or the two suras of taking refuge. Leemhuis 2006, pp. 153–154.

16 Blair and Bloom 2006.

17 Schaefer 2002, pp. 123–124.

Still it is evident that the modern mass production of the Qur'an has a much deeper impact on society. Refined and more efficient ways of reproducing and transmitting the holy text have led to new habits and attitudes towards it. Obviously this development has led to debates and conflicts of interest.[18] For example, according to an Egyptian informant quoted by the American anthropologist Gregory Starrett, the mass production of the Qur'an has among other things led to a more extensive use of the *mushaf* as a talisman for protection against car crashes:[19]

> Let me tell you something. That's a very bad habit, a very bad habit. The Qur'an is for reading only. If you're not reading it, you shouldn't have it around. It's not just to have around. Even in my own home, I'm not supposed to have more than a single mushaf. Just one. What's the use of more? … they're useless in my possession, and I should give them away to someone, or donate them to a mosque. In the car, look what happens: everything collects dust, and it gets dirty, and so on.
>
> As for stickers, they're also a very bad habit. There are only certain things that are allowable to put in the car, and only if they're there temporarily, and from the Qur'an. For example, there's short praying for travellers, and if a driver doesn't know it by heart, he can put that on the dashboard to read it before he drives, but that's it. It's not for showing, it's for *saying*. If it's not *said*, there's no point, so why just have the stickers there?
>
> *Saying* the prayer asks God to protect the driver, but it's not a preventative measure, it's a measure of devotion. God sends us accidents as test, and the more he loves us, the more he tests us …
>
> Besides, if I had stickers or something on the car, or a mushaf on the dashboard, what if I had just had sex with my girlfriend? … The Qur'an specifically says that after you've had sex you're not supposed to be touching or getting near the mushaf until you're pure … Or if I had a sticker there on the dashboard, my girlfriend could be sitting over there picking at its edges or something, and it would be getting dusty and dirty and so on … I can *say tasbih* [using prayer

---

18   Cf. O'Connor 2001.

19   In using the quotation from Gregory Starrett, I am not saying that the analysis advocated by the informant is correct. It is generally very difficult to compare the popularity of talismans in car windows with past epochs and former habits. Simply, we do not have enough sources that can give us a detailed account of the popularity and use of amulets and talismans for earlier and pre-modern periods. Most information about so-called popular religion is produced by critics and opponents who held these practices to be expressions of un-Islamic behaviours. An initiated discussion about Islam and popular belief is found in, for example, Berkey 2001; O'Connor 2001; Shoshan 1993 and Waardenburg 1979.

beads], thanking and praising God with my voice all I want, but the *sibha* [prayer beads] hanging from the mirror is pointless. It's not used.[20]

As this long quotation from Greogory Starrett's field notes from Egypt shows, it is clear that the Qur'an is not just a book that pious Muslims should read. The revelation should be handled with care and devotion, and the reader or listener must have a pure heart, a clean body and a good intention (*niyya*) when touching or inculcating the divine words.[21] Hence, the Qur'an is perceived as God's direct speech to mankind, and when Muslims are reciting or reading the holy text, they are not chanting words about God, but His own words. This fact makes the preservation, observation, study and transmission of the Qur'an a central aspect of Islam.[22] The importance of purity is, for example, clearly illustrated in both Islamic jurisprudence and the Qur'an. For instance, Q 5:6 contains direct references to how the believer should prepare for prayer.

> O YOU who have attained to faith! When you are about to pray, wash your face, and your hands and arms up to the elbows, and pass your [wet] hands lightly over your head, and [wash] your feet up to the ankles. And if you are in a state requiring total ablution, purify yourselves …

According to Islamic jurisprudence it is also important to distinguish between the minor ritual ablution (*wudu'*) and the major ablution (*ghusl*). Although it is possible to trace different opinions about how to perform the various forms of ablution and under which circumstances the believer should be ritually 'clean', it is evident that all '*ulama'* stress the importance of purity. When reading, handling or listening to the Qur'an, it is a prerequisite to be in a state of purity.[23] When attending the *salat* (the collective prayer) or reading or listening to the divine revelation, the believer must have a pure body and mind.

Purity and good intentions are also emphasised in the *hadith* literature. A classical example that stresses the importance of purity is attributed to the famous compiler Abu 'l-Husayn Muslim b. al-Hajjaj (*c.*817–875):

---

20   Starrett 1995, pp. 61–62. All emphases in the original.

21   Rules and regulations concerning purity and cleanliness before reading or listening to the Qur'an are, for example, to be found in Al-Kaysi 1989, pp. 103–105. Cf. Tayob 1995, pp. 370–372, and Robinson 2003, p. 21. On the concept of *niyya*, see Wensinck 1995, pp. 66–67.

22   Graham 1987, p. 87.

23   For example, Imam Malik ibn Anas places great emphasis on the necessity of ritual purity in his *Al-Muwatta'*. See, for example, pp. 8–23 and p. 76 (concerning purity in relation to the recitation of the Qur'an). On different attitudes and opinions concerning how to perform the prayer, see, for example, Fierro 1987.

Purity is half of faith. Al-hamdu lillah [praise be to Allah] fills the scales, and subhana 'illah [How far is Allah from every imperfection] and al-hamdu lillah [praise be to Allah] fills that which is between heaven and earth. Prayer is light; charity is a proof; patience is an argument for or against you. Everyone starts his day and is a vendor of his soul, either freeing it or bringing about its ruin.[24]

Ritual purity, however, is not enough: to be able to comprehend and know the Qur'an, it is also necessary to be able to read, listen and understand the revelation. Oral transmission is therefore viewed as the first prerequisite, and guarantee, of the sound transmission of the text. This conviction actually gives the printed or copied text a secondary status as compared to the oral message.[25] For example, the oral aspect is vital for the preservation of the text, especially since the earliest Qur'anic manuscripts do not have diacritics or signs of vocalisation.[26] The possibility of *tashif*, that is, that two words may have been written down wrongly or identically, was consequently perceived as a danger that could corrupt the word of God.[27] It was only by saying and hearing the word of God that it was possible for the believers to distinguish between so-called 'perfect' and 'sick' recitations. The Qur'an is therefore not only a book that the pious Muslim should read: the revelation must also be recited, listened to and commemorated by all Muslims in order to grasp God's message to humankind, according to most *'ulama'*.[28] The importance of oral transmission of knowledge is, for example, stressed by the famous jurist Muhammad Idris al-Shafi'i (767–820), to whom are attributed the words: 'Whoever learns jurisprudence (*fiqh*) from books alone loses sight of the law'.[29] The Qur'an makes a similar connection between hearing and learning/knowing (*sami' 'alim*),[30] while the *hadith* literature stresses the importance of reciting the Qur'an. According to one tradition, the Prophet Muhammad says 'Embellish the Qur'an with your voice', and in another place he says 'He who does not recite the Qur'an melodiously is not one of us'.[31] The positive effect of listening to the word of God is also clearly stressed in the Qur'an (cf. Q 7:204; 5:86; 9:6):

---

24   Quoted from An-Nawawi 1997, p. 79/English translation p. 78.

25   Cf. Graham 1987, p. 88 and pp. 96–109.

26   'The first vocalisation system then emerged, probably around the end of the Umayyad period and was based on the use of read dots: gradually *hamza* and orthoepic indicators (*sukun, shadda*) were marked down, albeit irregularly. The system as we know it today seems to have been introduced towards the end of the third/ninth century.' Déroche 2006, p. 175.

27   On this issue, see Rosenthal 1999, p. 347.

28   Robinson 2003, p. 9. See also van Gelder 2002.

29   Quoted from Labib al-Sa'id 1975, p. 54.

30   Van Gelder 2002, p. 406.

31   Quoted from Labib al-Sa'id 1975, p. 56. According to information provided by Labib al-Sa'id, the *hadith* is taken from Sunan al-Darimi, vol. II, pp. 471, 474 (Fadail al-Qur'an, No. 34).

Hence, when the Qur'an is voiced, hearken unto it, and listen in silence, so that you might be graced with [God's] mercy.' (Q 7:204)

And when they listen to the revelation received by the Messenger, thou wilt see their eyes overflowing with TEARS, for they recognise the truth: they pray: 'Our Lord! we believe; write us down among the witnesses. (Q 5:83)

Furthermore, the Qur'an also contains descriptions of how listeners react when they heard the recitation of the holy text. Those who listen to the Qur'an start to 'shiver', 'tremble' and 'cry' (cf. Q 5:83, 19:58, 17:107–109, 39:23).[32] From the quotations above and the discussion in this section, it is clear that on the one hand the mass production of the revelation contained new possibilities for spreading the word of God, while on the other hand also bringing new problems and challenges for the Muslim community. Since I have dealt with the discussion that followed the introduction of the printing press in an earlier chapter of this book, I will now turn directly to a *fatwa* that illustrates both the new possibilities and problems that the information and communication technologies gave rise to. It is time to turn to a legal discussion about the introduction of the phonograph in Batavia, Java, in the early nineteenth century.

The first sound recordings of the Qur'an

In his classic study of Islam and the phonograph, the Dutch Orientalist Christian Snouck Hurgronje (1857–1936) provides us with a clear illustration of how the introduction of the new information and communication technologies caused debate and conflict among the '*ulama*' from the end of the nineteenth century.[33] The debate was focused on the phonographic recordings of the recitation of the Qur'an, and more specifically on recordings of woman singers. The fact that the new technology attracted a lot of attention and that many Muslims also paid money to listen to recordings of the Qur'an troubled some of the '*ulama*' in Batavia.[34] On the one hand, the optimists suggested that a phonographic recording of the *adhan* (call to prayer) might replace the human voice in calling believers

---

32 On the effect of listening to recitations of the Qur'an, see, for example, Gade 2006, p. 482.

33 Snouck Hurgronje 1900. A much shorter version of this article was published in English in 1915. My discussion of the phonograph is based on both the German and English texts.

34 The problem of salaries for religious services is, for example, discussed by Muzammil Siddiqi, 'Can an Imam Receive a Salary for Leading the Prayers?', retrieved from http://www.islamonline.net/servlet/Satellite?pagename=IslamOnline-English-Ask_Scholar/FatwaE/FatwaEandcid=1119503548282 (printed 2008–10–10).

to prayer.[35] On the other hand, however, critics such as Sayyid Othman argued that the mechanical reproduction of the Qur'an was nothing but a profanation of the word of God. To resolve the problem and issue an Islamic opinion about the phonograph, he issued a *fatwa* on the subject. The following discussion is based primarily on Hurgronje's analysis and translation of this particular *fatwa*, but I will also discuss and relate the arguments to the general questions addressed in this chapter, that is, the impact that the introduction of the new information and communication technologies had on the transmission and use of the divine revelation. What was the problem according to Sayyid Othman? As a standard rule of *ifta'* — the process of giving a *fatwa* — his answer also contains a formulated question from an inquirer (*mustafti*):

> What is the statement of the scribes (whose wisdom may Allah allow us to enjoy continually!) concerning the box (*sanduq*), in which there are instruments that draw into its interior sounds created in its neighbourhood? [...] What then is the decision of the scribes concerning the exhibition of this box for payment, and what is the teaching of the sacred law regarding the hearing of such sounds as are received mechanically? Does the Moslem who hears recitations of the Koran reproduced in this way deserve any reward for the hearing? Is it permissible for Moslems to listen to the sounds of musical instruments thus reproduced, or to songs sung by an unknown woman (i.e., of a woman who is neither the listener's wife nor a relative with whom conversation is allowed). Give us your statement (*fetwa*) on these questions, and may Allah give you His reward.[36]

Before Sayyid Othman gives his answer, he has to place the question in its proper theological and social context. It is therefore essential to raise some general questions and relate them to the new technology. For example, can a pious Muslim earn his daily bread by selling recitations from the Qur'an? Does the mechanical reproduction of the recitation distort or change the word of God? If the phonographic reproduction is not equal to the human voice, is it then permissible to listen to the recordings of women's voices and even music?[37]

Although Sayyid Othman stresses that he is not automatically negative about new technological innovations, it is clear that he is sceptical about and even hostile to the phonograph. But in his conclusion, he states that it is the intention (*niyya*) of the believer that decides whether the recordings of the phonograph are good or bad. If the reproduction of the Qur'an is decent and follows the rules of *'ilm al-tajwid* (the art of reciting the Qur'an), and if it does not cause any harm, nor arouse

---

35   Snouck Hurgronje 1915, p. 159.

36   Translation taken from Snouck Hurgronje 1915, pp. 160–161.

37   Listening to music is a subject often dismissed by Muslim *'ulama'*. See, for example, Muhammad bin Abdul-Aziz al-Musnad's collection of *fatwas* on issues regarding women, which contains several examples of prohibitions against listening to music and rules for women to lower their voices in the public sphere. See pp. 324, 338–339, 371–373.

lustful passion, it is a 'neutral' (*mubah*) subject, according to Sayyid Othman.[38] However, the believer must be aware that he should not expect to receive any reward from listening to a mechanically produced recitation:

> for the thing heard is not the voice of man that recites the Koran, the hearing of which is commanded to us by God. The sounds have come away from the mouth of the reciter and are separated from him, and they arise anew from this instrument. There can be no question of a Koranic recitation, because the sounds of the Koran are no longer produced by the organs of speech destined for each one of them, and also because they do not possess the peculiar, legally demanded qualities, so that no heavenly reward can be give to the hearer.[39]

The quotation outlines a general rule that is applicable to all kinds of bad or improper recitation. Consequently, the basic rules of *'ilm al-tajwid* are applicable to all recitations of the divine revelation. For this scholar, it is obvious that the medium that transmitted the message has to be in congruence with the established tradition. If the laws of *'ilm al-tajwid* are not followed and applied, or if the *niyya* (intention) of the believer is bad, the recitation is improper, no matter whether the recitation is done by the human voice or with the aid of an artefact or a new technology.[40]

However, the debate over the mechanical sound reproduction of the Qur'an was not solved and did not come to an end because of Sayyid Othman's *fatwa*. The controversy was exemplified yet again by the debate that followed the recording of the recitation of the Qur'an for Radio Cairo that took place in the middle of the twentieth century.[41]

Radio Cairo and the recitation of the Qur'an

As already demonstrated in this chapter, the recitation and oral transmission of the Qur'an is a central feature of Islam, and from the previous backdrop it should come as no surprise that the decision to record a 'proper' recitation of the holy revelation was a delicate task that caused debate and potential conflicts among various *'ulama'*. To solve the problem and meet the public demand for a recitation of the Qur'an, Radio Cairo recorded and produced a set of long-playing

---

38   Translation taken from Snouck Hurgronje 1915, p. 163. On *'ilm al-tajwid*, see Denny 1995; Gade 2006; Graham and Kermani 2006; Nelson 2001.

39   Translation taken from Snouck Hurgronje 1915, p. 163. This opinion can also be compared with the pamphlet, *The Stations of Shaitaan: Polluting the Month of Ramadhan*.

40   The necessity of following the rules of *ilm al-tajwid* is stressed in Nelson 2001: see especially Chapter 6.

41   Snouck Hurgronje quotes an unnamed learned Arab from Singapore who rejected the *fatwa* given by Sayyid Othman; see Snouck Hurgronje 1915, pp. 164–165.

records of the Qur'an under the title *al-Mushaf al-Murattal* ('The recited text') in 1961. To guarantee the quality and soundness of the recordings, the project was conducted under the auspices of the Egyptian government, and the al-Azhar University gave the undertaking its blessing.[42]

> The project was initiated and headed by Labib al-Sa'id, at the time President of the General Association for the Preservation of the Glorious Koran.[43] The aim was to record a perfect oral recitation and transmission of the Qur'an to meet the new demand of the Egyptian radio audience. Al-Sa'id's concern for the art of recitation of the revelation was also closely linked to the changes that the Egyptian school system had gone through.[44] From the 1920s onwards, the educational system had been shaped and reformed along the lines of the Western secular model. According to Labib al-Sa'id, these changes had had a negative effect on the art of memorizing the Qur'an, and the popularity of religious schools was declining due to the new educational system. Even classical educational schools of higher Islamic learning, such as the al-Azhar in Egypt, had to adjust their curriculum and abandon the former policy of requiring that all pupils should know the whole Qur'an by heart before being enrolled in the school.[45]

To curb these negative trends and to create an alternative method for the memorisation of the Qur'an, it became essential to make use of the new information and communication technologies. This is an example of the fact that the media can be used to uphold old traditions and that traditionally oriented '*ulama*' can also embrace new technologies, that is, if they are for a higher cause – in this case, the preservation of the oral transmission of the Qur'an.

To produce an officially approved recording of the Qur'an that both met the demands of the '*ulama*' and could be 'played' on the radio, Labib al-Sa'id had to make twenty different recordings of the revelation, that is, a recording of the two versions of each of the ten accepted so-called readings (*qira'at*) of the Qur'an (both the seven canonical or *mutawatir* readings and the three widely known or *mashhur* readings).[46] It was al-Sa'id's ambition that his recording should be viewed as a modern collection of the Qur'an (that is, a *jam'*) resembling the collection that was presumably undertaken by the third caliph 'Uthman b. 'Affan (d. 656) in the

42 *Majallat al-Azhar* 1959, vol. 30, p. 926.

43 The recording included both the recitation style of the Hafs transmission of 'Asim and the Warsh transmission of Nafi'. The recording was executed by the Egyptian Shaykh of the Qur'an reciters, Mahmud Khalil al-Husari, who died in 1980. Leemhuis 2006, p. 152.

44 The changes to the school system in the Middle East and in India/Pakistan are described, for example, in Hefner and Zaman 2007. See also Waardenburg 1995.

45 Labib al-Sa'id 1975, p. 66.

46 Weiss 1974, pp. 134–135. See also Gade 2006, pp. 483–484 and Leemhuis 2006, pp. 149–151.

early and formative history of Islam.[47] As mentioned earlier, the aim of the project was also to stop the decline of the art of reciting the Qur'an and to promote the oral tradition. Hence, in the words of Fred Leemhuis, the 'contemporary development is reviving the diversity of what is essentially an oral tradition'.[48]

Furthermore, Labib al-Sa'id wished to introduce and promote novel didactical methods for learning how to recite the text. This aim could also be used as an excuse for recording the Qur'an and could legitimise it. This is an example of how broadcasting technologies can be used for a higher purpose.

The recorded text of the Koran could, by being broadcast over the media and by being made available to the public in the form of readily purchasable records, serve as an omnipresent 'teacher,' through which ordinary people could not only memorize the Koran but also master the technique of chanting. Those who learn the Koran from the records would be spared those problems of orthography which learning from the written or printed text entails.[49]

The recordings made by Radio Cairo in the 1960s should also be seen as a reaction to the mass production of printed versions of the Qur'an. It was Labib al-Sa'id's firm belief that the broadcast recitation could be used like a traditional teacher who helps the members of the Muslim community memorize the Qur'an.[50] Instead of sitting at the feet of a sheikh – the traditional method of learning the Qur'an – the 'modern' Muslim could put on a record at home and learn the words of God by heart at any time. From this point of view, the recording of the revelation was a method for the preservation of Islamic knowledge and classical Arabic, as well as a tool for the modernization of the Muslim audience. Hence, the recorded recitations of the Qur'an are an example of how modern media technologies could be used for the protection of the classical education among Muslims, as well as to spread the word of God.

The ideal recitation

The importance of striving for an ideal recitation of the Qur'an is a topic that we have already discussed earlier in this chapter. The holy revelation should, for example, be recited in a beautiful voice, and believers should always aim for perfection when reading or chanting the Qur'an. With the development of information and communication technologies and their ability to record and preserve the recitation, the questions of perfection and control have become more clearly manifest.

---

47   He even compares his work to the codification of the Qur'an that was conducted under the rule of the third Caliph, 'Uthman b. 'Affan. Weiss 1974, p. 135.

48   Leemhuis 2006, p. 153.

49   Labib al-Sa'id 1975, p. 71.

50   Weiss 1974, p. 135 and p. 139.

The link between perfection and recording technologies is, for example, highlighted by Kristina Nelson in her groundbreaking work, *The Art of Reciting the Qur'an*. Following these technological developments, Nelson argues, it became more important for the Egyptian state to control and shape the sound of the ideal recitation. For example, in order to be given a permit to work as an authorised reciter (that is, a reciter approved by the state), it is necessary to undergo a difficult test examining the candidate's qualities. Furthermore, it is also clear that the recording technology and the radio and television broadcasting of Qur'anic recitations have become very important in 'shaping audience expectations and popularising reciters', as well as for setting standards for how the text 'should' be read.[51] Hence, in order to control the quality and live up to certain standards, the *Lajnat al-Qurra'* (Reciters' Committee) was set up. This body has a responsibility for all recitations that are broadcast on the radio, as a result of which they have great direct and indirect influence on the perception of how the ideal recitation should sound. The committee is also important because it has a responsibility for the official ranking of reciters, organising auditions and evaluating candidates who wish to become 'professional reciters'. The importance of the recording technology is clearly illustrated by the following quotation that describes how an audition may be conducted in Egypt. Karen Nelson summarises the procedure as follows:

> The audition follows a set procedure: the candidate is led into the recording booth, where he recites a section of text of his own choosing in the *mujawwad* style. This is amplified so that the committee can evaluate his recorded voice quality as well as his general musicality. The candidate is then seated before the committee, which proceeds to examine him in *hifd*, and *tajwid*. Testing for *hifd*, Sayx Muhammad Mursi 'Amir or Sayz Rizq Habbah will begin a phrase of the text and ask the reciter to complete it. Or they may ask him to locate a particular phrase in the text and complete it. The reciting in this context is in the *murattal* style.[52]

Without commenting on Nelson's informative discussion and analysis of the art of recitation, the quotation clearly shows the complex interplay between control, power and the new information and communication technologies. On the one hand, with the aid of the recording technology, it seems as if it has become easier to control and set the standard for how the Qur'an should be recited. On the other hand, however, the mass production of tape cassettes, CDs and DVDs has made it easier to challenge the established order and to make room for alternative interpretations or more 'unusual voices' that could, for example, recite the Qur'an. Even though both developments are present in

---

51   Nelson 2001, p. 143.
52   Nelson 2001, p. 145.

the source material, it is clear that the new media are playing a central role in debates over the ideal recitation of the Qur'an.

New attitudes, new forms of behaviour

However, the fact that the recitation of the Qur'an was broadcast via the radio gave rise to new attitudes and modes of behaviour. For example, Charles Hirschkind argues that the broadcasts and recordings of famous reciters on cassettes and CDs has changed the conditions in respect of how people listen to the Qur'an. The recitation has become a kind of commercialised popular entertainment that can be mixed with popular and secular music and 'ordinary' forms of entertainment. Cassette tapes with passages from the Qur'an are nowadays being used as a kind of 'background music' in order to create a sort of religious atmosphere.[53]

> Qur'an tapes are often played at the same times and in the same locations as other popular entertainment media, recordings of the Qur'anic recitation have come to function as a kind of background sound, one that signals the religious commitment of the store owner or taxi driver, but does not demand the sort of attention traditionally associated with practices of recitation.[54]

Although this analysis is balanced by, for example, Kristina Nelson, who argues that the recitation of the Qur'an is something more than just persuasive background music,[55] it is clear that these technological developments have embedded the Qur'an in a new social context. This concern is, however, not only limited to the use of the new information and communication technologies for the reproduction of the Qur'an. Similar concerns are also expressed in the discussion of so-called Qur'an recitation competitions. On these highly popular occasions, the reciters are often venerated and treated as pop stars, and the most appreciated reciters are almost equivalent to megastars in Arabic-speaking and Islamic environments. Even though it is a matter of great esteem to recite the Qur'an, it is not too far-fetched to argue that these occasions come very close to a form of public entertainment and represent a proliferation of the holy text. If this analysis is correct, as I believe it is, it shows that the boundary between 'correct' and 'incorrect' behaviour is very thin. The difference has on the one hand to do with the setting and context of the recitation, and on the other with the intention of the performance.

---

53   Hirschkind 2003, pp. 345–346.
54   Hirschkind 2003, p. 346.
55   Nelson 2001, p. xxviii.

Furthermore, when it is broadcast over the radio, the Qur'an is not framed in a religious or sacred tradition, as is the case in, for example, a mosque or a *madrasa* institution. The critics of the *al-Mushaf al-Murattal* described above therefore argue that the recording of the revelation was nothing more than 'an unjustifiable innovation prompted by irresponsibility and self-interest'.[56] Not surprisingly, the views of this critic were strongly rejected by Labib al-Sa'id, who convincingly argued that the printed or written version of the Qur'an (which is accepted by most Muslims) is also 'a kind of innovation in that there was no clear mandate for it [that is, the written or printed text] in the Koran or the Tradition of the Prophet'.[57] It was argued that, since the great majority of Muslims accept the printed Qur'an, they should have no problems with recordings of the revelation. It could even be argued that the latter is closer to the original intention of the text. The classical way of transmitting the Qur'an and the sound recording are both based on oral communication and hearing, as compared to the printed text, which requires the individual to be able to read Arabic.[58] This prerequisite is, for example, at odds with the fact that the Prophet Muhammad was an *ummi* (that is, an illiterate individual who could not read or write according to Islamic historiography).[59] This way of putting the argument is highly interesting because it is a good illustration of how the *'ulama'* can adjust their arguments and theological interpretations to fit the prevailing context. If the written word was acceptable for writing down the Qur'an, there should be no obstacle to accepting other kinds of information and communication technologies according to Labib al-Sa'id.[60]

Labib al-Sa'id's view is supported by the fact that there are today 'in principle no objections to printing the Koran in Arabic'.[61] But it should, however, be underlined that modern editions of the Qur'an still try to emulate the handwritten manuscript. Harald Bobzin writes:

> This can be seen not only in the ornamentation of the first two facing pages customary in printed editions, but also above all in the fact that no movable type is used to set the pages, which are, instead, always based on a calligraphically designed text which is reproduced either by lithography or by photomechanical processes.[62]

---

56   Labib al-Sa'id 1975, p. 75.
57   Labib al-Sa'id 1975, pp. 75–76.
58   Cf. Van Gelder 2002.
59   On the concept of *ummi* and the Qur'an, see Günter 2002.
60   A similar analogical reasoning is, for example, used in support of using the telescope to observe the new moon. See Yusuf al-Qaradawi, 'Sighting the Moon of Ramadan During the Daytime', retrieved from http://www.islamonline. net/servlet/Satellite?pagename=IslamOnline-English-Ask_Scholar/FatwaE/ FatwaE&cid=1119503544558 (printed 2008–10–10).
61   Bobzin 2002, p. 171.
62   Bobzin 2002, pp. 171–172.

With the development of computer technologies, it has also become possible to combine both text and sound in new creative and powerful ways. But since several '*ulama*' have been engaged in a long debate about the suitability of and problems with the information and communication technologies, it seems that the transmission and digitalisation of the Qur'an by means of computers has caused few if any new debates. As we shall see below, the same pros and cons are more or less repeated and rehashed in the debate over the digitalisation and computerisation of the Qur'an.

The Qur'an in the age of computers

The rapid development of computers and the new information and communication technologies has had a strong effect on the distribution, use and exegesis of the Qur'an. The development of computer software for reading and writing Arabic has also been stimulated by the demand for Islamic texts on the Internet.[63] From this point of view, computerised Islamic texts bear a resemblance to Gregory Starrett's discussion about religious commodities. Today, for example, it is possible to buy a CD-ROM for a small sum of money that contains the Qur'an in Arabic, as well as translations of the holy text into numerous languages, books of commentary (that is, *tafsir*) and even *hadith* traditions.

One example is the transnational electronic and computer company Enmac, which was started in 2002. The business goal of this company is to sell the latest products in communication and computer software. Besides 'ordinary' computer items, they are also selling a vast number of different mobile phones and Ipods or MP3 players that contain digitalised versions of the Qur'an. One example from their online catalogue is the so-called Color Digital Qur'an player iCQ 505.[64] According to the information on the webpage, this product includes the following possibilities and services that can be related to a Muslim way of life:

- Complete Holy Qur'an Text and Audio (Voice of Sheikh Suddais and Sheikh Sharaim)
- Colourful images, Text and Super High Quality Audio
- Qur'an Translation in English, French, German, Turkish, Malaysian, Indonesian and Urdu
- Prayer Times and Qibla Direction for World Cities with Adhan Alarm
- Complete Tafseer ibn Katheer Book (Arabic)
- Complete Riyadh As-Saliheen Book (Arabic)
- Names of Allah (images and Audio)
- Surah and Verse number will be saved even after shutdown
- Voice Recorder (10 minutes duration)

---

63 Cf. Anderson and Gonzalez-Quijano 2004, p. 66.
64 On the iCQ, see http://www.enmac.com.hk/icq505.htm (printed 2008–04–03).

- Daily supplications with audio and English Translation
- Doaa Khatam al-Qur'an (Voice of Sheikh Suddais)
- Surah/Verse Menu, Book-marking and Repeat functions
- Beautiful Full-Screen Clock Styles with 5 User Alarm Settings other than Prayer Alarms
- Built-in Speaker and Colour LCD with more then 65,000 Colours
- Dual Charging: AC/DC Adapter and PC USB
- Replaceable Battery like Mobiles

Furthermore, the iCQ 505 also contains no fewer than seven translations of the Qur'an.

- Urdu: Maulana Fateh Muhammad Jalandhry
- English: Dr Mohsin Khan French
- French: King Fahad Complex for printing of The Holy Qur'an, Saudi Arabia
- German: Ministry of Islamic Affairs, Da'wah and Guidance, Saudi Arabia
- Malaysian: Ministry of Islamic Affairs, Da'wah and Guidance, Saudi Arabia
- Indonesian: Ministry of Islamic Affairs, Da'wah and Guidance, Saudi Arabia
- Turkish: Diyanet Isleri Baskanligi

According to the homepage of Enmac, the company is authorised to sell digital products that contain recitations of the Qur'an and other Islamic products on the Internet by the Islamic Affairs and Charitable Activities Department in the United Arab Emirates.[65] This approval indicates that the company is not seeking to break Islamic rules and regulations, but it can also be seen as a guarantee to the buyers that the company and its technical equipment are serious and in line with Islamic theology.[66] If we apply Starrett's terminology to this development, however, the above-named product is nothing but a religious commodity that should be situated within the expanding market of computer software.

Although digitalised and computerised Islamic texts are a relatively new and unexplored field, it is evident that cheap CD-ROM copies of the Qur'an and searchable databases containing the Qur'an and Islamic commentary literature on the Internet will have an effect on the Muslim community.[67] On the one hand, these sources can be seen as tools able to make the text and its interpretation

---

65   See http://www.enmac.com.hk/images/download/UAE%20Certificate%20all%20 models.JPG (printed 2008–04–03).

66   A similar support or guarantee was also given by the Al-Azhar in Cairo, Egypt, to the animated film *Muhammad: The Last Prophet*, which I discussed in Chapter 3.

67   Berg 2001; Rippin 2000.

available to greater numbers of Muslims.[68] This view is, for example, embraced by the Thesaurus Islamic Foundation in Liechtenstein, which supports the publication and setting up of *The Sunna Project. Encyclopaedia of Hadith: The Ihsan Network*. Among other things, this project is developing a searchable *hadith* database using the most authoritative sources (that is, the collectors of *hadith*). The aim of the project is to prevent the manuscript tradition from declining and to raise Muslim awareness of the importance of the *hadith* literature with the aid of the new information and communication technologies:

> The rise of computer technology in recent years, however, offers promising means of transforming this situation. It has become possible to process enormous quantities of data in a matter of seconds, and software supporting an almost infinite variety of search methods may open up whole new horizons for the researcher. The hadith texts, previously consulted only by a fairly narrow category of specialists, now become accessible to people with an interest in virtually any aspect of Islamic studies, who can make use of them without the need to acquire a detailed familiarity with the format and peculiarities of each text.[69]

However, and this is the other side of the coin, this process could also foster a kind of relativism and a privatisation of the interpretation of Islam, a development not automatically supported by the religious elite.[70] As discussed in an earlier section of this book, the homepage of MSA (the Muslim Student Association) in the United States and its searchable *hadith* collections of Bukhari, Muslim, Abu-Dawud and Malik provide a clear example of this concern. This webpage stress that it is important not to confuse information with knowledge and that to be able to use a search engine or the Internet is not the same as possessing a 'sound' knowledge of Islamic traditions.[71]

It is therefore doubtful whether the new possibility to digitise and computerise Islamic texts is supported by all of the '*ulama*'. The necessity to study with a master is, for example, strongly stressed by the followers of the Deoband tradition, as well as by '*ulama*' belonging to other traditions. As Muhammad Khalid Masud points out, to be called an '*alim*, a student must have studied with a proper teacher

---

68   On this development see, for example, Anderson 2003; Anderson and Gonzalez-Quijano 2004; Eickelman 2003; Hirschkind 2006 and Sardar 2003.

69   *The Sunna Project. Encyclopaedia of the Hadith: The Ihsan Network*, pp. 3–4.

70   Furthermore, it should also be noted that the *The Sunna Project. Encyclopaedia of Hadith: The Ihsan Network* is not free of charge, but is rather expensive. The practice of charging money for a religious service, in this case for copies of Islamic texts, ties into the discussion about money and religion. In other words, is it lawful or forbidden to earn money from the selling of Islamic texts? See Muzammil Siddiqi, 'Can an Imam Receive a Salary for Leading the Prayers?', retrieved from http://www. islamonline.net/servlet/Satellite?pagename=IslamOnline-English-Ask_Scholar/FatwaE/ FatwaE&cid=1119503548282 (printed 2008–10–10).

71   http://www.usc.edu/dept/MSA/reference/searchhadith.html.

who is knowledgeable in the sciences of Islam. The importance of studying with a teacher is clearly illustrated in the collection entitled *Fatawa Deoband*, one of the most authoritative sources for the followers of the Deoband tradition:

> It becomes clear that notwithstanding the volume of information one may acquire from the books, their study alone cannot make a person an authority. Unless one learns the religious science from authoritative scholars of religion in a regular manner, one remains an ignorant and uneducated layman.[72]

Despite the warning issued by the MSA and the recommendations of the *Fatawa Deoband*, it is clear that several '*ulama*', such as Yusuf al-Qaradawi, whom we have discussed extensively in several of the earlier chapters, have little or no hesitation in using the latest modern information and communication technologies in spreading the word of God.[73] In making this remark, I am not saying that he has not received a 'classical' Islamic education – on the contrary, as pointed out earlier, he gained his formal education from the al-Azhar in Cairo and holds a PhD in Islamic theology. Even though he has no issues with the latest technologies, the question is whether the users (that is, those who watch his television shows and browse the Internet) have the same classical training as Yusuf al-Qaradawi. In other words, can the 'ordinary' Muslim be expected to have enough education and knowledge of the tradition to comprehend, interpret and apply Islam in a 'proper' and 'sound' way?

By using the latest technological developments and by setting up international organisations, Yusuf al-Qaradawi has become a sort of global or transnational *mufti* who could claim a kind of global authority.[74] Besides his activities on al-Jazeera and the Internet, al-Qaradawi is also associated with a number of international and global Islamic organisations.[75] Even though it is not possible to find a uniform opinion about this development or any anonymous support for Yusuf al-Qaradawi and his interpretation of Islam, to the best of my knowledge there are few signs of strong opposition to the digitisation and computerisation of the Qur'an. To put the Qur'an on the Internet or to produce a CD-ROM of it does not automatically violate or break the rules of *tajwid* (recitation) or corrupt the beauty of the text (that is, the calligraphy). On the contrary, for the enthusiast, the computer or the CD-ROM could even be used as a tool or a teacher for learning the classical traditions of '*ulum al*-Qur'an (that is, the science of the Qur'an).[76] Today it is even possible

---

72   The quotation from the *Fatawa Deoband* is taken from Masud 1984, p. 136.

73   It is, however, important to stress that both IslamOnline.net and Qaradawi.net are free of charge.

74   See Gräf 2007, 2008, Mariani 2006 and Skovgaard-Petersen 2004.

75   He is closely associated with the European Council for Fatwa and Research (ECFR) and the International Association of Muslim Scholars (IAMS). On these organisations, see Gräf 2007.

76   Cf. Labib al-Sa'id.

to incorporate 'recitational requirements' digitally, such as the *ta'awwudh* (a call for God's protection before reading the Qur'an)' in the e-Qur'an.[77]

From this point of view, the latest developments are in line with the ambition and ideas of Labib al-Sa'id and the Radio Cairo recordings of the recitation of the Qur'an discussed above. As with Labib al-Sa'id's way of putting the argument, a computerised text can be used for pedagogical purposes and to learn the correct pronunciation and recitation of the Arabic text in an efficient and proper way.[78] Furthermore, the new technologies can also be used by both Muslim and non-Muslim researchers for exploring the Qur'an. This is, however, a topic that creates possibilities as well as problems, a discussion I will return to later in this chapter.[79]

At the same time, it is evident that the digitalisation of the Qur'an, the large corpus of different *tafsir* books and the *hadith* literature can dissolve and challenge the classical boundaries between different law schools and mix up incompatible discourses or interpretations.[80] The fear of *talfiq*, or the 'piecing together' of views from the different schools of law to formulate a legal principle or rule, is a classical topic in Islamic jurisprudence.[81] With the introduction of hypertexts and hypermedia, the linear sequential structure of a written text or an oral message can easily be dissolved and questioned by a layperson who has not been trained according to the classical requirements of higher Islamic learning. Since hypertexts are textual bodies (including pictures and sounds) with links to other texts, the internal order of, for example, a book (which is structured according to chapters and sections and bound together by a cover) becomes more fluid and flexible. In the end, it is the reader who decides the order and structure of the hypertext, that is, which sites he or she chooses to visit. Unlike a written text found outside cyberspace, the online text is generally divorced from its social, political and theological contexts. To a higher degree, it is the reader who browses the Internet who has control over the interpretation of the text. This 'unorthodox' way of approaching the classical sources is also enhanced by the anonymity of the Internet. Without physical contact and with a strong feeling of anonymity, it is easier both to ask unpleasant questions and to challenge a religious authority. For example, it is much easier to ask questions about sensitive issues, such as Islamic views on homosexuality and sexual relationships before marriage, on the Internet than in a 'real', offline, face-to-face situation. Even though the influence of the media should be analysed carefully – it is, for example, not easy to demonstrate

---

77   Berg 2001, p. 391.

78   See, for example, Hirschkind 2006.

79   Berg 2001, p. 392. Cf. *The Sunna Project. Encyclopaedia of the Haidth: The Ihsan Network*. Via the Internet it is, for example, possible to get access to different manuscripts of the Qur'an.

80   Cf. Anderson and Gonzalez-Quijano 2004, p. 61.

81   Netton 1997, p. 244. To combine interpretations and rulings from various law schools in a way that makes the action, outcome or behaviour unacceptable to any law school is also defined as *talfiq*.

whether it is the 'media' or general changes in the social climate that is leading the believer to ask 'unpleasant' questions – academic studies have clearly demonstrated that the Internet is a powerful tool that can be used for alternative interpretations and to question the religious authorities.[82] It is generally easier to question the establish order and to test alternative opinions online than offline. The social costs – that is, the loss of social capital, to use the terminology of the French sociologist Pierre Bourdieu – is much higher in a situation of face-to-face contact than it is in an anonymous cyber milieu.[83] Hence, it is possible to describe the Internet as an identity laboratory for the creation of a vast number of contesting identities.

For Muslims, the developments described above can be seen as showing that the interpretation of Islam has become more relativistic and is more in the hands of lay Muslims. If this interpretation is correct, the traditional religious authorities are running the risk of losing their power and influence over the interpretation. This development is clearly enhanced by the new information and communication technologies, educational reforms and social developments associated with processes of modernisation and globalisation. However, it is clear that, for example, hyperlinks and meta-texts on the Internet do not make any difference between Sunni Muslim *tafsirs* and other texts. These commentaries can easily be attached to others on contradictory webpages or databases that belong to, for example, Shi'a groups or other so-called sectarian groups, such as the *Nation of Islam* or the *Ahmadiyya*. This shows that these technological developments may actually create a new context for Islamic and Qur'anic exegesis that stretches and even dissolves the boundaries of the classical *tafsir* tradition.[84]

If we listen to the '*ulama*' who are trained in accordance with the classical *madrasa* institutions, the new technologies have made it more difficult to control and guarantee the quality of an online text compared to an offline text. In a polemical address against so-called Salafi tendencies on the Internet, the British imam Abdal-Hakim Murad says:

> Salafist Islam is itself a kind of web, with few physical signs. It is non-sacramental, if we exclude the practice of Qur'anic cantillation. It has no need of local pilgrimages, or physical dab in the presence of a spiritual director. Just as the Internet abolished geography, and replaces it with a shifting space of categories; just as it has no memory, apart from the conditional survival of the usenet conversations; so too scriptural fundamentalism in the Abrahamic religions generally, are uninterested in diversities of tradition which might accrue to the deposit of faith. The isnad, or ijaza, has no obvious extension in cyberspace; in the language of traditional usul al-hadith, every text is acquired by wijada, not by sama'. A 'depthless' Islam may ensue; and the ulema will be

---

82   Thomsen Højsgaard 2006.
83   See Bourdieu 1977 for a more developed discussion of symbolic capital.
84   Berg 2001, pp. 392–393.

hard pressed to resist it in this new medium which takes the scriptures so entirely out of their control.[85]

For good or evil, the development and refinement of the technology has made it easier and cheaper for lay persons to publish their own translations and analysis on the Internet. This process has troubled the traditional religious elite into thinking that they have lost their control over the originality and authenticity of the text.[86] Even more demanding is the fact that it has become possible to publish false or polemical texts about the Qur'an on the Internet.[87] Manuscripts of what the '*ulama*' perceive as texts of low quality can easily be used to circulate ideas about Islam that can be harmful to the Muslim community, at least according to the critical '*ulama*' discussed in this chapter. Even though there are important differences, the contemporary debate over the digitalisation of the Qur'an resembles the early discussions that I have analysed in the previous chapters (for example, especially the chapter on Islam and printing). From the sixteenth century onwards, the Qur'an was printed in Arabic script in Europe.[88] These editions were, however, of low quality and contained many errors. To prevent this, it became necessary for Muslims to acquire control over the publishing and printing of the holy text. This was one of arguments used to convince the Sultan to accept the introduction of the printing press in the Ottoman Empire in 1726.[89] From this point of view, the insecurity that the '*ulama*' display when faced with the computerisation of the holy revelation and the Islamic literature resembles the worry that many '*ulama*' had regarding the printing press in the eighteenth century.[90]

Conclusion

From the discussions and examples presented in this chapter, it is evident that the great majority of the '*ulama*' regard the rapid development of the information and communication technologies as a set of new tools for learning more about Islam and the Qur'an. As with the use of cassettes, the advance of various forms of digitalisations of the Qur'an and other forms of database containing Islamic

---

85   Quotation from Larsson 2006b, pp. 95–96.

86   One illustration of this development is a *fatwa* issued by Sano Koutoub Moustapha called 'Online Muftis: Who Is Eligible?', retrieved from http://www.islamonline.net/servlet/Satellite?cid=1218558415726&pagename=IslamOnline-English-Ask_Scholar%2F FatwaE%2FFatwaEAskTheScholar (printed 2008–08–22).

87   Cf. Bunt 2000. An analysis of how the Internet can be used to spread Islamophobia and anti-Muslim opinions can be found in Larsson 2007, which analyses the content of the portal *WikiIslam*.

88   On the printing of the Qur'an in Europe, see Déroche 2006, pp. 183–184.

89   Cf. Chapter 2.

90   Cf. Chapter 2.

texts can be used as efficient tools for calling people to Islam (that is, for doing *da'wa*). For example, in one *fatwa* issued by Sheikh Ahmad Kutty, whom we have discussed in earlier chapters, it is emphasised that CDs and cassettes are useful for learning the art of *tajwid* and for memorising the Qur'an.[91] Yet again, if the technology is being used for a good purpose, there is no problem in Muslims using electronic artefacts. But if the technology is used for negative purposes or with bad intentions, it is problematic and dangerous for all Muslims. For example, the Internet can be used to search out illicit and destructive information (for example, pornography), games and other kinds of meaningless activities. Judging from the *'ulama'* I have included in my discussions, the Internet is often viewed as a waste of important time that could be used to learn more about Islam and God.

The printing, recording and digitalisation of the Qur'an have made the revelation more accessible and easier to use for a larger number of individuals, both Muslims and non-Muslims. Recording the Qur'an is particularly important because the literacy rate is low in many countries and regions dominated by Islam. Nonetheless it is clear that the mass production of the Qur'an has raised a number of new questions. Is mass production leading to a proliferation of the revelation? Is it even possible to view the printed, recorded and digitalised Qur'an as a religious commodity? Do Muslims obtain the same feeling and reward from reading, listening or looking at the mass-produced Qur'an that they would if they were listening to a recitation of the text in a mosque? Even though these questions can be answered in many different ways, it is evident from the examples given in this chapter that these and similar questions are of great concern to the *'ulama'* included in this study. Nonetheless it is clear that most contemporary *'ulama'* are content with the fact that the new information and communication technologies can be of great help to the Muslim community provided they are used for what they believe is the right purposes. This positive interpretation is, for example, present in the writings of Labib al-Sa'id. By recording the recitation of the Qur'an, he even compares himself to the Caliph 'Uthman and his authoritative collection of the Qur'an in the early history of Islam. Al-Sa'id argues convincingly that Muslims should not be afraid of accepting the recitation in recorded form. If they (that is, Muslims) are prepared to accept the printed version of the Qur'an, they should not be reluctant to listen to its recording. The Prophet Muhammad is never reported to have said that he approved of printing, a technique that had not even been invented in his lifetime – but still Muslims accept the printed version of the Qur'an as a true and sound reproduction. So if they accept the printed text, they should have no problems in accepting the recorded version. But even though most Muslims have no hesitation in accepting the printed text or the recorded recitation, it is possible to find a small minority of Muslim *'ulama'* arguing that recorded or broadcast recitations do not provide the same degree of merit as oral recitation in

---

91 'How to Learn the Qur'an on My Own', retrieved from http://www. islamonline.net/servlet/Satellite?pagename=IslamOnline-English-Ask_Scholar/FatwaE/ FatwaE&cid=1119503547818 (printed 2008–10–10).

a mosque. This opinion was, for example, voiced at the time of the introduction of the phonograph in Java.[92] A similar criticism is also expressed by the Mujlisul Ulama of South Africa, who argue in their publications that recitations of the Qur'an broadcast on the radio are inferior, not equal to the live recitations that take place in the mosque.[93] This opinion is, however, not the usual attitude of the '*ulama*' I have analysed. It seems that most of the '*ulama*', no matter what theological tendency they belong to, are willing to embrace any kind of new information and communication technologies that can help Muslims to spread, reproduce and support learning.

One issue that causes some debate and concern is the fact that the new communication technologies may erode the authority of the established '*ulama*' and place it in question. With the aid of the Internet and digitalised databases, it is both very easy and tempting for Muslims to search and come up with an interpretation that fits current demands. This way of handling the sources is not automatically supported by or in line with the beliefs of the classically trained '*ulama*'. Several examples have been included in this chapter to illustrate how concerned the '*ulama*' are regarding the fact that, according to them, the new possibilities that have been created by these technological developments are not the same as those produced by classical training and a so-called sound knowledge of Islamic theology. From this point of view, it is clear that the printing, recording and digitalisation of the Qur'an have placed the authority of the '*ulama*' in question. The discussion regarding how to interpret Islam and who should do so have therefore become a public concern, and more voices are heard in the debate today (not least on the Internet). Even though it is very difficult to determine whether this development is the result of the new information and communication technologies or of changes in society more generally, it is evident (as demonstrated by this and several other studies) that these technological developments can be seen as providing support to those who want to question the interpretations of the religious elite. That said, it is also important to underline that those in power can also use the technologies discussed in this book. It is, however, easy to demonstrate that the interpretation of any particular theologian is not beyond question. From this point of view, it is clear that the information and communication technologies are facilitating and supporting a more pluralistic discussion and are opening up public debate, as well as contributing to the globalisation of the discussion over how to interpret and who has the authority to interpret. This deterritorialisation is a complex and multidimensional process that, among other things, includes the development of the information and communication technologies. The outcome of this process, to put it in the words of Olivier Roy, is that 'Islam is less and less ascribed to a specific territory and civilisational area'.[94]

---

92   See Snouck Hurgronje 1915, p. 163.

93   See *The Radio Stations of Shaitaan: Polluting the Month of Ramadhan*. Retrieved from http://www.themajlis.net/books-index-req-view_book_details-bkid-27.html.

94   Roy 2004, p. 18.

Conclusions

The aim of this book has been to analyse how Muslim '*ulama*' have discussed and debated the introduction of various modes of communication and information technologies, successively the printing press, photography, the cinema, radio and television, the telephone and the Internet. The '*ulama*' I have analysed and studied belong to different time periods, geographical localities and theological and political camps. One the one hand I have included '*ulama*' who could be linked to the reform tradition that had emerged by the end of the nineteenth century. Representatives of this group include Muhammad Abduh and Muhammad Rashid Rida, as well as more contemporary figures such as Yusuf al-Qaradawi and other followers of the ideology of the Muslim Brothers, a movement that also could be linked to the reform thinkers named above. On the other hand, I have included '*ulama*' who have discussed the influence of colonialism, modernity and the new technologies from a different point of view. Together with the reform tradition in the Middle East, a number of other movements or interpretations were also developed in the eighteenth and nineteenth centuries. Two examples are the Wahhabi and Deoband traditions, which became influential in Saudi Arabia and on the Indian subcontinent respectively. Resembling the reform thinkers in the Levant, they too sought to find solutions to modern problems and ways of developing an Islamic answer to the rise of modern society. While the followers of the reform traditions had few objections to technological innovations, the followers of the Wahhabi and Deoband traditions generally had more objections.

However, by closely analysing a large number of *fatwas* issued by the 'two' camps, one clear conclusion is that it is not possible to find any *one* Islamic point of view about the new information and communication technologies. The debate is complex, and the answers of the '*ulama*' are often linked to questions of power, prevailing local contexts and a general fear that the '*ulama*' will lose their position and power regarding the interpretation of Islam. From a general point of view, the debates over the information and communication technologies encompass larger questions about colonialism, western influences, modernity, freedom of expression, democracy, the rise of the secular society and the position of Islam in the modern world. The examples can therefore be read either as close analyses of how Muslim '*ulama*' debate specific technologies or as a meta-history describing the transformation that the Middle East has gone through from the colonial period up until the present day.

What is the problem?

In order to understand the debate about information and communication technologies, it is first essential to understand what kinds of problems and possibilities the '*ulama*' have associated with the new media. The following table shows the most frequently discussed problems and possibilities with the media.

Table C.1   Media, Problems and Possibilities

Media	Problems	Possibilities
The printing press	Oral transmission is a better guarantee for transmitting Islamic knowledge than printing. The Islamic system for the transmission of knowledge was threatened by the mass production of text. Printed texts could easily end up in wrong and indecent places (e.g., a copy of the Qur'an could be placed in a non-religious context). The printing press was often cleaned with the help of pig's bristles (a procedure that polluted the printed word). The copyists' guild protested against the mechanical reproduction of text. The printing press was often associated with western or colonial influences.	The possibility to mass-produce texts (both religious and non-religious texts). It was necessary to adopt printing, otherwise the printing of religious texts would be in the hands of Europeans. The printing press could be used to counter Christian missionaries, who used the printing press to proselytise among Muslims.
Photography	Theological objections against images – God is the only 'shaper of form'. The negative view of images and image-makers in the *hadith* literature. The use of images is an imitation of non-Muslim traditions. Images may be objects of worship (i.e., they may become idols).	Photography is positive if it is used for identity cards or for passports that can be used for business trips or religious pilgrimages (especially for the *hajj*).

Media	Problems	Possibilities
The cinema (film)	Theological objections against images – God is the only 'shaper of form'. The negative view of images and image-makers in the *hadith* literature. The use of images is an imitation of non-Muslim traditions. The film industry is filled with non-Islamic traditions and Western values (e.g., immorality, nudity, alcohol, violence). The cinema theatre is a public sphere where the sexes can meet with little or no social control (i.e., what happens when the lights are turned off?).	The film medium can be a tool for the education of Muslims if the content is inline with Islamic theology and moral. The film medium can be used to counter negative and stereotypical images of Islam and Muslims. Muslims are today producing 'Islamic' films with the aim of creating Muslim alternatives (especially for Muslim families).
Radio and television	The ability to listen to and watch non-Islamic programmes (i.e., programmes of no value for Muslims). Non-Islamic radio and television are a waste of time. Radio and television are both filled with non-Islamic content (music, dancing, entertainment and other kinds of immoralities). The ability to hear the voice of women with whom you are not related or married. Even religious programmes can become a problem if they are broadcast to an audience that is not focused on the programme (i.e., they are not in a religious mode or in a state of ritual purity).	The ability to broadcast recordings of the recitation of the Qur'an and other Islamic lectures. The ability to broadcast educational programmes and issue *fatwas* on radio and television. Via satellite television, it has become possible to send 'Islamic programmes' targeting Muslims living in countries or regions not dominated by Islam or Muslim culture (e.g., in Europe and the United States).

Media	Problems	Possibilities
The telephone	Is *shaytan* responsible for the transmission of sound from A to B? The telephone can be used to make contact with the opposite sex without the proper permission of the family. Telephone sex is a problem. The use of Islamic ring tones is a problem. Music used as ring tones is a problem. The ability to obtain a divorce by SMS is a problem.	The telephone can be used for Islamic counselling and the issuing of *fatwas*. The telephone can be used for emergency calls, for business transactions and to keep in touch with family and friends (provided that the telephone calls are decent and follow the laws of Islam).
The Internet	The Internet contains mainly indecent texts, forbidden images and immoral videos. The ability to break Islamic rules concerning dating and flirtation online via chatting, discussion groups, etc. is a problem. The easy access to alternative interpretations could be a problem for Muslim '*ulama*' who stress the necessity of following one tradition.	The ability to publish 'correct' information about Islam (and regimes in the Middle East). The ability to organise and set up online *fatwa* services is positive.

In reading the above table, it is important to stress that different '*ulama*' can have different opinions about these media, and that some of the problems addressed by '*ulama*' are of a more general nature. Some of them relate to theological objections, while others are more closely linked to social or ritual aspects (that is, how to live as a good Muslim). It should also be stressed that there is continuity in the perception and discussion of the pros and cons of the information and communication technologies. The table therefore provides an outline of some of the most frequently addressed problems and possibilities associated with the new media.

What is the solution?

To understand Islamic debates about information and communication technologies, it is important to stress that it is not possible to find any *one* answer to or opinion about the problems and possibilities posed by the new media. The debate is therefore complex, and different *'ulama'* have different answers to these technological developments. It is clear, however, that most *'ulama'* have a tendency to accept the new technologies over time. For example, when photography was introduced and the cinema was developed, there were plenty of discussions and objections regarding Islamic opinions about images, but today, when the television and the Internet are both being used by Muslim *'ulama'*, there is little objection or discussion about the ability of these technologies to transfer and reproduce images. This conclusion – that is, that contemporary Muslim *'ulama'* have a tendency to accept earlier technologies, even when they are resistant to new ones – does not, however, mean that Muslims are free to use older technologies with no restrictions.

Most of the *'ulama'* included in this study (no matter what theological camp they belong to) argue that technology is not good or bad in itself: it is what you do with it that counts, and the intention of the user is generally a focus of the debate. For example, the Internet is a powerful tool for finding out and learning more about Islamic theology, but the technology can also be used with bad intentions, such as exploring un-Islamic sites and breaking the laws of Islam. From a very general point of view, the *'ulama'* are engaged in developing an Islamic ethics covering the purposes for which Muslims are allowed to use the latest information and communication technologies and how to use them. If, in the words of Roger Silverstone, Eric Hirsch and David Morley, the technologies can be 'domesticated' to comply with the 'moral economy of the household', they can be used for a good purpose.[1] Muslims can even learn more about Islam with the aid of these technologies, and they can be used to attract people to Islam.

Even though some *'ulama'*, especially some of those who are influenced by Wahhabi interpretations, are more critical of information and communication technologies than other *'ulama'* (for example, those who are closer to the reform tradition), it is evident that Muslims cannot avoid the new media entirely. Even Saudi Arabia, which has banned the cinema, cannot prevent the influx of the new media. Like most people in the West, who have access to the latest communication technologies, the people of this country are today using the Internet for online flirtation, downloading films and visiting 'improper' sites on the Net. It is evident that the *'ulama'* are having great problems in trying to prevent this development.[2] From the examples in this study, it seems that several *'ulama'* have surrendered to the power of the new media under the assumption that, 'if you can't beat 'em,

---

1   Silverstone et al. 1992.

2   This problem is, however, not unique to Muslims. See, for example, Black 1997 and Åberg 2003, pp. 189–191.

join 'em'. Several leading '*ulama*' have therefore started to employ the new media to spread their messages and interpretations of Islam to believers. As we saw in earlier chapters, maybe the best known example of this development is the Egyptian theologian Yusuf al-Qaradawi, who has made extensive us of the Internet and satellite television to spread his interpretation of Islam to a global audience.

Media, authority and power

As indicated in the previous section, the new media embody the power to liberate the masses and make them more active in the formulation and interpretation of Islam. From this point of view, the mass media and the latest communication technologies have the potential to make the discussion more open, liberal and democratic, while at the same time it has become easier to express and find alternative interpretations and voices questioning the established order. For the '*ulama*' included in my study, this development is generally perceived as a serious problem. Consequently, it could be argued that the information and communication technologies have led to a privatisation of the religious code, and '*ulama*' can easily be side-stepped by other individuals who have taken the interpretation of Islam into their own hands. Even though '*ulama*' encourage believers to learn more about Islam, it is evident that many of them are worried that the latest interpretations found on, for example, the Internet are not grounded in a proper schooling. On the Internet, for example, while it is easy for believers to shop around for alternative interpretations, it is also generally very difficult for believers to check the validity of the answers given in an online forum.

It is also evident that the information and communication technologies have changed conditions for '*ulama*' in a very practical way. In earlier periods (at least in theory) the Muslim scholar who received a question from a believer was generally acquainted with the social, economic and cultural situation of the individual who was asking him for advice. With the printing, broadcasting or online publication of *fatwas*, however, it is clear that the conditions for answering questions changed. From then on, the Muslim scholar often had no knowledge of the social background of the questioner and little or no ability to find anything out; as a result he could not tailor his answers to meet individual requirements. For example, why was he/she asking this question? What are the characteristics of the questioner? Is he/she a firm believer or someone who takes the laws of Islam in an easy fashion? Should the answer be general (universal) or specific? In the new situation, the Muslim scholar had to rely on the information provided by the questioner, and it was generally more difficult to check the validity of the information he or she provided. Furthermore, the theologian who is supposed to answer the question could be living in another country or even another part of the world. Hence, with the mass production of Islamic *fatwas* the answer had to be adjusted to the new conditions set by modern society and the media. From a very practical point of view, the answer had to be more general or universal when compared to the 'traditional' answer, which was more tailored to meet individual demands or specific contexts. This is a clear illustration of how the new media have changed the context for the giving of Islamic answers.

Another side effect of these developments is that the questioner may well be able to seek out new alternatives if he or she is not satisfied with the answer given by the theologian who was consulted initially. This development is clearly also linked to questions of authority and power. That said, however, it is important to stress that Muslim '*ulama*' who have written about the giving of *fatwas* often emphasise that Muslims have always had this possibility. Even if this conclusion is correct, it is evident that the new media have increased this possibility still further, becoming a matter of degree rather than kind.

Is the Islamic debate unique?

This study is focused on '*ulama*' discussing the impact, reception and use of the information and communication technologies in both historical and contemporary periods. From the answers and recommendations given by these '*ulama*', we can easily draw the impression that Muslims are different and that their reactions are distinct from those of other religious groups. In order to avoid this interpretation, below I have included some comparative examples to create a more balanced impression. Even though this is not the focus of the present study, it is important to stress that the debates that occur among the '*ulama*' can easily be found among non-Muslim religious leaders too. For example, the Catholic theologians has often been reluctant to accept the new information and communication technologies because of their alleged ability to challenge the authority of the church. Hence, the Catholic Church wanted to control the printing press (as demonstrated by the Fifth Lateran Council of 1512–1517), and it also intervened in debates over the impact of the cinema. When the cinema was introduced in the Middle East, it is clear that both Muslim and Christian leaders were concerned about the negative impact of the film industry. Similar reactions and opinions have also been expressed by ultra-Orthodox Jews, the Amish and Mennonites over use of the telephone, television or the Internet. From these examples, it is clear that most religious groups have been concerned with the negative side effects of many information and communication technologies. But like the contemporary '*ulama*' included in my study, most Christian, Jewish, Hindu or other religious leaders are today using these technologies to spread their messages and their interpretations of their respective holy traditions. From this point of view, these media also embody the ability of the established order to uphold its position and defend its specific interpretations.

Back to the future

From the existing literature on religion and the information and communication technologies, it is evident that more systematic research is needed. It is therefore necessary to collect more data and to create models for how to analyse the content and use of these new media. From this point of view, I hope that this study will encourage more researchers to develop and refine the study of religion, media and culture. On the basis of earlier research, it is also evident that we need to focus on new topics and questions in order to understand how various 'believers' discuss and use the new media in relation to so-called religious topics.

According to my understanding, there is also a need for more studies that focus on the discussion, reception and use of the new media. A larger number of articles and books have documented how religious groups are making use of such media to communicate their beliefs, but there is little analysis of how and why they are using these technologies. For example, in this study I have made extensive use of printed, broadcast and online *fatwas*, but we still have very little knowledge about what Muslims actually do with the large number of Islamic answers that exist on, for example, the Internet. What kinds of questions are they asking, and why are they asking them? What do they do with the answers they receive? Do they follow them? Do they negotiate with the answer to find a solution that agrees with non-religious and religious norms? Do they shop around for yet more answers, or do they stick to one tradition or a specific school of thought?

More comparative studies covering several religious traditions in one project should also be initiated. Even though I have made some comparative remarks, it is evident that there is a need for more studies. The study of religion, media and culture has predominantly focused on Christians or followers of New Age traditions and their discussions and use of the new media. There are, of course, exceptions, but to the best of my knowledge there are few attempts that have tried to make systematic comparisons over time and across religious boundaries. Hence, I think that the future study of religion and the media must produce more comparative studies that focus on how various religious leaders have discussed, debated and used information and communication technologies.

I therefore hope that this final section will be understood as a call for more research and for increased cooperation between researchers interested in the interplay of media, religion and society.

References

Biographical references to sources retrieved from the Internet are given in the footnotes.

*EI*² = *Encyclopaedia of Islam*. Leiden: Brill, 1960–2002, vol. I–XI.

'Abduh, M. (1980) *The Theology of Unity*. English translation of *Risalat al-tawhid* by Musahad, I. and K. Cragg. New York: Books for Libraries.

Abdulrazak, F.A. (1990) *The Kingdom of the Book: The History of Printing as an Agency of Change in Morocco between 1865 and 1912*. Boston: Boston University.

Abrahamov, B. (1998) *Islamic Theology: Traditionalism and Rationalism*. Edinburgh: Edinburgh University Press.

Abu-Lughod, L. (1989) 'Bedouins, Cassettes and Technologies of Public Culture', *Middle East Report*, vol. 159, pp. 7–11.

Abu-Lughod, L. (1997) 'Finding a place for Islam: Egyptian television serials and the national interest'. In: Boyd-Barret, O. et al. (eds) *Media in Global Context: A Reader*. London and New York: Arnold, pp. 311–322.

Abu-Lughod, L. (2005) *Dramas of Nationhood: The Politics of Television in Egypt*. Chicago: University of Chicago Press.

Abu-Lughod, L. (2006) *Local Contexts of Islamism in Popular Media*. Amsterdam: ISIM Papers/Amsterdam University Press.

Akrami, J. (1987) 'The Blighted Spring: Iranian Cinema and Politics in the 1970s'. In: Downing, J.D.H. (ed.) *Film and Politics in the Third World*. New York: Autonomedia, Inc., pp. 131–144.

Akrami, J. (1991a) 'Cinema (Feature Films)'. In: Yarshater, E. (ed.) *Encyclopaedia Iranica*. Costa Mesa: Mazda Publishers, vol. V, pp. 572–579.

Akrami, J. (1991b) 'Cinema (Film Censorship)'. In: Yarshater, E. (ed.) *Encyclopaedia Iranica*. Costa Mesa: Mazda Publishers, vol. V, pp. 585–586.

Albin, M.W. (1995) 'Book Publishing'. In: Esposito, J.L. (ed.) *The Oxford Encyclopedia of the Modern Islamic World*. New York: Oxford University Press, vol. 1, pp. 226–229.

Albin, M.W. (2004) 'Printing of the Qur'an'. In: McAuliffe, J.D. (ed.) *Encyclopaedia of the Qur'an*. Leiden and Boston: Brill, vol. IV, pp. 264–276.

Allievi, S. (2003) 'Islam in the Public Space: Social networks, media and neo-communities'. In: Allievi, S. and J.S. Nielsen (eds) *Muslim Networks and Transnational Communities in and across Europe*. Leiden: Brill, pp. 1–27.

al-Andalusi, Said (1991) *al-Tabaqat al-'Umam*. English translation by Salem, S.I. and A. Kumar. Austin: University of Texas Press.

Anderson, J.W. (2003) 'The Internet and Islam's New Interpreters'. In: Eickelman, D.F. and J.W. Anderson (eds) *New Media in the Muslims World: The Emerging Public Sphere*. Bloomington: Indiana University Press, pp. 45–60.

Anderson, J.W. (2005) 'Wiring Up: The Internet Difference for Muslim Networks'. In: Cooke, M. and B.B. Lawrence (eds) *Muslim Networks from Hajj to Hip Hop*. Chapel Hill and London: The University of North Carolina Press, pp. 252–263.

Anderson, J.W. and Y. Gonzalez-Quijano (2004) 'Technological Mediation and the Emergence of Transnational Muslim Publics'. In: Salvatore, A. and D.F. Eickelman (eds) *Public Islam and the Common Good*. Leiden: Brill, pp. 53–71.

Arab Human Development Report 2003: *Building a Knowledge Society*. New York: United Nations Development Programme.

Arberry, A.J. (1964) *The Koran Interpreted*. London: Oxford University Press.

Armbrust, W. (2000) 'The Golden Age before the Golden Age: Commercial Egyptian Cinema before the 1960s'. In: Armbrust, W. (ed.) *Mass Mediations: New Approaches to Popular Culture in the Middle East. Berkeley*: University of California Press, pp. 292–327.

Armbrust, W. (2005) 'Synchronizing Watches: The State, the Consumer, and Sacred Time in Ramadan Television'. In: Meyer, B. and A. Moors (eds) *Religion, Media and the Public Sphere*. Bloomington: Indiana University Press, pp. 207–226.

Armes, R. (1995) 'Cinema'. In: Esposito, J.L. (ed.) *The Oxford Encyclopedia of the Modern Islamic World*. New York: Oxford University Press, vol. 1, pp. 286–290.

Armes, R. (1997) 'The Arab World'. In: Nowell-Smith, G. (ed.) *The Oxford History of World Cinema*. New York: Oxford University Press, pp. 661–666.

Arnold, T.W. (1965) *Painting in Islam: A Study of the Place of Pictorial Art in Muslim Culture*. New York: Dover Publications, Inc.

Ayalon, A. (1995) *The Press in the Arab Middle East: A History*. New York and Oxford: Oxford University Press.

Babinger, F. (1919) *Stambuler Buchwesen in 18. Jahrhundert*. Leipzig: Deutscher Verein für Buchwesen und Schrifttum.

Bakker, F.L. (2009) *The Challenge of the Silver Screen: An Analysis of the Cinematic Portraits of Jesus, Rama, Buddha, and Muhammad*. Leiden: Brill.

Baljon, J.M.S. (1994) 'Indian *Muftis* and the Prohibition of Images', *Islamic Studies*, vol. 33, pp. 479–484.

Bæk Simonsen, J.S. (2008) *Politikens bog om islam*. København: JP/Politikens Forlagshus A/S.

Barak, O. (2005) *Names Without Faces: From Polemics to Flirtation in Islamic Chat-Room Nicknaming*. Uppsala: Swedish Science Press.

Baune, I. (2005) 'Youth in Morocco: How Does the Use of the Internet Shape the Daily Life of the Youth and What Are its Repercussions?' In: Baek Simonsen, J. (ed.) *Youth and Youth Culture in the Contemporary Middle East*. Aarhus: Aarhus University Press, pp. 128–139.

Bear, G. (1968) 'Urbanization in Egypt, 1820–1907'. In: Polk, W.R. and R.L. Chambers (eds) *Beginnings of Modernization in the Middle East: The Nineteenth Century*. Chicago: University of Chicago Press, pp. 155–169.

Bektas, Y. (2000) 'The Sultan's Messenger: Cultural Constructions of the Ottoman Telegraphy, 1847–1880', *Technology and Culture*, vol. 41, no. 4, pp. 669–696.

Bentzin, A. (2003) 'Islamic TV programmes as a forum of a religious discourse'. In: Allievi S. and J.S. Nielsen (eds) *Muslim Networks and Transnational Communities in and across Europe*. Leiden: Brill, pp. 170–193.

Berg, H. (2001) 'Computers and the Qur'an'. In: McAuliffe, J.D. (ed.) *Encyclopaeida of the Qur'an*. Leiden and Boston: Brill, vol. 1, pp. 391–395.

Berkes, N. (1971) 'Ibrahim Müteferrika'. In: *EI²*, vol. III, pp. 996–998.

Berkey, J. (2001) *Popular preaching and religious authority in the medieval Islamic Near East*. Seattle: University of Washington Press.

Bernard, J. (2007) 'Media'. In: von Stuckrad, K. (ed.) *The Brill Dictionary of Religion*. Leiden: Brill, vol. III, pp. 1190–1197.

Beyer, P. (2006) *Religions in Global Society*. London: Taylor & Francis Ltd.

Black, G.D. (1998) *The Catholic crusade against the movies, 1940–1975*. Cambridge: Cambridge University Press.

Blair, S. and J. Bloom (2006) 'Inscriptions in art and architecture'. In: McAuliffe, J.D. (ed.) *The Cambridge Companion to the Qur'an*. Cambridge: Cambridge University Press, pp. 163–178.

Bloom, J. (2006) 'Paper Manufacture'. In: Meri, J.W. (ed.) *Medieval Islamic Civilization: An Encyclopaedia*. London and New York: Routledge, vol. 2, pp. 592–593.

Bobzin, H. (1993) 'Latin Koran Translations: A Short Overview', *Der Islam*, vol. 70, pp. 193–206.

Bobzin, H. (2002) 'Von Venedig nach Kairo: Zur Geschichte arabischer Korandrucke (16. – frühes 20. Jahrhundert)'. In: *Sprachen des Nahen Ostens und die Druckrevolution. Eine interkulturelle Begegnung*. Westhofen: WVAVerlag Skulima, pp. 151–176.

Bosworth, C.E. (1976) *The Mediaeval Islamic Underworld: The Banu Sasan in Arabic Society and Literature*. Leiden: Brill Academic Publishers.

Bourdieu, P. (2000) *Om Televisionen*. Swedish translation by Mats Rosengren. Stockholm: Symposion/Brutus Östlings bokförlag.

Bourdieu, P. (1977) 'Sur le pouvoir symbolique', *Annales. ESC.*, vol. 32, pp. 405–411.

Boyd, D.A. (1975) 'Development of Egypt's Radio: "Voice of the Arab's" under Nasser', *Journalism Quarterly*, vol. 52, no. 4, pp. 645–653.

Boyd, D.A. (1982) *Broadcasting in the Arab World: A Survey of Radio and Television in the Middle East*. Philadelphia: Temple University Press.

Boyd, D.A. (1998) 'Television in the Arab World'. In: Smith, A. (ed.) *Television: An International History*. London: Oxford University Press, 1998, pp. 182–187.

Boyd, D.A. and A. Morad (1991) 'Transnational Radio Listening Among Saudi Arabian University Students', *Journalism Quarterly*, vol. 68, no. 1–2, pp. 211–215.

Bray, J. (2006) 'Adab'. In: Meri, J.W. (ed.) *Medieval Islamic Civilization: An Encyclopedia*, vol. I. New York and London: Routledge, pp. 13–14.

Briggs, A. and P. Burke (2002) *A social history of the media: from Gutenberg to the Internet*. Cambridge: Polity.

Brown, J.P. (1849) 'The Corr. Secretary read letters: From Mr *John P. Brown*, relative to an exhibition of Professor *Morse*'s magnetic telegraph before the Sultan', *Journal of the American Oriental Society*, vol. 1, no. 4, pp. liv–lvii.

Buchele, N. (2003) ' "The Matrix" Like its Cold War Predecessors, Reflects Pervasive Anxieties of Our Time', *Arab News* 17/5–2003.

al-Bukhari (1997) *The Translation of the Meanings of Sahih Bukhari*. Riyadh: Darussalam, vol. I–9.

Bulliet, R.W. (1987) 'Medieval Arabic Tarsh: A Forgotten Chapter in the History of Printing', *Journal of the American Oriental Society*, vol. 107, pp. 427–438.

Bunt, G.R. (2000) *Virtually Islamic: Computer-Mediated Communication and Cyber Islamic Environments*. Cardiff: University of Wales Press.

Bunt, G.R. (2003) *Islam in the Digital Age: E-Jihad, Online Fatwas and Cyber Islamic Environments*. London: Pluto Press.

Bunt, G.R. (2004) ' "Rip. Burn. Pray": Islamic Expressions Online'. In: Dawson, L.L. and D.E. Cowan (eds) *Religion Online: Finding Faith on the Internet*. New York and London: Routledge, pp. 123–134.

Bustani Salah al-Din (1986) *Bonaparte's Egypt in picture and word: 1798–1801*. Cairo: Arab Bookshop.

Cahen, C. and M. Talbi (1971) 'Hisba', *EI²*, vol. III, pp. 485–489.

Campbell, H. (2007) ' "What Hath God Wrought?" Considering How Religious Communities Culture (or Kosher) the Cell Phone', *Continuum*, vol. 21, Issue 2, pp. 191–203.

Carlson, E. and C.F. Höpken (1735) 'Beskrifning öfwer tryckeriets inrattning i Constantinople samt dess nowarande tilstand'. Turkish and English trans. In: Akbulut, M. (ed.) *Ibrahmim Müteferrika basimevi ve bastiÿi ilk eserler*. Ankara: Türk Kütüphaneciler Derneπi, pp. 27–30.

Carter, T.F. (1943) 'Islam as a Barrier to Printing', *The Moslem World*, vol. 33, Issue 3, pp. 213–216.

Castells, M. (2001) *The Internet Galaxy: reflections on the Internet, business, and society*. Oxford: Oxford University Press.

Centlivres, P. and M. Centlivres-Demunt (2006) 'The Story of a Picture. Shiite Depictions of Muhammad', *ISIM Review*, no. 17, pp. 18–19.

Chamberlain, M.M. (2002). *Knowledge and Social Practice in Medieval Damascus: 1190–1350*. Cambridge: Cambridge University Press.

Chevedden, P.E. (1984) 'Making Light of Everything: Early Photography in the Middle East and Current Photomania', *Middle East Studies Association Bulletin*, vol. 18, no. 2, pp. 151–174.

Clogg, R. (1979) 'An Attempt to Revive Turkish Printing in Istanbul in 1779', *International Journal of Middle Eastern Studies*, vol. 10, no. 1, pp. 67–70.

Constable, O.R. (1996) *Trade and traders in Muslim Spain: The commercial realignment of the Iberian peninsula, 900–1500*. Cambridge: Cambridge University Press.

Cragg, K. (1995) ' 'Abduh, Muhammad'. In: Esposito, J.L. (ed.) *The Oxford Encyclopedia of the Modern Islamic World*. New York: Oxford University Press, vol. 1, pp. 11–12.

Cunningham, K.J. (2002) 'Factors Influencing Jordan's Information Revolution: Implications for Democracy', *Middle East Journal*, vol. 56, no. 2, pp. 240–256.

Davis, E. (1983) *Challenging Colonialism: Bank Misr and Egyptian Industrialization, 1920–1941*. Princeton, New Jersey: Princeton University Press.

Davison, R.H. (1990) 'The Advent of the Electric Telegraph in the Ottoman Empire'. In: Davison, R.H. (ed.) *Essays in Ottoman and Turkish History, 1774–1923: The Impact of the West*. Austin: University of Texas Press, pp. 133–165.

Delanoue, G. (1971) 'Al-Ikhwan al-Muslimun', *EI²*, vol. III, pp. 1068–1071.

Delanoue, G. (1991) 'Al-Marsafi, Al-Husayn'. In: *EI²*, vol. VI, p. 602.

Denny, W.B. (1995) 'Aesthetic Theory'. In: Esposito, J.L. (ed.) *The Oxford Encyclopedia of the Modern Islamic World*. New York and Oxford. Oxford University Press, vol. 1, pp. 21–23.

Déroche, F. (2006) 'Written Transmission'. In: Rippin, A. (Ed.) *Blackwell Companion to the Qur'an*. Oxford: Blackwell, pp. 172–186.

Devictor, A. (2002) 'Classic Tools, Original Goals: Cinema and Public Policy in the Islamic Republic of Iran (1979–1997)'. In: Tapper, R. (ed.) *The New Iranian Cinema. Politics, Representation and Identity*. London: I.B. Tauris, pp. 66–85.

Dodds, J.D. (ed.) (1992) *Al-Andalus. The Art of Islamic Spain*. New York: Metropolitan Museum of Art.

Doumato, E.A. (1995) 'Marriage and Divorce: Modern Practice'. In: Esposito, J.L. (ed.) *The Oxford Encyclopedia of the Modern Islamic World*. New York and Oxford: Oxford University Press, vol. 3, pp. 50–54.

Dwyer, R. (2006) *Filming the Gods: religion and Indian cinema*. Abingdon: Routledge.

Dönmez-Colin, G. (2004). *Women, Islam and Cinema*. London: Reaktion.

Dönmez-Colin, G. (ed.) (2007) *The Cinema of North Africa and the Middle East*. London: Wallflower Press.

Eddy, W.A. (1963) 'King Ibn Sa'ud: "Our Faith and Your Iron" ', *The Middle East Journal*, Volume XVII, no. 3, pp. 257–263.

Eickelman, D.F. (1978) 'The Art of Memory: Islamic Education and its Social Reproduction', *Comparative Studies in Society and History*, vol. 20, no. 4, pp. 485–516.

Eickelman, D.F. (1992) 'Mass Higher Education and the Religious Imagination in Contemporary Arab Societies', *American Ethnologist*, vol. 19, no. 4, pp. 643–655.

Eickelman, D.F. (2003) 'Communication and Control in the Middle East: Publication and its Discontents'. In: Eickelman, D.F. and J.W. Anderson (eds) *New Media in the Muslim World: The Emerging Public Sphere*. Bloomington: Indiana University Press, pp. 33–44.

Elbendary, A. (2003) 'Matrix Undone', *Al-Ahram Weekly Online* 19–25 June 2003, Issue no. 643 (printed 28–01–2004).

El-Enany, R. (2006) *Arab Representations of the Occident: East-West encounters in Arabic fiction*. London: Routledge.

Ende, W. (1995) 'Rashid, Rida'. In: *EI²*, vol. VIII, pp. 446–448.

El Fadl, K.A. (2001) *Speaking in God's Name: Islamic Law, Authority and Women*. Oxford: Oneworld Publications.

Fahd, T. (1971) 'Hatif'. In: *EI²*, vol. III, p. 18.

Fahd, T. (1995) 'Nusub'. In: *EI²*, vol. VIII, pp. 154–155.

Fatawa Islamiyah: Islamic Verdicts (2002). Riyadh: Darussalam, vol. 1–8.

Fatawa Sirat-e-Mustaqeem (1998) Compilation by Maulana Mahmood Ahmed Mirpuri. Riyadh: Darussalam.

Fierro, M. (1987) 'La polemique a propos de raf 'al-yadayn fi 'salat dans al-Andalus', *Studia Islamica*, vol. 65, pp. 69–90.

Fifth Lateran Council (1512–1517). Studies on its membership, diplomacy and proposals for reform. Edited by Minnich, Nelson H. (1993). Aldershot: Variorum.

The Ferman of Ahmed III on printing. English translation by C.M. Murphy. In Atiyeh, G.N. (ed.) (1995) *The Book in the Islamic World: The Written Word and Communication in the Middle East*. Albany: State University of New York Press, pp. 284–285.

Floor, W.M. (1980) 'The First Printing-Press in Iran', *ZDMG*, vol. 130, pp. 368–371.

Gade, A.M. (2006) 'Recitation'. In: Rippin, A. (ed.) *Blackwell Companion to the Qur'an*. Oxford: Blackwell, pp. 481–493.

Gaffary, F. (1991) 'Cinema (History of Cinema in Persia)'. In: Yarshater, E. (ed.) *Encyclopaedia Iranica*. Costa Mesa: Mazda Publishers, vol. V, pp. XX.

Gal Berner, L. (2002) 'Hearing Hannah's Voice: The Jewish Feminist Challenge and Ritual Innovation'. In: Haddad, Y.Y. and J.L. Esposito (eds) *Daughters of Abraham: Feminist Thought in Judaism, Christianity, and Islam*. Gainesville: University Press of Florida, pp. 35–49.

Gardell, M. (1995) *Countdown to Armageddon: Minister Farrakhan and the Nation of Islam in the Latter Days*. Stockholm: Stockholms Universitet.

van Gelder, G.J.H. (2002) 'Hearing and Deafness'. In: McAuliffe, J.D. (ed.) *Encyclopaedia of the Qur'an*. Leiden and Boston: Brill, vol. II, pp. 405–406.

Gellens, S.I. (1990) 'The Search for Knowledge in Medieval Muslim Societies: a comparative approach'. In Eickelman, D.F. and J. Piscatori (eds) *Muslim travellers: pilgrimage, migration, and the religious imagination*. London: Routledge, pp. 50–65.

Gieling, S. (1998) 'The Iconography of the Islamic Republic of Iran', *ISIM Newsletter*, no. 1, p. 16.

Gilliot, C. (2000) 'Ulama'. In: *EI²*, vol. X, pp. 801–805.

Gilliot, C. (2002) 'Exegesis of the Qur'an: Classical and Medieval'. In: McAuliffe, J.D. (ed.) *Encyclopaedia of the Qur'an*. Leiden and Boston: Brill, vol. V, pp. 99–124.

Glass, D. and G. Roper (2002) 'Part I: The Printing of Arabic Books in the Arab World'. In: Hanebutt-Benz, E. et al. (eds) *Middle Eastern Languages and the Print Revolution: A Cross-cultural Encounter: A Catalogue and Companion to the Exhibition*. Westhofen: WVA-Verlag Skulima/Gutenberg-Museum Mainz, pp. 177–206.

Goborieau, M. (2000) 'Tablighi Djama'at'. In: *EI²*, vol. X, pp. 38–39.

Gonzalez-Quijano, Y. (2003) 'The Birth of a Media Ecosystem: Lebanon in the Internet Age'. In: Eickelman, D.F. and J.W. Anderson (eds) *New Media in the Muslim World: The Emerging Public Sphere*. Bloomington: Indiana University Press, pp. 61–79.

Grabar, O. (1954) 'The Painting of the Six Kings at Qusayr 'Amrah', *Ars Orientalis*, vol. I, pp. 185–187.

Grabar, O. (1959) 'The Umayyad Dome of the Rock in Jerusalem', *Ars Orientalis*, vol. III, pp. 33–62.

Graber, O. and M. Natif (2003) 'The Story of Portraits of the Prophet Muhammad', *Studia Islamica*, vol. 96, 19–36.

Graham, W.A. (1987) *Beyond the Written Word: oral aspects of scripture in the history of religion*. Cambridge: Cambridge University Press.

Graham, W.A. and N. Kermani (2006) 'Recitation and aesthetic reception'. In. McAuliffe, J.D. (ed.) *Cambridge Companion to the Qur'an*. Cambridge: Cambridge University Press, pp. 115–144.

Gräf, B. (2007) 'Sheikh Yusuf al-Qaradawi in Cyberspace', *Die Welt des Islams*, vol. 47, no. 3–4, pp. 403–423.

Gräf, B. (2008) 'IslamOnline.net: Independent, interactive, popular', *Arab Media and Society*, retrieved from http://www.arabmediasociety.com/?article=576.

Gräf, B. and J. Skovgaard-Petersen (eds) (2009) *Global Mufti: The Phenomenon of Yusuf al-Qaradawi*. London: Hurst & Company.

Günay, A.K. (1991) 'Matba'a. 2. In Turkey'. In: *EI²*, vol. VI, pp. 799–803.

Günter, S. (2002) 'Muhammad, the Illiterate Prophet: An Islamic Creed in the Qur'an and Qur'anic Exegesis', *Journal of Qur'anic Studies*, vol. IV, Issue 1, pp. 1–26.

Hackett, R. (2006) 'Mediated Religion in South Africa: Balancing airtime and rights claims'. In: Meyer, B. and A. Moors (eds) *Religion, Media, and the Public Sphere*. Bloomington: Indiana University Press, pp. 166–187.

Halldén, P. (2001) *Islamisk predikan på ljudkassett. En studie i retorik och fonogramologi*. Stockholm: Almqvist & Wiksell International.

Halldén, P. (2006a) 'Från Muhammad till mp3'. In: Larsson, G. et al.(eds) *Religion och medier. Några perspektiv*. Lund: Studentlitteratur, pp. 81–101.

Halldén, P. (2006b) 'Militant Salafism on the Internet: "Alneda.com" and the legacy of Yusuf al-'Ayyiri'. In: Larsson, G. (ed.) *Religious Communities on the Internet: Proceedings form a conference*. Uppsala: Swedish Science Press, pp. 62–85.

Hammam, M.Y. (1951) 'History of Printing in Egypt', *Gutenberg-Jahrbuch*, pp. 156–159.

Hammond, A. (2005) *Pop Culture Arab World! Media, Arts, and Lifestyle*. Santa Barbara: ABC-Clio.

Hamzawy, A. (2000) 'Processes of Local Deconstruction of Global Events, News, And Discursive Messages: Case Studies from Egypt'. In: Utvik, B.O. and K.S. Vikør (eds) *The Middle East in a Globalized World. Papers from the Fourth Nordic Conference on Middle Eastern Studies, Oslo 1998*. Bergen: Nordic Society for Middle Eastern Studies, pp. 130–149.

Hanan, D. (1997) 'Indonesian Cinema'. In: Nowell-Smith, G. (ed.) *The Oxford History of World Cinema*. New York: Oxford University Press, pp. 690–692.

Hanebutt-Benz, E.-M. (ed.) (2002) *Middle Eastern Languages and the Print Revolution: A cross cultural encounter: A catalogue and companion to the exhibition*. Westhofen: WVA-Verl. Skulima.

Hashim Kamali, M. (1987) 'Qiyas'. In: Eliade, M. (ed.) *The Encyclopedia of Religion*. New York and London: MacMillan Publishing Company, vol. 12, pp. 128–129.

Hawting, G. (2002) 'Idols and Images'. In: McAuliffe, J.D. (ed.) *Encyclopaedia of the Qur'an*. Leiden and Boston: Brill, vol. I, pp. 481–484.

Hefner, R.W. and M.Q. Zaman (eds) (2007) *Schooling Islam: The culture and politics of modern Muslim education*. Princeton, NJ: Princeton University Press.

Helland, C. (2005) 'Online Religion as Lived Religion: Methodological Issues in the Study of Religious Participation on the Internet', *Online – Heidelberg Journal of Religions on the Internet*, vol. 1.1.

Herring, S. (1996) 'Posting in a Different Voice: Gender and Ethics in CMC'. In Ess, C. (ed.) *Philosophical Perspectives on Computer-Mediated Communication*. Albany: State University of New York Press, pp. 115–146.

Heyworth-Dunne, J. (1940) 'Printing and Translations under Muhammad "Ali of Egypt: The Foundation of Modern Arabic" ', *The Journal of the Royal Asiatic Society*, no. 3, pp. 325–349.

Hirschkind, C. (2003) 'Media and the Qur'an'. In: McAuliffe, J.D. (ed.) *The Encyclopaedia of the Qur'an*. Leiden and Boston: Brill, vol. 2, pp. 341–349.

Hirschkind, C. (2006) *The Ethical Soundscape: Cassette sermons and Islamic counterpublics*. New York: Columbia University Press.

Hourani, A. (1946) *Syria and Lebanon: A Political Essay*. New York: Oxford University Press.

Högfeldt, K. et al. (2008) *Muhammed-karikatyrer och rondellhundar: reaktioner, bakgrund och sammanhang.* Göteborg: Social resursförvaltning, Göteborgs stad.

Ilal, E. (1987) 'On Turkish Cinema'. In: Downing, J.D.H. (ed.) *Film and Politics in the Third World.* New York: Autonomedia, Inc., pp. 119–129.

Imam Malik ibn Anas (1989) *Al-Muwatta of Imam Malik Ibn Anas. The first formulation of Islamic law.* English translation by Aisha Abdurrahman Bewley. London: Kegan Paul.

Issawi, C. (1988) *The Fertile Crescent 1800–1914: A Documentary Economic History.* New York and Oxford: Oxford University Press.

Al-Jabarti, 'Abd al-Rahman (1993) *Napoleon in Egypt: Al-Jabartî's chronicle of the French occupation of Egypt, 1798.* English translation by Smuel Moreh, with an introduction by Robert L. Tignor. Princeton: M. Wiener Publications.

James, L.M. (2006) 'What Voice? Nasser, the Arabs, and "Sawt al-Arab Radio" ', *Transnational Broadcasting Studies*, vol. 16. Retrieved from http://www.tbsjournal.com/James.html.

Jeffery, A. (1960) 'Aya'. In: *EI²*, vol. I, pp. 773–774.

Jomier, J. (1960) 'Al-Azhar'. In: *EI²*, vol. I, pp. 813–821.

Jonker, G. (2000) 'Islamic Television "Made in Berlin" '. In: Dassetto, F. (ed.) *Paroles d'Islam. Des nouveauz Discourses islamiques in Europe.* Strasbourg: Gallimard, pp. 267–280.

Juynboll, G.H.A. (1969) *The Authenticity of the Tradition Literature: Discussions in Modern Egypt.* Leiden: E.J. Brill.

Juynboll, G.H.A. (2007) *Encyclopedia of Canonical Hadith.* Leiden: Brill.

Kaplan, Y. (1997) 'Turkish Cinema'. In: Nowell-Smith, G. (ed.) *The Oxford History of World Cinema.* New York: Oxford University Press.

Kaptein, N. (1993) *Muhammad's Birthday Festival: early history in the central Muslim lands and development in the Muslim west until the 10th/16th century.* Leiden: Brill.

Karic, E. (2002) 'Gambling'. In: McAuliffe, J.D. (ed.) *The Encyclopaedia of the Qur'an.* Leiden and Boston: Brill, vol. II, pp. 280–282.

Kassis, H.E. (1983). *A Concordance of the Qur'an.* Berkeley: University of California Press.

Al-Kaysi, M.I. (1989) *Morals and Manners in Islam: A Guide to Islamic Adab.* Leicester: The Islamic Foundation.

Keddie, N.R. (1995) 'al-'Afghani, Jamal al-Din'. In: Esposito, J.L. (ed.) *The Oxford Encyclopedia of the Modern Islamic World.* New York: Oxford University Press, vol. 1, pp. 23–27.

Kennerberg, O. (1996) *Innanför och utanför. En studie av församlingsstrukturen i nio svenska frikyrkoförsamlingar.* Uppsala: Uppsala universitet.

Kepel, G. (1985) *The Prophet and Pharaoh: Muslim Extremism in Egypt.* London: Al Saqi Books.

Khalid, A. (1994) 'Printing, Publishing, and Reform in Tsarist Central Asia', *International Journal of Middle East Studies*, vol. 26, no. 2, pp. 187–200.

Khatib, L. (2004) 'The Orient and its Others: Women as Tools of Nationalism in Egyptian Political Cinema'. In: Sakr, N. (ed.) *Women and Media in the Middle East: Power Through Self-Expression*. London and New York: I.B. Tauris, pp. 72–88.

Khomeini, Imam Ruhullah al-Musavi (1981) *Islam and Revolution: Writings and Declarations of Imam Khomeini*. Translated and annotated by Hamid Algar. Berkeley: Mizan Press.

Kilgour, F.G. (1998). *The Evolution of the Book*. New York: Oxford University Press.

Kreiser, K. (2001) 'Causes of the Decrease of Ignorance? Remarks on the Printing of Books in the Ottoman Empire'. In: *The Beginnings of Printing in the Near and Middle East: Jews, Christians and Muslims*. Wiesbaden: Harrassowitz, pp. 13–17.

Kuhn, A. (1989) *Cinema, Censorship and Sexuality, 1909–1925*. London and New York: Routledge.

Kunin, S.D. (2002) 'Judaism'. In: Woodhead, L. (ed.) *Religions in the modern world: traditions and transformations*. London: Routledge, pp. 128–152.

Krämer, G. (2006) 'Anti-Semitism in the Muslim World: A Critical Review', *Die Welt des Islams*, vol. 46, no. 3, pp. 243–276.

Lahiji, S. (2002) 'Chaste Dolls and Unchaste Dolls: Women in Iranian Cinema since 1979'. In: Tapper, R. (ed.) *The New Iranian Cinema: Politics, Representation and Identity*. London. I.B. Tauris, pp. 215–226.

Lambert, Y. (2003) 'New Christianity Indifference and Diffused Spirituality'. In: McLeod, H. and W. Ustorf (eds) *The Decline of Christendom in Western Europe, 1750–2000*. Cambridge: Cambridge University Press, pp. 67–78.

Landau, J.M. (1958) *Studies in the Arab Theater and Cinema*. Philadelphia: University of Pennsylvania Press.

Landau, J.M. (1965) 'Cinema'. In: *EI²*, vol. II, pp. 39–40.

Landau, J.M. (1971) *The Hejaz Railway and the Muslim Pilgrimage: A Case of Ottoman Political Propaganda*. Detroit: Wayne State University Press.

Landau, J.M. (2000) 'Taswir' [In the sense of photography]. In: *EI²*, vol. X, pp. 363–364.

Landman, N. (1997) 'The Islamic Broadcasting Foundation in the Netherlands: Platform or Arena?'. In Vertovec, S. and C. Peach (eds) *Islam in Europe: The Politics of Religion and Community*. London: Macmillan, pp. 224–244.

Lane, E.W. (1908) *The Manners and Customs of the Modern Egyptians*. London: J.M. Dent & Co.

Lane, E.W. (1973) *An Account of the Manners and Customs of the Modern Egyptians*. Facsimile of the 1860 edition with a new introduction by Jon Manchip White. New York: Dover Publications Inc.

Larkin, B. (1999) 'Cinema Theatres and Moral Space in Northern Nigeria', *ISIM/ Newsletter*, no. 3, p. 13.

Larkin, B. (2002) 'The Materiality of Cinema Theaters in Northern Nigeria'. In: Ginsburg, F.D. et al. (eds) *Media Worlds: Anthropology on New Terrain.* Berkeley: University of California Press, pp. 319–336.

Larsson, G. (2003) *Ibn Garcá's shu'ubiyya Letter: Ethnic and Theological Tensions in Medieval al-Andalus.* Leiden: Brill.

Larsson, G. (2004a) 'Don't Believe the Hype. Musik, identitet och religion bland unga muslimer'. In: Häger, A. (ed.) *Tro, pop och kärlek.* Åbo: Åbo Akademi, pp. 81–92.

Larsson, G. (2004b) 'Islam Online', *Internationella studier*, Nr 4, pp. 3–7.

Larsson, G. (2005) 'The Death of a Virtual Muslim Discussion Group', *Online – Heidelberg Journal for Religions on the Internet.* Retrieved from http://www.online.uni-hd.de/

Larsson, G. (2006a) 'Animerad film i islams tjänst'. In: Larsson, G. et al. (eds) *Religion och medier. Några perspektiv.* Lund: Studentlitteratur, pp. 103–119.

Larsson, G. (2006b) 'Sidrat ul-Muntaha: an Alternative Voice for Swedish Muslims in Cyberspace'. In: Larsson, G. (ed.) *Religious Communities on the Internet: Proceedings form a conference.* Stockholm and Uppsala: Swedish Science Press, pp. 86–105.

Larsson, G. (2007) 'Cyber-Islamophobia? The Case of WikiIslam', *Contemporary Islam*, vol. 1, pp. 53–67.

Larsson, G. (2010) 'Yusuf al-Qaradawi and Tariq Ramadan on Secularisation: Differences and Similarities'. In: G. Marranci (ed.), *Muslim Societies and the Challenge of Secularization: An Interdisciplinary Approach.* Dordrecht: Springer, pp. 47–63.

Larsson, G. (in print) ' "It's all About Magic": A fatwa on Harry Potter: Online fatawa, wasatiyya, and new challenges for the Global Muslim Community'. In: Stenberg, L. (ed.) *Science, Technology and Entrepreneurship in the Muslim World.* Utah: Utah University Press.

Larsson, G. and L. Lindekilde (2009) 'Muslim Claims-making in Context: Comparing the Danish and the Swedish Muhammad Cartoons Controversies', *Ethnicities*, vol. 9, no. 3, pp. 361–382.

Leaman, O. (ed.) (2001) *Companion Encyclopedia of Middle Eastern and North African Film.* London: Routledge.

Leemhuis, F. (2006) 'From Palm Leaves to the Internet'. In. McAuliffe, J.D. (ed.) *Cambridge Companion to the Qur'an.* Cambridge: Cambridge University Press, pp. 145–162.

Livingstone, J.W. (1995) 'Muhammad Abduh on Science', *Muslim World*, vol. 85, no. 3, pp. 215–234.

Lewis, B. (1996) *Cultures in Conflicts: Christians, Muslims and Jews in the Age of Discovery.* New York: Oxford University Press.

Lewis, B. (1999) *Semites and Anti-Semites: An Inquiry into Conflict and Prejudice.* New York: Norton & Company, INC.

Lewis, B. (1937) 'The Islamic Guilds', *The Economic History Review*, pp. 20–37.

Linant de Bellefonds, Y. (1965) 'Darura'. In: *EI²*, vol. II, pp. 163–164.

Livingston, J. (1997) 'Shaykhs Jabarti and 'Attar: Islamic Reaction and Response to Western Science in Egypt', *Der Islam*, vol. 74, no. 1, pp. 92–106.

Lohlker, R. (2000) *Islam im Internet: Neue Formen der Religion im Cyberspace*. Hamburg: Deutsches Orient-Institut.

Lukes, S. (1974) *Power – a radical view*. London: MacMillan.

Maamouri, M. (2008) 'Literacy'. In: Versteegh, K. (ed.) *Encyclopedia of Arabic Language and Linguistics*, vol. III. Leiden: Brill, pp. 74–80.

Mahdi, M. (1995) 'From the Manuscript Age to the Age of Printed Books'. In: Atiyeh, G.N. (ed.) (1995) *The Book in the Islamic World: The Written Word and Communication in the Middle East*. New York: State University of New York Press, pp. 1–16.

Majallat al-Azhar (1959) Al-Mushaf al-Murattal, vol. 30, p. 926.

Mandaville, P. (2001) 'Reimagining Islam in Diaspora: The Politics of Mediated Community', *Gazette*, vol. 63, no. 2–3, pp. 169–186.

Mariani, E. (2006) 'The Role of States and Markets in the Production of Islamic Knowledge On-Line: the Example of Yusuf al-Qaradawi and Amru Khaled'. In: Larsson, G. (ed.) *Religious Communities on the Internet: Proceedings from a Conference*. Uppsala: Swedish Science Press, pp. 131–149.

Marin, M. (1992) *Individuo y sociedad en al-Andalus*. Madrid: Mappfre.

Markussen, H.I. (2005) 'En studie av muslimsk dekor i frisörsalonger i Bergen: Teoretiske og metodologiske implikasjoner'. In: Markussen, H.I. and R.J. Natvig (eds) *Islamer i Norger*. Uppsala: Swedish Science Press, pp. 33–37.

Markussen, H.I. (2006) 'Feltarbeid som metodisk strategi i motet med masseproduserte religiose bilder'. In: Kraft, S.E. and R.J. Natvig (eds) *Metode i religionsvitenskap*. Oslo: Pax Forlag A/S, pp. 162–180.

Masud, M.K. (1984) '*Adab al-Mufti*: The Muslim Understanding of Values, Characteristics, and Role of a Mufti'. In: Metcalf, B.D. (ed.) *Moral conduct and authority: the place of adab in South Asian Islam*. Berkeley: University of California Press, pp. 124–151.

Masud, M.K. et al. (1996) 'Muftis, Fatwas, and Islamic Legal Interpretation'. In: Masud, M.K. et al. (eds) *Islamic Legal Interpretation: Muftis and Their Fatwas*. Cambridge, Massachusetts: Harvard University Press, pp. 3–32.

McLuhan, M. (1964) *Understanding Media: The extensions of man*. London: Routledge.

Messick, B. (1996) 'Media Muftis: Radio Fatwas in Yemen'. In: Masud, M.K. et al.(eds) *Islamic Legal Interpretation: Muftis and Their Fatwas*. Cambridge, Massachusetts: Harvard University Press, pp. 311–320.

Messick, B. (1997) 'On the Question of Lithography', *Culture and History*, vol. 16.

Metcalf, B.D. (1982) *Islamic Revival in British India: Deoband, 1869–1900*. New Jersey: Princeton University Press.

Metcalf, B.D. (ed.) (1984) *Moral Conduct and Authority: The place of adab in South Asian Islam*. Berkeley: University of California Press.

Metcalf, B.D. (ed.) (1996a) *Making Muslim Space in North America and Europe*. Berkeley: University of California Press.

Metcalf, B.D. (1996b) 'Introduction: Sacred Words, Sanctioned Practice, New Communities'. In: Metcalf, B.D. (ed.) *Making Muslim Space in North America and Europe*. Berkeley: University of California Press, pp. 1–27.

Mirbakhtyar, S. (2006). *Iranian Cinema and the Islamic Revolution*. Jefferson, N.C.: McFarland.

Mirpuri, M.M.A. (1998) *Fatawa: Sirat-e-Mustaqeem*. Riyadh: Darussalam.

Mitchell, T. (1991) *Colonising Egypt*. Berkeley: University of California Press.

Mitchell, R.P. (1993) *The Society of the Muslim Brothers*. Oxford: Oxford University Press.

Mostyn, T. (2002). *Censorship in Islamic societies*. London: Saqi.

Mowlana, H. (1995a) 'Communications Media'. In: Esposito, J.L. (ed.) *The Oxford Encyclopedia of the Modern Islamic World*. New York: Oxford University Press, vol. 1, pp. 300–304.

Mowlana, H. (1995b) 'Radio and Television'. In: Esposito, J. (ed.) *The Oxford Encyclopedia of the Modern Islamic World*, vol. 3. New York: Oxford University Press, vol. 3, pp. 405–407.

Al-Munajjid, Muhammad Salih (2004) *Muharramat. Forbidden Matters Some People Take Lightly*. Riyad: International Islamic Publishing House.

Muslim, Imam (1990) *Sahih Muslim. Rendered into English by Abdul Hamid Siddiqi*. Lahore: Sh. Muhammad Ashraf Booksellers & Exporters, 8 vols.

Mühlböck, M. (1988). 'Die Entwicklung der Massenmedien am Arabischen Golf'. Unpublished doctoral dissertation, University of Wien, Austria.

Müteferrika, I. (1727) *Vesiletu-t Tibaa*. English translation by Murphy, C.M. In: Atiyeh, G.N. (ed.) (1995) *The Book in the Islamic World: The Written Word and Communication in the Middle East*. Albany: State University of New York Press, pp. 286–292.

Möller, A. (2005) *Ramadan in Java: The Joy and Jihad of Ritual Fasting*. Lund: Lunds Universitet.

Naficy, H. (1995) 'Cassettes'. In: Esposito, J. (ed.) *The Oxford Encyclopedia of the Modern Islamic World*, vol. 1. New York: Oxford University Press, vol. 1, pp. 265–270.

Naficy, H. (2002) 'Islamizing Film Culture in Iran: A Post-Khatami Update'. In: Tapper, R. (ed.) *The New Iranian Cinema. Politics, Representation and Identity*. London: I.B. Tauris, pp. 26–65.

Naguib, S.-.A. (2001) *Mosques in Norway. The Creation and Iconography of Sacred Space*. Oslo: Novus forlag.

Nasr, S.H. (1999) *A Young Muslim's Guide to the Modern World*. Cambridge: The Islamic Text Society.

An-Nawawi, Abu Zakariya Yahya Ibn Sharaf (1997) *Forty Hadith: An Anthology of the Sayings of the Prophet Muhammad*. Cambridge: Islamic Text Society.

El-Nawawy, M. and A. Iskander (2002) *Al-Jazeera: How the Free Arab News Network Scooped the World and Changed the Middle East.* Cambridge, MA: Westview Press.

Nelson, K. (2001). *The Art of Reciting the Qur'an.* Cairo: American University in Cairo Press.

Netton, I.R. (1997) *A Popular Dictionary of Islam.* Richmond: Curzon.

Netton, I.R. (2003) 'Nature as Signs'. In: McAuliffe, J.D. (ed.) *Encyclopaedia of the Qur'an.* Leiden and Boston: Brill, vol. III, pp. 528–536.

O'Connor, K.M. (2001) 'Amulets'. In: McAuliffe, J.D. (ed.) *Encyclopaedia of the Qur'an.* Leiden and Boston: Brill, vol. I, pp. 77–79.

Oman, G. (1991) 'Matbaʿa. 5. In the *Maghrib*'. In: *EI²*, vol. VI, pp. 798–799.

Otterbeck, J. (2004) 'Music as a Useless Activity: Conservative Interpretations of Music in Islam'. In: Korpe, M. (ed.) *Shoot the Singer: Music Censorship Today.* London and New York: Yed Books, pp. 11–16.

Owen, R. and Pamuk, S. (1998) *A History of Middle East Economies in the Twentieth Century.* London: I.B. Tauris.

Parker, A. and Neal, A. (1995) *Hajj Paintings: Folk Art of the Great Pilgrimage.* Washington and London: Smithsonian Institution Press.

Pearl, David (1987). *A Textbook on Muslim Personal Law.* London: Croom Helm.

Pedersen, J. (1946) *Den arabiske bog.* København: Fischers forlag.

Peters, R. (1980) 'Idjtihad and Taqlid in 18th and 19th Century Islam', *Die Welt des Islams*, vol. XX, no. 3–4, pp. 131–145.

Peters, R. (1986) 'Religious Attitudes Towards Modernization in the Ottoman Empire: A Nineteenth Century Pious Text on Steamship, Factories and the Telegraph', *Die Welt des Islams*, vol. XXVI, no. 1–4, pp. 76–105.

Peters, R. (1996) 'The Lions of Qasr al-Nil Bridge: The Islamic Prohibition of Images as an Issue in the "Urabi Revolt"'. In: Masud, M.K. et al. (eds) *Islamic Legal Interpretation: Muftis and their Fatwas.* Cambridge, MA: Harvard University Press, pp. 214–220.

Peters, R. (2002) 'Zina'. In: *EI²*, vol. XI, pp. 509–510.

Pitt-Rivers, J. (1968) 'Honor'. In: Sills, D.L. (ed.) *International Encyclopedia of the Social Sciences*, vol. 5. New York and London: The MacMillan Company & The Free Press, pp. 503–511.

Plato (2002). *Phaedrus.* Translated with an introduction and notes by Robin Waterfield. Oxford: Oxford University Press.

al-Qaradawi, Y. (1985/2001) *The Lawful and the Prohibited in Islam.* Cairo: Al-Falah.

al-Qaradawi, Y. (without year) *Diversion and Arts in Islam.* Cairo: Islamic Inc. Publishing & Distribution.

al-Qaradawi, Y (without year) *Time in the Life of the Muslim.* Cairo: Al Falah Foundation.

Ramadan, T. (2002) *To Be a European Muslim: A Study of Islamic Sources in the European Context.* Leicester: The Islamic Foundation.

Ramadan, T. (2004) *Western Muslims and the Future of Islam*. Oxford: Oxford University Press.

Ramsey, G. (2007) 'Speaking up with Yahoo: An Arabic e-mail novel'. In: Isaksson, B. et al. (eds) *The Professorship of Semitic Languages at Uppsala University 400 years: Jubilee Volume from a Symposium held at the University Hall, 21–23 September 2005*. Uppsala: Studia Semitica Upsaliensia 24, pp. 179–190.

Rashid Rida (1908) 'Suwar al-yad wa 'l-suwar al-shamsiyya', *Al-Manar*, vol. XI/4, 30 May, pp. 277–278.

Repp, R.C. (1997) 'Shaykh al-Islam (In the Ottoman Empire)', *EI²*, Vo. IX. Leiden: Brill, pp. 400–402.

Rippin, A. (2000) 'The Study of Tafsir in the 21st Century: E-Texts and Their Scholarly Use'. Retrieved from http://www.mela.us/MELANotes/MELANotes6970/tafsir.html.

Roald, A.-S. (1999) 'Evas andra ansikte – muslimska kvinnoaktiviteter'. In: Svanberg, I. and D. Westerlund (eds) *Blågul islam? Muslimer i Sverige*. Nora: Nya Doxa, pp. 123–139.

Roald, A.-S. (2001) 'The Wise Men: Democratisation and gender equalisation in the Islamic message: Yusuf al–Qaradawi and Ahmad al–Kubaisi on the air', *Encounters* 7:1. pp. 29–55.

Roald, A.-S. (2003) 'Polygamy on the Air: Reactions to the Egyptian TV Serial Al-hajj Mutwalli', *Social Compass*, vol. 50, pp. 47–57.

Roald, A.-S. (2004) 'Arab Satellite Broadcasting – The Immigrants' Extended Ear to their Homelands'. In: Malik, J. (ed.) *Muslims in Europe: From the Margin to the Centre*. Münster: LIT-Verlag, pp. 207–226.

Robinson, F. (1993) 'Technology and Religious: Islam and the Impact of Print', *Modern Asian Studies*, vol. 27, no. 1, pp. 229–251.

Robinson, N. (2003) *Discovering the Qur'an: a contemporary approach to a veiled text*. Washington, DC: Georgetown University Press.

Rohnström, J. (1988) 'The Turkish Incunabula in the Royal Library, Stockholm: A Catalogue'. In: Ehrensvärd, U. (ed.) *Turcica et Orientalia: Studies in Honour of Gunnar Jarring on his Eightieth Birthday, 12 October 1987*. Stockholm: Almqvist & Wiksell International, pp. 121–138.

Rosenthal, F. (1970) *Knowledge Triumphant: The concept of knowledge in medieval Islam*. Leiden: Brill.

Rosenthal, F. (1986) 'La'ib'. In: *EI²*, vol. V, pp. 615–616.

Rosenthal, F. (2000) 'Tashif'. In: *EI²*, vol. X, pp. 347–348.

Rooke, T. (2003) *Den nya arabiska översättningsrörelsen – ett svenskt perspektiv*. Trelleborg: Svenska Institutet i Alexandria.

Roy, O. (1994) *The Failure of Political Islam*. Cambridge, Massachusetts: Harvard University Press.

Roy, O. (2004) *Globalised Islam: The Search for a New Ummah*. London: Hurst & Company.

Roy, O. (2008) *The Politics of Chaos in the Middle East*. New York: Colombia University Press.

Rugberg Rasmussen, T. (1994) 'The Ideology of Gharbzadegi'. In: Erslev Andersen, L. (ed.) *Middle East studies in Denmark*. Odensen: Odense University Press, pp. 171–179.

Rugh, W.A. (2004) *The Arab Mass Media: newspapers, radio, and television in Arab politics*. Westport, CT: Praeger.

The Ruling on Tasweer (2002) Riyadh: Darussalam.

Sadoul, G. (ed.) (1966) *Les Cinémas des pays arabes*. Beyrouth: Centre Interarabe du Cinéma et la Television.

Saʻid, Labib (1975). *The recited Koran: a history of the first recorded version*. Princeton, NJ.

Sakr, N. (2001) *Satellite Realms: Transnational Television, Globalization and the Middle East*. London and New York: I.B. Tauris.

Salvatore, A. (1997) *Islam and the Political Discourse of Modernity*. Reading: Ithaca Press.

Sardar, Z. (2003) 'Paper, Printing and Compact Discs: The Making and Unmaking of Islamic Culture'. In: Inayatullah, S. and G. Boxwell (eds) *Islam, Postmodernism and Other Futures: A Ziauddin Sardar Reader*. London: Pluto Press, pp. 89–105.

AlSayyad, N. (ed.) (1992) *Forms of Dominance: on the architecture and urbanism of the colonial enterprise*. Aldershot: Avebury.

Schacht, J. (1960a) 'Ashab al-Ra'y'. In: *EI²*, vol. I, p. 692.

Schacht, J. (1960b) 'Ahl al-Hadith'. In: *EI²*, vol. I, pp. 258–259.

Schacht, J. (1995a) 'Nikah (In Classical Islamic Law)'. In: *EI²*, vol. VIII, pp. 26–29.

Schacht, J. (1995b) 'Zina'. In: Gibb, H.A.R. and J.H. Kramers (eds) *Shorter Encyclopaedia of Islam*. Leiden: E.J. Brill, pp. 658–659.

Schaeffer, K. (2002) 'Arabic Printing before Gutenburg: Block-printed amuletes'. In: Hannebutt-Benz, E. et al. (eds) *Sprachen des Nahen Ostens und die Druckrevolution; eine interkulturelle Begegnung*. Westhofen: WVA-Verlag Skulima, pp. 123–128, 475–478.

Schimmel, A. (1987) 'Islamic Iconography'. In: Eliade, M. (ed.) *The Encyclopedia of Religion*. New York: Macmillan Publishing Company, vol. 7, pp. 64–67.

Schleifer, Abdallah S. (2004) 'Interview with Sheikh Yusuf al-Qaradawi', *Transnational Broadcasting Studies*, no. 13/Fall 2004. Retrieved from http://www.tbsjournal.com/Archives/Fall04/interviewyusufqaradawi.htm

Schulze, R. (1997) 'The Birth of Tradition and Modernity in 18th and 19th Century Islamic Culture – The Case of Printing', *Culture and History*, vol. 16, pp. 29–72.

Şeker, N. (2009) *Die Fotografie im Osmanischen Reich*. Würzburg: Ergon Verlag.

Sellheim, R. (1995) 'Samaʻ '. In: *EI²*, vol. VIII, pp. 1018–1020.

Shafik, V. (2000) *Arab Cinema: History and Cultural Identity*. Cairo: The American University in Cairo Press.

Shahba, M. (2005) 'Iqra: Channel with a Mission', *Transnational Broadcasting Studies*, no. 14/Spring 2005. Retrieved from http://www.tbsjournal.com/ Archives/Spring05/shaba.html

Shaheen, J.G. (2001) *Reel Bad Arabs: How Hollywood Vilifies a People.* New York: Olive Branch Press.

Shahin, E.E. (1994) *Through Muslim Eyes: M. Rashid Rida and the West.* Herndon, Virginia: International Institute of Islamic Thought.

Shahin, E.E. (1995) 'Salafiyah'. In: Esposito, J.L. (ed.) *The Oxford Encyclopedia of the Modern Islamic World.* New York: Oxford University Press,, vol. 3, pp. 463–469.

Shakir, Abu Muhamed Abdur-Ra'uf (without year) *The Islamic Ruling Concerning Tasweer.* Philadelphia, PA: Zakee Muwwakkil's Books & Articles, CWP Publishers.

Shinar, P. (1995) 'Salafiyya'. In: *EI²* vol. VIII, pp. 900–906.

Shoshan, B. (1993). *Popular culture in medieval Cairo.* Cambridge: Cambridge University Press.

Sikand, Y. (2006) 'Deoband's War on Television: Fury over a fatwa', *ISIM Review*, vol. 17, pp. 48–49.

Silverstein, A.J. (2007) *Postal Systems in the Pre-Modern Islamic World.* Cambridge: Cambridge University Press.

Silverstone, R. et al. (1992) 'Information and communication technologies and the moral economy of the household'. In: Silverstein, R. and E. Hirsch (eds) *Consuming Technologies: Media and Information in Domestic Spaces.* London and New York: Routledge, pp. 15–31.

Skovgaard-Petersen, J. (1997a) *Defining Islam for the Egyptian State: Muftis and Fatwas of the Dar al-Ifta.* Leiden: Brill.

Skovgaard-Petersen, J. (1997b) 'Fatwas in Print', *Culture and History*, vol. 16, pp. 73–88.

Skovgaard-Petersen, J. (2001) 'Introduction. Public Places and Public Spheres in Transformation – The City Conceived, Perceived and Experienced'. In: Korsholm Nielsen, H.C. and J. Skovgaard-Petersen (eds) *Middle Eastern Cities 1900–1950. Public Places and Public Spheres in Transformation.* Aarhus: Aarhus University Press, pp. 9–19.

Skovgaard-Petersen, J. (2004) 'The Global Mufti'. In: Stenberg, L. and B. Schaebler, B. (eds) *Globalization and the Muslim World: Culture, Religion, and Modernity.* New York: Syracuse University Press, pp. 153–165.

Snouck Hurgronje, C. (1889) *Bilder aus Mekka. Mit kurzem erläuterndem Texte.* Leiden: Brill.

Snouck Hurgronje, C. (1900) 'Islam and the Phonograph', *Tijdschritt Indische T.L.V.*, Vol. XLII, pp. 392–427.

Snouck Hurgronje, C. (1915) 'Islam and the Phonograph', *Moslem World*, vol. 5, Issue 2, pp. 159–165.

Snouck Hurgronje, C. (1970/1931) *Mekka in the latter part of the 19th century: daily life, customs and learning, the Moslims of the East-Indian-archipelago.* Leiden: Brill.

Sonbol, A.A. (2002) 'Rethinking Women and Islam'. In: Haddad, Y.Y. and J.L. Esposito (eds) *Daughters of Abraham: Feminist Thought in Judaism, Christianity, and Islam.* Florida: University Press of Florida, pp. 108–146.

Soucek, P.P. (2000) 'Taswir'. In: *EI²*, vol. X, pp. 361–365.

Sreberny-Mohammadi, A. and A. Mohammadi (1994) *Small Media, Big Revolution: Communication, culture, and the Iranian revolution.* Minneapolis: University of Minnesota Press.

Starrett, G.S. (1995) 'The Political Economy of Religious Commodities in Cairo', *American Anthropologist*, vol. 97, no. 1, pp. 51–68.

Starrett, G.S. (1996) 'The Margins of Print: Children's Religious Literature in Egypt', *The Journal of the Royal Anthropological Institute*, vol. 2, no. 1, pp. 117–139.

Steger, M.B. (2003) *Globalization: A Very Short Introduction.* Oxford: Oxford University Press.

The Sunna Project: *Encyclopaedia of Hadith: The Ihsan Network.* Liechtenstein: Thesaurus Islamicus Foundation (no year).

Tal (1971) 'Responsa'. In: *Encyclopaedia Judaica*. Jerusalem: Keter Publishing, vol. 14, pp. 83–95.

Tamari, I.J. (2001) 'Jewish Printing and Publishing Activities in the Ottoman Cities of Constantinopel and Salonik at the Dawn of Early Modern Europe'. In: *The Beginnings of Printing in the Near and Middle East: Jews, Christians and Muslims*. Wiesbaden: Harrassowitz.

Tapper, R. (ed.) (2002) *The New Iranian Cinema. Politics, Representation and Identity.* London: I.B. Tauris.

Tash, A.Q. (2004) 'Islamic Satellite Channels and Their impact on Arab Societies: Iqra channel – a Case Study', *Transnational Broadcasting Studies*, no. 13/Fall 2004. Retrieved from http://www.tbsjournal.com/Archives/Fall04/tash.html.

Tauber, E. (1990) 'The Press and the Journalist as a Vehicle in Spreading National Ideas in Syria in the Late Ottoman Period', *Die Welt des Islams*, vol. XXX, no. 1/4, pp. 163–177.

Tayob, A.I. (1995) 'Purification'. In: Esposito, J.L. (ed.) *The Oxford Encyclopedia of the Modern Islamic World.* New York: Oxford University Press, vol. 3, pp. 370–372.

Tayob, A.I. (2006) 'Caricatures of the Prophet: European integration', *ISIM Review*, no. 17, p. 5.

Teitelbaum, J. (2002) 'Dueling for Da'wa: State Vs. Society on the Saudi Internet', *Middle East Journal*, vol. 56, no.2, pp. 222–239.

Thompson, E. (2000) *Colonial Citizens: Republican Rights, Paternal Privilege and Gender in French Syria and Lebanon.* New York: Columbia University Press.

Thompson, E. (2001) 'Sex and Cinema in Damascus. The Gendered Politics of Public Space in a Colonial City'. In: Korsholm Nielsen, H.C. and J. Skovgaard-Petersen, J. (eds) *Middle Eastern Cities 1900–1950. Public Places and Public Spheres in Transformation*. Aarhus: Aarhus University Press, pp. 89–111.

Thomsen Højsgaard, M. (2006) 'Connecting without Belonging: Interfaith Dialogue and Religious Conflict within Oline Settings'. In: Larsson, G. (ed.) *Religious Communities on the Internet*. Uppsala: Swedish Science Press, pp. 164–179.

Thoraval, Y. (1990) *Den Egyptiska filmens historia 1895–1905*. Swedish translation by Annika Gegenheimer. Lund: Alhambra Förlag.

Thurfjell, D. (2003) *Living Shi'ism: Instances of Ritualisation Among Islamist men in Contemporary Iran*. Uppsala: Uppsala University.

Turner, J.P. and T.H. Hower (2006) 'Buyids'. In: Meri, J.W. (ed.) *Medieval Islamic Civilization: An Encyclopedia*. New York and London: Routledge, vol. I, pp. 124–125.

Umble, D.Z. (1994) *Holding The Line: The Telephone in Old Order Mennonite and Amish Life*. Baltimore: Johns Hopkins University Press.

Vacca, V. (1935) 'Movimennto per vietare alle donne musulmane di frequentare i cinematografia el-Ladhiqiyyah', *Oriente Moderno*, no. 3, Marzo.

Vacca, V. (1939) 'Voti della 'Società dei sostenitori della virtù' a Damasco', *Oriente Moderno*, no. 4, Aprile.

Vajda, G. (1971) 'Idjaza'. In: *EI²*, vol. III, pp. 1020–1021.

Varzi, R. (2002) 'A Ghost in the Machine: The Cinema of the Iranian Sacred Defence'. In: Tapper, R. (ed.) *The New Iranian Cinema: Politics, Representation and Identity*. London: I.B. Tauris, pp. 154–166.

Vatikiotis, P.J. (1991) *The History of Moden Egypt: From Muhammad Ali to Mubarak*. London: Weidenfeld and Nicolson.

Vertovec, S. and A. Rogers (eds) (1998) *Muslim European Youth: Reproducing ethnicity, religion, culture*. Aldershot: Ashgate.

Voll, J.L. (1987) 'Wahhabiyah'. In: Eliade, M. (ed.) *The Encyclopedia of Religion*. New York and London: MacMillan Publishing Company, vol. 15, pp. 313–316.

Waardenburg, J. (1979) 'Official and Popular Religion as a Problem in Islamic Studies'. In: P.H. Vrijhof and J. Waardenburg (eds) *Official and Popular Religion. Analysis of a Theme for Religious Studies*. Hague: Mouton, pp. 340–386.

Waardenburg, J. (1995) 'The Mosque in Education'. In: Esposito, J.L. (ed.) *The Oxford Encyclopedia of the Modern Islamic World*. New York: Oxford University Press, vol. 3, pp. 147–151.

al-Wahhab, Muhammad 'Abd (1994) *Kitab al-Tawhid*. Riyadh: International Islamic Publishing House.

Walbiner, C.-M. (2001) 'The Christians of *Bilad al-Sham* (Syria): Pioneers of Book Printing in the Arab World'. In: *The Beginnings of Printing in the Near and Middle East: Jews, Christians and Muslims*. Wiesbaden: Harrassowitz, pp. 11–12.

Waines, D. (2002) 'Islam'. In: Woodhead, L. et al. (eds) *Religion in the Modern World*. London and New York: Routledge, pp. 182–203.

Watt, W.M. (1998) *The Formative Period of Islamic Thought*. Oxford: Oneworld.

Wehr, H. (1976) *A Dictionary of Modern Written Arabic*. Wiesbaden: Otto Harrassowitz.

Weiss, B. (1974) 'Al-Mushaf al-Murattal: A modern phonographic 'collection' (jam') of the Qur'an', *The Muslim World*, vol. LXIV, Issue 20, pp. 134–140.

Wennö, N. (2003) 'Matrix Reloaded stoppad av censuren i Egypten', *Dagens Nyheter* 12/6–2003.

Wensinck, A.J. (1927) *A Handbook of Early Muhammadan Tradition: Alphabetically arranged*. Leiden: Brill.

Wensinck, A.J. (1995) 'Niyya'. In: *EI²*, vol. VIII, pp. 66–67.

Wheeler, D.L. (2004) 'Blessings and Curses: Women and the Internet Revolution in the Arab World'. In: Sakr, N. (ed.) *Women and Media in the Middle East: Power Through Self-Expression*. London and New York: I.B. Tauris, pp. 138–161.

Wickens, G.M. (1956) 'Al-Jarsifi on the Hisba', *Islamic Quarterly*, vol. 3, pp. 176–187.

Wiebe, D. (2000) 'Modernism'. In: Braun, W. and McCutcheon R.T. (eds) *Guide to the Study of Religion*. London and New York: Cassell, pp. 351–364.

Williams, R. (2001) *TV, teknik och kulturella former*. Lund: Arkiv förlag.

Wise, L. (2003) *'Words from the Heart': New Forms of Islamic Preaching in Egypt*. Oxford: St Anthony's College, Oxford University.

Wise, L. (2004) 'Amr Khaled: Broadcasting the Nahda', *Transnational Broadcasting Studies*, no. 13/Fall 2004.

Wright, M.J. (2007). *Religion and Film: An introduction*. London: I.B. Tauris.

Woodhead, L. (ed.) (2002) *Religions in the Modern World: Traditions and transformations*. London: Routledge.

Al-Yassini, A. (1995) 'Wahhabiyah'. In: Esposito, J.L. (ed.) *The Oxford Encyclopedia of the Modern Islamic World*. New York and Oxford: Oxford University Press, vol. 4, pp. 307–308.

Zaman, M.Q. (2004) 'The Ulama of Contemporary Islam and their conceptions of the Common Good'. In: Salvatore, A. and D.F. Eickelman (eds) *Public Islam and the Common Good*. Leiden: Brill, pp. 129–155.

Zayani, M. (ed.) (2005) *The al-Jazeera Phenomenon: Critical Perspectives on New Arab Media*. Boulder: Paradigm Publishers.

Zeghal, M. (2007) 'The "Recentering" of Religious Knowledge and Discourse: The Case of al-Azhar in Twentieth-Century Egypt'. In: R.W. Hefner and M.Q. Zaman (eds) *Schooling Islam: The Culture and Politics of Modern Muslim Education*. Princeton: Princeton University Press, pp. 107–130.

Zetterstéen, K.V. (1914) *Det Muhammedanska universitetet El-Azhar i Kairo*. Uppsala and Stockholm: Almqvist & Wiksells.

Åberg, Johan (2003). *Det föreställda ghettot: ultraortodox gränsdragning och identitetskonstruktion i the Jewish Observer 1983–2002*. Lund: Lunds universitet.

Index